Blood, Sweat, and My Rock 'n' Roll Years

Is Steve Katz a Rock Star?

Steve Katz

Guilford, Connecticut

An imprint of Rowman & Littlefield

Distributed by NATIONAL BOOK NETWORK

British Library Cataloguing in Publication Information Available

Library of Congress Cataloging-in-Publication Data

Katz, Steve, 1945- author.
  Blood, sweat, and my rock 'n' roll years : is Steve Katz a rock star? / Steve Katz.
    pages cm
  Includes index.
  ISBN 978-1-4930-9999-3 (hardcover)
  1. Katz, Steve, 1945- 2. Blood, Sweat, and Tears (Musical group) 3. Guitarists—United States—Biography 4. Rock musicians—United States—Biography. I. Title.
  ML419.K375A3 2015
  782.42166092—dc23
  [B]
                              2014048518

♾™ The paper used in this publication meets the minimum requirements of American National Standard for Information Sciences—Permanence of Paper for Printed Library Materials, ANSI/NISO Z39.48-1992.

For Alison

CONTENTS

INTRODUCTION

A One and a Two and a . . .

Once upon a time, I had an incredibly passionate and somewhat dysfunctional affair with Mimi Fariña. When that went south, I had a fling with Joni Mitchell. Jim Morrison's girlfriend Pam used to come over to make love when Jim was drunk and abusing her. And it all seemed normal.

I almost got into a fight with Bob Dylan—and I did many times with Lou Reed. And of course, Al Kooper—a formerly nice Jewish boy like me, and my partner in the Blues Project and then Blood, Sweat & Tears, who became Dylan's sidekick and dined out for years telling the story of how he crashed the *Highway 61* recording session to play the organ on "Like a Rolling Stone"—well, we spent half a lifetime trying to kill each other.

I played at Monterey and Woodstock—not to mention one of those crazy Murray the K shows with the Who and Cream and Wilson Pickett—and partied with Groucho Marx, Sidney Poitier, Elizabeth Taylor, and the '69 Mets.

Somewhere around my house here in the foothill of the Berkshires I have three Grammy Awards—not bad out of ten nominations. I have a few *DownBeat* Readers Poll Awards, which are awesome, but also contributed to the downfall of Blood, Sweat & Tears when the jazz guys in the band thought that was their cue to take over and start blowing "serious shit," promptly driving our rock 'n' roll audience away. I've got three gold albums and one that went quadruple platinum. All together I've sold something like 29 million records. My neighbors don't have a clue.

I've done tours with Miles Davis and Nina Simone, did my damnedest to teach Sammy Davis Jr. how to roll a serviceable joint, and eventually became everything I hated—a suit at a record company.

Occasionally I gig, but never again with the guys who seemingly defined my career: Al Kooper, Lou Reed, and the woman-beating, arrogant Blood, Sweat & Tears singer David Clayton-Thomas.

Of the three, though, Lou was the real poison pill. He was the catalyst for me falling out with my brother, who was head of Artists and Repertoire at RCA, and Lou's putative boss. I produced two pretty good records for Lou and pretty much saved him from a career as a cult figure living on the margins.

A magazine once published a feature story called "Blood, Sweat & Blintzes." The subtitle on the cover was "Is Steve Katz a Rock Star?" It was a fairly accurate portrait of me. There I was, listening to show tunes and leaving my parents' house with a week's worth of supplies— "stuffed cabbage, chicken soup with rice, salad with sour cream dressing, pot roast, potato kugel, corn on the cob, and in-case-you-are-still-hungry roast chicken," not to mention a bag full of clean linens.

I was, and am, kind of a nerd. I never wore cool on my sleeve like some guys could, and never tried. Jimi Hendrix once asked me if he could borrow my horn section for his next record; how much cooler did I need to be? Too bad he died before he got around to it.

I got lucky. It's kind of hard to imagine now just how big Blood, Sweat & Tears was back then—smash records, traveling the world on private jets, too much money and sex to keep track of. And as proud as I am of our big hits—"You've Made Me So Very Happy" and "And When I Die" (I never liked "Spinning Wheel")—unfortunately, we get blamed for a lot of bad jazz-rock fusion. (I swear I had nothing to do with that; I'm a rock 'n' roll guy.)

I was a product of the times in which I lived, but thankfully, I wasn't a casualty. Talking about drugs in that magazine article, I sound like an idiot: "It's great to play when you are stoned on grass—the psychic vibrations are much stronger." And then there was my mom, right there in the story, asking me if I ever took LSD, and me confessing that I had, but promising her I would never do it again. I guess it's kind of ironic that I ended up working with a notorious pincushion like Lou Reed.

Rock stardom, real or imagined, drives people to some pretty weird places. I'm one of the fortunate ones. I walked through that door and, for the most part, stayed fairly sane.

But boy, do I have a story to tell you . . .

CHAPTER 1

The Birth of the Blues

MINEOLA HIGH SCHOOL WAS CLOSE TO BEING TORN DOWN WHEN I first arrived. It was 1960. Vietnam was just the tiniest tempest in a teapot, and prior to the protests and riots to come, colleges were strictly where one went to get an education.

Mineola High was an old brick behemoth and, like most high schools of the time, smelled of Brylcreem and body odor. It would be a while before the boys room was filled with pot smoke.

The school housed four kinds of kids—jocks, hoods (post-greaser punks, Sharks and Jets who kept their cigarettes rolled up in their T-shirt sleeves), the kids not smart enough to consider college who majored in woodshop, and the few weirdoes who went out for drama. Music at Mineola was pretty much nonexistent, and probably thought of by the administration to be totally off-the-wall, if not dangerously extreme. Rock music was still considered a threat.

As a nice Jewish boy with beatnik tendencies, I didn't really fit in to any of those four categories (I didn't know it then, but I was just waiting for the '60s to *really* get started), so I quickly had to find a way to survive high school without being shunned by the entire student body and doomed to acute social depression and greater than normal teen angst.

I decided to become a journalist—not the "news" kind of journalist, more like the "gossip" kind of journalist—reporting on the comings and goings of the underbelly of our little postpubescent adolescent society. I took journalism class and somehow talked my way into getting my own column in the school newspaper. I would become the J. J. Hunsecker of Mineola High School. Why on earth would I want to have a column? To blackmail my fellow classmates. What could I possibly gain by putting everybody's dirty laundry out to dry? Security. I would use my column to blackmail the physically threatening hoods and pompously condescending jocks so that they would allow me to survive in this depressing teenage jungle that I was stuck in, and in return they would not have to suffer the humiliation that my malevolent little world of gossip and innuendo could offer.

My column was called, appropriately, "Steve's World." I felt like Stalin's NKVD. People would come to me with stories of other people. They would name names, point accusing fingers at their fellow classmates, entitle me with juicy tales from parties past and of pregnancies future. I was king of the rumor mill. I loved it. I not only survived, I thrived. If a girl looked at me the wrong way, I would write that she was about to do a butter commercial in New York for the "seventy-cent spread." If a hood threatened to beat my brains in, I would report on good authority that his muffler sported a "a three-inch tailpipe," thereby establishing myself as Mineola's king of the double entendre. Once my classmates were subdued and my power trip no longer a novelty, I went on to use my column as a weekly diary to record my journeys into Manhattan.

I had been singing unprofessionally since I was five years old, sometimes in the courtyard in front of our garden apartment in Queens, sometimes for my elementary school classmates, and sometimes on local live TV. I felt I needed something to accompany my growing a cappella repertoire, so I rented a ukulele. But at the risk of sounding like a miniature Arthur Godfrey, I gave it up, little realizing that I was only two strings away from my future vocation. I didn't just want to sing—I wanted to be a musician.

It was the era of folk music, The Kingston Trio and The New Christy Minstrels. College kids were the fashionistas of the time—cool jazz, sick humor, coffeehouses with real-life beatniks. I wanted to be part of it and not just another square peg in Mr. Rhinehalter's math class.

Away from school, I was becoming more and more introspective, turning away from social and family obligations and leaning toward the arts for solace and inspiration. I hitched a ride to Greenwich Village one evening with my brother. Dennis and a friend of his wanted to spend some time checking out the coffeehouses. They wanted to see the White Horse Tavern where Dylan Thomas supposedly drank himself to death, and to find out what the beatniks were up to—maybe catch a Shakespeare sonnet over a cup of cappuccino or a "union" anthem or two by some ex–merchant marine at Gerdes Folk City.

MacDougal Street was where we found the coffeehouses—the Figaro, Rienzi's, the Fat Black Pussycat—all within a stone's throw from each other, and where local chess players hovered over their tiny espresso cups in smoke-infested, softly lit amber palaces of the Beat Generation. Right in the middle, and just across from Minetta Lane, was a small conglomerate of storefronts that were at the heart of the pure folk music movement in New York. Downstairs was the Gaslight Cafe, to its left was the Kettle of Fish, a bar that was the folk music equivalent of the literary crowd's White Horse Tavern, and, upstairs, occupying a small, old, musky floor-through, was Israel Young's Folklore Center. Outside, on the street that was usually packed with suburban kids on weekend nights, you could take in the scent of coffee, filterless French cigarettes, and freshly grilled sausage and onions.

The Folklore Center was the meeting place of the New York folk music crowd and all its attendant émigré folk musicians. Owned by Israel Young, known around the block as "Izzy," the Folklore Center was the place to pick up obscure records that you couldn't find anywhere else, where you could peruse *Broadside* and *Sing Out* magazines and linger around walls of traditional fretted instruments that would one day gain tenfold in value. But most of all, the Folklore Center, along with Allan Block's Sandal Shop on West Fourth Street, was the place to hang out, to talk folk music and politics—to meet people and to jam. The store manager when Izzy wasn't around was a skinny young man by the name of Jack Ballard. Jack, whose real name was Jack Prelutsky, and who later was to become America's poet laureate for children, was an excellent guitarist. I practically begged Jack to rent me a guitar and give me lessons and he agreed, so I took home an old Martin and began a journey from which I have never turned back.

I started taking the train on my own into the city. I especially loved the Village. I loved the beatniks and the leftists, the minstrels and the intellectuals. It was everything that my school wasn't, so I traveled into Manhattan frequently and reported on it almost weekly in my column.

⁓

I began going in at night, mainly to hang out at the Gaslight Cafe. For a brief period, my homework consisted of learning chords and basic fingerpicking rudiments. I had to actually find time for school, although I disliked it more and more, and at times even resented going as my immersion into Manhattan grew. The Gaslight was also an antique floor-through just like the Folklore Center upstairs. It was dark and worn like a musty old antique and, like most of the cafes at the time, did not have a liquor license. The Gaslight offered "hootenanny" nights with an emcee who organized the talent for the evening. And most of the time, the emcee was grungy-voiced Dave Van Ronk, later known as "The Mayor of MacDougal Street." When he wasn't hosting, Dave would forfeit the role to Noel Stookey, later to become Paul of Peter, Paul and Mary.

Van Ronk, still only in his twenties but nonetheless a cynical old socialist, could frighten the holy bejesus out of a little kid from Long Island with his near-violent interpretations of "House of the Rising Sun" and Bessie Smith's "Mean Old Bed Bug Blues." I was transfixed. I listened to sets by Tom Paxton, Mark Spoelstra, Ramblin' Jack Elliott, Patrick Sky, and Len Chandler while slowly sipping my cappuccino. I heard songs that I never knew existed, obscure blues, old-timey murder ballads, and original songs of protest and love—songs from all over the world. It took me a couple of weeks, but I finally asked Dave if he would give me lessons, and, like Jack Prelutsky, his answer, in his world-weary voice that probably meant *I can't believe I have to do this to earn a living*, was that he would. I floated home that night.

The next day I carried my rented guitar down to the station and took the Long Island Railroad into Manhattan, where I would hop a subway downtown to West Fifteenth Street, to Dave Van Ronk's top-floor walk-up apartment and where, in the early afternoon, a sleepy Bob Dylan would just be waking up on Dave's living room couch. Dylan had recently arrived in New York from the Midwest and was couch-hopping, mainly at the Van Ronks'. Dave and his wife, Terri Thal, a tall raven-haired beauty who was also managing Dave at the time, had taken Dylan under their wing, gave him shelter for a time, and unwittingly gave him some of Dave's songs and arrangements to boot.

Van Ronk, a walrus of an Irishman and one of the few remaining members of the Industrial Workers of the World, the Wobblies, would be sipping his coffee and smoking his first filterless Picayune cigarette of the day, his long straight sandy-blond hair falling wispily over one eye. He would stomp around the apartment in an old T-shirt and bare feet, trying to remember where he left his guitar, a large Gibson J-200 that looked like it belonged more in an upscale rodeo than in a lower Manhattan walk-up. Surrounded by African art and old ragtime and early jazz records, we would begin my lesson. With the help of Dave's own homemade tablature, I learned how to back-pick an old New Orleans chestnut, a metaphor about prostitution called "Candy Man." I had to practice like mad for the rest of the week so I wouldn't have to endure Van Ronk's intimidating evil eye all through our next session. Obviously Dave would have been happier doing other things, but not me.

For a while, Dave and Terri also took me under their wing. I once joined them at a Young Socialist League meeting—or was it Young *People's* Socialist League meeting? These were the two factions of young socialists in New York at the time. Both were adjuncts of the American Socialist Party. I was told that the two groups did not get along. I imagined them having it out on Fourteenth Street, each nerdy faction, as in Kurosawa's *Yojimbo*, taking their positions at either end of the block, all these kids with long black curly hair and impossibly thick glasses apprehensively running toward each other while tossing missiles of folded Trotskyite and Stalinist pamphlets like they were inventing a new sport up at City College. It was too difficult for me to understand, and to be honest, I really didn't care. I just wanted to hang with Dave and Terri and meet girls. After an hour or so at the party, people would try to sign me up for membership while Terri batted them away with a stern look of disapproval, me being only seventeen and a political naïf.

Meanwhile, Dylan, with the help of some of the arrangements he had boosted from Van Ronk, got himself a record deal. One day while I was taking my lesson, he came rushing up the stairs to Dave and Terri's from Columbia Records uptown with the final proof of the album's artwork. He was as excited as a little kid and couldn't get over the fact that in the cover photo, the strings of his guitar were backwards. I didn't ask why, but Columbia obviously flipped the photo around for their own reasons, which didn't seem to bother Bob at all.

Dave and Terri made love constantly. Sometimes I had to wait in their small living room while the two of them would thump away in the bedroom, a living metronome for my upcoming lesson. I loved going to Dave and Terri's. The lessons were work, but hanging with the two of them was both joyful and educational. I wanted them to be my parents. Dave and Terri opened a world for me that I never wanted to leave. Sadly, in later years, I felt a coldness from Dave, possibly because of my own success and Dave's bitterness at not being as successful in his lifetime as he should have been.

Usually, before my lessons with Dave, I would stop in at the Sam Goody Midtown record store. Goody had racks of cheap Folkways records without their sleeves. I never understood why the sleeves were missing, but I always found some great music to take home. On Sundays I would join the weekly folk music gatherings at Washington Square Park.

One summer Sunday, while casually walking around the large circle that enveloped the fountain, I heard what sounded like Reverend Gary Davis's guitar. I walked around the fountain until I found a tall bespectacled kid playing his own sunburst Gibson J-200, the same as Van Ronk's, and playing just like Reverend Davis himself. One of the most influential records for me at the time, and one that's been in my top-ten list for most of my life, was *Blind Gary Davis: Harlem Street Singer*. Gary played his guitar like a gospel organ. His voice was the earthy, sometimes painful, sometimes powerful, and sometimes humorous voice of the poor black South. No wonder Van Ronk, Stefan Grossman, David Bromberg, Pete Seeger, and everyone else who knew or learned from Reverend Davis idolized him as much as they did.

When I first met him in 1963, Blind Gary Davis was singing on the streets of Harlem. Playing music in the streets was one of the few ways that impoverished blind black musicians were able to make a living in the 1920s through the early 1960s. Both in the South and in the major urban areas of the North, great blues singers like Blind Boy Fuller, Blind Blake, Blind Lemon Jefferson, and Blind Willie McTell created an art form out of their will to survive.

I became lifelong friends with Stefan Grossman, one of the guys I met in Washington Square Park. Stefan was enrolled at Cooper Union and living with his parents in Gramercy Park. I was still living with my parents in Roslyn Heights, and about to commute to C. W. Post College in Brookville, part of Long Island University. (I somehow managed to graduate high school, though I didn't even attend my own graduation. I had the school put my diploma in the mail.)

Stefan was very close to Reverend Davis and felt that it would be good for me to travel up to the Bronx for a few lessons with the master himself. My fingerpicking was improving, and I needed to have a decent instrument—not just to play, but to impress all my folky friends around the fountain. Van Ronk and Stefan both played Gibson J-200s, so I had to have one as well. But it meant getting a job in the "straight" world.

The job I found was as stock boy and sometime salesman in the record department of the Westbury branch of E. J. Korvette. One of the larger chains of department stores in the New York metro area at the time, Korvettes was the 1950s and '60s Long Island version of Walmart. I felt lucky to have landed a job in the record department of a major department store, even though I first started out the summer stocking albums and loading and unloading boxes of LPs. At least I was doing something that was somewhat close to music. Ironically, I was stocking Bob Dylan's first album—schlepping the boxes up the conveyer belt, along with multiple volumes of *Persuasive Percussion* and *The Sound of Music*, and adding them to the bins and shelves.

Typically corporate, when Korvettes hired the guys who worked in their record department, including myself, they should have known better. There were four of us. The other three, unlike myself, were adults with families to support and bills to pay. As diverse as we were, we all had one thing in common: a deep love and appreciation for music and records. Stanley was the manager of our department; Jerry and Hal were the salesmen. Stanley was a middle-aged Jewish guy whose specialty was old-time jazz and bebop from the 1930s and '40s. Jerry was the bluegrass and country maven—Bill Monroe, the Stanley Brothers, George Jones. Hal was a skinny little black guy who loved R&B—John Lee Hooker and Jimmy Reed. I was the obscure folk music kid—lover of records that didn't sell, or, according to my newfound politically correct phrase of choice, records that didn't *sell out*. The four of us were purists. There was a sound system in our department where we were encouraged by management to play the top LPs of the day for the customers that wandered through and who hopefully picked up a few records to take home—*West Side Story*; Tony Bennett's *I Left My Heart in San Francisco*; *Peter, Paul and Mary*; and anything by Frank Sinatra.

Instead we played what we liked. People would wander in, crinkle their noses at the speakers above, shake their heads, and walk out. This was especially true whenever I played Bob Dylan's first album. People did not know what to make of it, and so, as if a giant golem had just farted in our little corner of the store, they would continue on to Kitchenware, Lawn Care, Young Sophisticates, or the parking lot.

One day an elderly Jewish man came up to me and asked if we had a copy of Richard Wagner's *Götterdämmerung*, the last opera in Wagner's *Ring Cycle*. Wagner, of course, was an infamous anti-Semite, but this in itself did not deter my customer, who, when told the only version we had in stock was on the esteemed German label Deutsche Grammophon, informed me that he would not buy anything on a German label, stormed out of the store, got into his Mercedes, and left, probably stopping at the local deli for some potato salad and knockwurst before heading back.

At home my few friends and I lived a normal teenage existence, smoking and drinking when the parents weren't looking, gossiping, and immersing ourselves in rock and roll. For me, it was like leading a double life, learning and practicing folk songs and blues in the evening and listening to The Shirelles in my spare time. Every night before going to sleep, I turned on my radio to hear Jean Shepherd and his colorful stories about growing up in the Midwest. Shepherd's stream of consciousness was hip, intensely creative, and wonderfully entertaining. He was the Mark Twain of the early 1960s, and helped to develop my own somewhat cynical sense of humor. Shepherd was best known for writing and narrating *A Christmas Story*, now a staple of TV every holiday season. I tried not to wake my brother in the next room because he was studying for a degree at Fordham Law School, across from the new Lincoln Center. I lowered the volume, put the radio close to my ear, turned the dial, and bathed in the hard bop of *The Symphony Sid Show* until I drifted off.

———

It was time to make an appointment to see Reverend Davis. I was a little scared, but I couldn't wait to meet him. I would take the subway up to the South Bronx and walk up a rickety flight of stairs to his little clapboard shanty that was abutted on either side by two large tenements. The Reverend's lovely wife, Annie, treated me like royalty, and for a five-dollar fee, Reverend Davis would tease and cajole me into playing my new big blond Gibson like I was entertaining at a Saturday-night fish fry in the Carolinas, circa 1935. Blind Gary Davis was a genius, and I feel honored to this day to have spent time with and learned from him. He taught me his own version of "Candy Man," front-picking, unlike Van Ronk's version, although Van Ronk professed to have learned it from Gary. I was now a "Candy Man" expert, backward *and* frontward.

Soon we took the lessons with Gary Davis on the road. Stefan and I would drive him to gigs and lead him around, as did a few other lucky kids. I would drive Gary up to Woodstock, Saratoga, and other folk venues where, at whatever lodging we were staying, I would bother the Reverend for some stories, songs, and hopefully a riff or two that I could pick up along the way. One of the funniest people I've ever known, Gary would always give in to my demands in return for a pinch of gin that I had promised Annie I would withhold from him.

Annie and the Reverend eventually moved from the South Bronx to Queens, thanks to some long-overdue royalty checks for "If I Had My Way," recorded by Peter, Paul and Mary. Reverend Davis recorded the song for Prestige Records as "Samson and Delilah," also a staple of Van Ronk's repertoire.

One day I got a call from Annie, who asked if I could pick up Reverend Davis on an upcoming Saturday night. Sonny Terry and Brownie McGhee were opening for Roland Kirk at the Village Gate, and Gary wanted to say hello to his old friend Sonny. Their friendship went back decades to the early blues days in North Carolina. I picked up the Reverend and we went down to Bleecker Street, to the Village Gate. Sonny and Brownie played a set, and the Reverend and I went backstage where Roland Kirk was hanging around as well, waiting to go on.

Now, Reverend Davis is blind, Sonny Terry is blind, *and* Roland Kirk is blind. So Reverend Davis bumps into Roland Kirk and, thinking it's his old friend Sonny, gives Roland Kirk a big bear hug, and of course Roland Kirk thinks it's an old friend of his and returns the hug through yet another bout of tears as I am trying desperately, like a referee at a heavyweight boxing match, to pull the two apart. Things then settled down and Sonny and Reverend Davis finally had their own tearful reunion.

Whenever Van Ronk, Dylan, and Phil Ochs wanted to go somewhere and not pay for a cab, I would get a call from Dave. "Hey, can you get the car tonight?" So I would ask my parents for the car, and four or five of us would go uptown to hang out with Paul Rothchild, Prestige Records' house hipster and producer. We then journeyed back down to the Village, our safe harbor from anything above Fourteenth Street. I recall one night when we all went to the Kettle of Fish, the bar adjacent to the Gaslight Cafe. The Kettle was small, with sawdust on the floor. Van Ronk, Dylan, and Ochs wanted to have a few drinks, and I had my phony ID (I was still underage). Dylan was regaling us with tales of how he was being booked on tours, traveling from city to city to do shows and *actually being paid for it.*

Touring and actually getting paid for it was completely beyond everyone's scope of comprehension. It was not something that West Village folksingers did. It was the kind of thing that Sammy Davis Jr.

did, and God knows, you would never catch Sammy passing the hat at Caesars Palace. And here was Dylan talking about having played at a college in Georgia to thunderous applause, months before Martin Luther King's "I Have a Dream" speech in Washington and the Freedom Rides of 1964. At this point in his career, Dylan was mentored by the ghost of Hank Williams and proclaimed to his friends, ironically, that he was nonpolitical, and that he was as flabbergasted as the rest of us by his newfound fame and growing reputation as a guru of the coming counterculture.

I was now hanging out at the Gaslight Cafe most of the time. The stage, which had started out against a long wall, was later moved to the back of the room—a room that was small to begin with but never ergonomically comfortable enough for a fan base that was growing by the week. I remember Bob Dylan and John Sebastian playing together one evening, a night when I introduced myself to Al Jardine of the Beach Boys, who had decided to take a trip downtown to the Bohemian enclaves of Greenwich Village. I was sitting with Al when Dylan came on and did "Hey, Mr. Tambourine Man," the first time I had heard it. In between songs, Jardine leaned over and asked me if Dylan was "straight." I said, "Yes," but I couldn't tell if Al was asking about Dylan's drug use or his sexual habits. In retrospect, I probably should have answered "It's complicated" and left it at that.

The memories I treasure most from the Gaslight were meeting some of the blues greats that were "rediscovered" by Dick Waterman and Tom Hoskins, a couple of guys from the Washington, DC, area. When I first heard an old 78 rpm record of Skip James doing "Devil Got My Woman," I couldn't believe what I was hearing. It was spooky, ethereal, almost not from this world. This was not the casual twelve- or eight-bar blues of Big Bill Broonzy and Brownie McGhee. This was something completely far out. Skip James had a high-tenor, almost-falsetto quality in his voice and sang over a complex guitar part that introduces the song for a chorus, and that I later learned was in an open D-minor tuning. The first line—*I'd rather be the devil, than be that woman's man*—exemplifies why the Delta blues was as poetic and mysterious as anything in American literature. Eric Clapton understood this when Cream featured Skip James's "I'm So Glad" in their repertoire.

I met Skip James at the Gaslight. Along with Mississippi John Hurt, he was one of the gentlest people I've ever met, at once living up to the mystery of his recordings and revealing himself to be a fine poet and musician. He was the antithesis of Son House, who could be nasty and irascible like his songs. Son House's music was also poetry, but of a different kind.

Gerdes Folk City had three locations during its long and storied life in New York City. In the early and mid-'60s, it was across the street from the building that later housed The Bottom Line, at the corner of West Fourth and Mercer. The bluegrass people would be there, the singer-songwriters, the blues crowd, the traditional folkies. I used to go there because that was where so many of my future bandmates and some of my favorite "roots" musicians would hang out—Winnie Winston, David Grisman, John Sebastian, Stefan Grossman, Red Allen and Frank Wakefield, the Greenbriar Boys with John Herald and Ralph Rinzler, and Eric Andersen. Reverend Gary Davis would often play there, and Bob Dylan would be lurking around as well, or thumbing through the *New York Times*, looking for song ideas. Downstairs at Gerdes was folk music's equivalent of the Round Table at the Algonquin Hotel. One gas explosion in that basement in 1963 would have completely changed the course of folk music history—but Dylan wouldn't have been around to write about it.

⌐╼ ╾⌐

I was part of the generation of folkies that preceded Dylan, Van Ronk, Ochs, and all the other heroes of our crowd. It consisted of future luminaries like Sebastian, Grisman, Maria D'Amato, Stefan, and

Joshua Rifkin, who later interpreted Scott Joplin rags on his own hit Nonesuch album, and then proceeded to become one of the world's leading Bach experts and conductors. In our coming jug band, however, Rifkin would play kazoo, and sometimes piano when the opportunity presented itself.

We would trade licks at Marc Silber's Fretted Instruments on Sixth Avenue, a second-floor walk-up next to the Waverly Theater, where you could try out a guitar without attracting the suspicious glares you would get from the uptight salesmen in the music stores of squaresville Midtown. Some of us were devotees of the blues, and some were bluegrass and old-timey enthusiasts, but all of us wanted to play music together. We found our common denominator in jug band music.

The Even Dozen Jug Band was my first group. It was late spring of 1963. We were mostly local kids who loved traditional folk music, *real* folk music. We got acquainted with each other at jam sessions in Washington Square Park. After sundown, some of us reconvened to play at old-time fiddler Allan Block's Sandal Shop on West Fourth Street, run by the father of the great folk-blues musician Rory Block. Sometimes we were ten, or sometimes thirteen, depending on who showed up to any given gig or rehearsal. The core lineup that also recorded the only album we ever did came to thirteen people—not exactly an even dozen, but rather, a baker's dozen:

> Stefan Grossman—vocal, guitar, six-string banjo
> Peter Jacobson—vocal, guitar, six-string banjo
> Peter Siegel—vocal, guitar, five-string banjo
> Frank Goodkin—five-string banjo
> David Grisman—mandolin
> Fred Weisz—fiddle
> Steve Katz—vocal, washboard
> Joshua Rifkin—vocal, piano, kazoo

John Sebastian—harmonica, kazoo

Danny Lauffer—jug

Peggy Haines—jug

Maria D'Amato—vocal, fiddle

Bob Gurland—hand trumpet

We were all in college, New York's adolescent answer to the older and more-experienced Jim Kweskin Jug Band out of Cambridge, Massachusetts. We idolized Cannon's Jug Stompers and the Memphis Jug Band. None of us were religious, yet we prayed at the altar of Bill Monroe, Charley Patton, and the Carter Family. We subsisted on 78 rpm records that were discovered in the shacks and hovels of the rural South by collectors like Harry Smith, Nick Perls, and Alan Lomax. Along with Sam Charters's collection, *The Country Blues*, on Folkways, it was Harry Smith's *Anthology of American Folk Music*, a three-box set of LPs, also on Folkways, that originally inspired my love for American roots music. I listened to these records as if I were diving into a pomegranate—for me, each seed was a perfect song, a perfect story, and a perfect work of art. Listen to "Statesboro Blues" by Blind Wille McTell, "Maggie Campbell Blues" by Tommy Johnson, or "Devil Got My Woman" by Skip James, and you will understand.

As it turned out, the Even Dozen Jug Band had too many guitar players, so I found myself an old washboard, brushed up on what I knew from playing my bongos, and saddled up for ragtime. We rehearsed anywhere we could, including Victoria Spivey's apartment. Victoria Spivey, an old-time jazz singer in the style of Bessie Smith, recorded mainly in the 1930s and was cast in King Vidor's first sound film, *Hallelujah!* Ms. Spivey had taken us under her wing, a very generous and brave act considering how many we were. We worked up a bunch of string band tunes and rags. Most of us sang, and Maria and I did a couple of duets. We did sensitive songs, like "Evolution Mama," or songs that touched the heart, like "Take Your Fingers Off It."

We "signed" to Victoria Spivey's label, Spivey Records, in the summer of 1963, but later, when Vanguard Records signed the Jim Kweskin Jug Band, Elektra Records made a bid for the Even Dozen Jug Band in anticipation of a jug band music fad. Elektra bought out the contract with Spivey Records in early October 1963 (our advance was an extravagant $1,000, split twelve ways, minus management's cut—management being Israel Young, who owned the Folkore Center on MacDougal Street).

The jug band wars were about to begin. In the time that it took a messenger to bicycle down Sixth Avenue to the Village, contracts in hand, we were in the studio and recording our only album, *The Even Dozen Jug Band*. It took us two days to record and was released in December of 1963, a month after our "rival," the Jim Kweskin Jug Band, released *their* first album. Our producer, the aforementioned Paul Rothchild, who moved on to Elektra and was later to produce The Doors, Love, the Paul Butterfield Blues Band, Tim Buckley, Fred Neil, Phil Ochs, and Judy Collins, had us form a large circle around two microphones for the newly ubiquitous "stereo" effect. All takes were done live without any overdubs, and yet both the performance and recording still sound good today—except for a bizarre Jimmy Durante impersonation that I did on the last verse of "Come On In."

Speaking of impersonations, Izzy Young did his version of a manager, though I honestly can't remember what Izzy ever did aside from telling us where to be and at what time. In order to facilitate an image, we dressed ourselves in uniforms of dungarees, blue work shirts, and black vests—and that is how we look on the album cover. The photo was taken by Elektra art director Bill Harvey atop a building in Midtown, where we were sprawled out under a huge water tower. There is one person on the cover, I believe her name was Marlene, who was a friend of some of the band members and not in the band at all.

Marlene didn't even play an instrument. The missing members from the photo were Peter Jacobson and Peggy Haines.

Things were pretty loose in those days. We played a few live gigs, including two at Carnegie Hall and two nationally televised TV shows. The first TV show we did was *The Tonight Show* with Johnny Carson on Friday, January 17, 1964. Because of union rules at the time, the show could not afford more than five of us, so John Sebastian, myself, Stefan, Peter Siegel, and Maria came, in uniform, to Radio City's NBC studios, where we were joined onstage by Johnny Carson on kazoo and baseball great Leo Durocher on comb.

On Saturday, February 22, 1964, we performed on a nationally aired folk music exploitation TV show called *Hootenanny*, emceed by Art Linkletter's son, Jack. Had the band been political, we would have joined the pickets that night outside of Fordham University's Bronx campus, who were protesting Pete Seeger's exclusion from the series because of Pete's leftist leanings. A Fordham priest in full attire came up to me in the cafeteria. Thinking I was a student, he looked at my old-timey dungaree outfit and, in the tone of a nasty Dickensian schoolmaster, asked me, "What are you doing dressed like that?" to which I answered, while mustering all the Jewishness I could in the form of answering a question with a question, "What are you doing dressed like *that*?" I was lucky not to have been expelled.

We suffered a small bout of jug band crossbreeding. Maria D'Amato met Geoff Muldaur (of the Kweskin Jug Band) at a party that the record companies threw at our rehearsal space next to the Chelsea Hotel, on West Twenty-Third Street. Maria got plastered that night and threw up all over Geoff. They were engaged not long after, and she became Maria Muldaur. We lost Maria to the competition.

The rest is jug band history. Elektra wanted us to quit college and play full-time professionally. We had an audition with the William Morris Agency. They wanted us to go on the road, competing with acts like the New Christy Minstrels, but we all thought that quitting school would be foolish so, in May of 1964, after one year, two nationally televised TV shows, two appearances at Carnegie Hall, and one appearance at the Lajos Kossuth's First Hungarian Reformed Church on the Upper East Side of Manhattan, we decided to call it quits. We took a vote by hand one day outside of our rehearsal hall. John Sebastian wanted to perform. John was in the musicians' union and not in school at the time, and that's why he used his middle name, "Benson," on the album credits. None of the rest of us were union members. All of us but John wanted to go back to school. So that day, to the dismay of our agency, record company, and the few fans that we had, was the day we voted the Even Dozen Jug Band out of existence.

I continued my commute to school every day, now from Douglaston, Queens, where my parents had moved. I majored in English and minored in history. I was in the slow lane to law school, but I missed the band and the "glitz" of show business. Playing in a jug band had really given me the bug.

In the summer of 1964, after the break-up of the Even Dozen, Stefan and Marc Silber and I decided to drive out to California in Marc's red 1952 Mercury, which was accessorized with an ailing fuel pump and a broken rear signal light. Never having been west of the Hudson River, this was to be the adventure of a lifetime. We were going to spend the summer in Berkeley, trading instruments, jamming, and looking for the odd gig at whatever folk music venues were available. The car was filled with acoustic instruments that we would sell along the way, possibly to Harry Tuft at the Folklore Center in Denver, or maybe to McCabe's Guitar Shop in Santa Monica. And we knew we would be hanging out at Jon Lundberg's Fretted Instruments on Dwight Way in Berkeley. Jon specialized in restoring, building, and selling acoustic instruments.

On our way out, we were stopped in Vernal, Utah, by two officers of the Utah State Police. Our car was filled with acoustic instruments. Oh, and then there was the Buffalo Bill look-alike carnival guy in the backseat who we'd picked up hitchhiking outside of Omaha, who, when asked where he was going, had shrugged his shoulders and said "Oh, I dunno; where're you boys headin' to?"

This was the year of the Freedom Rides, of long-haired left-wing punks who were asking for trouble just by passing through and stirring things up with their fancy banjo tunes and early Welsh murder ballads. I was driving at the time we were pulled over and was asked to sit in the backseat of the patrol car.

The first officer came back after a quick search of the Mercury and said to his partner, "Think we should have them play us a song?" My knees began to shake. The biggest fear at that moment was not spending some time in a local cell; my biggest fear was that I was about to pee in my pants right there in the patrol car and get their backseat all wet, in which case we probably wouldn't have even made it into town for an arraignment. Luckily, we were saved from major humiliation and possible personal injury when the other officer answered, "Nah, shift's ending; let's go home," and let us off with a warning to get our taillight fixed.

So we proceeded on our way, me driving with my eyes out the side window so I could get a good glimpse of the mesas at sunset, something I was not used to seeing in Queens. Stefan and Marc begged me to keep my eyes on the road, but I knew these were sights that you would only get to see maybe once in a lifetime. They did make it clear, however, that my lifetime probably wouldn't last more than an hour or two more if I kept driving with my head out the window.

The interstates were not yet finished. We saw America from its secondary roads, and what we saw was an America that no longer exists, where local businesses were owned by families and small-town entrepreneurs, and each locality had not yet lost their own unique accents and identity. We ate local meat and vegetables, and for breakfast had fresh eggs that were as big as tennis balls. As we drove, we listened to local radio stations that were not yet programmed by "professionals," but were dictated by the tastes of people from diverse ethnic areas all across the country. And people were friendly all over; Vietnam and the Nixon administration had not yet divided the nation.

We arrived in Berkeley the summer before the student demonstrations of Mario Savio and the Berkeley Free Speech Movement, a foreshadowing of the antiwar demonstrations that would occur on campuses across the country throughout the remaining decade and beyond. We couldn't have cared less about campus protests at the time, although you could cut the vibe in that summer's Berkeley air with a dull knife. We were there to see Lightnin' Hopkins and Big Mama Thornton at the Cabale, to hang out with John Fahey at the Jabberwock, and to jam with Jerry Garcia and Pigpen at Lundberg's Fretted Instruments.

I was living all that summer on one hundred hard-earned dollars and subsisted on cheap footlong hot dogs and milk shakes from the counter of the drugstore across the street from Lundberg's. I spent my Sundays in an African-American Baptist church near the Cabale, where I first watched and listened from the back row. By the end of the summer, I wound up near the front, banging a tambourine and singing my heart out. Stefan and I played at the Jabberwock a few times. We would ask the audience from the stage if they had any room to put us up for the night, and so, long story short, at nineteen, I lost my virginity. I *loved* show business.

Before heading home, that July we took a side trip to LA, my first time in an airplane, where we were met at the airport by a friend of Stefan's, blues guitarist Steve Mann. Steve met us at the arrivals building and welcomed us to LA with a grocery bag filled with pot. My first days in LA were spent meeting some local folk musicians and hanging out at McCabe's Guitar Shop. I dropped in on Chris Hillman, who was living on Fountain Avenue, not far from Sunset. Chris was a bluegrass mandolin player then, just before he picked up a bass and joined the Byrds.

My first evening was spent at a coffeehouse on Sunset called the Fifth Estate. Jim (Roger) McGuinn, also a future Byrd, was there with his twelve-string guitar, wearing a suit, sporting a goatee, and playing Beatles songs. McGuinn wasn't performing that night, though. The Fifth Estate was the kind of place where people just sat around, played, and traded songs. I was telling a few people that one of my dreams was to see Hollywood and Vine, so they piled me into a car and we drove down Sunset to Hollywood Boulevard. We smoked some dope and drove around all four blocks that circumvented the famous intersection. I not only got to see Hollywood and Vine—I saw it from every direction. The night was relatively young—for musicians, that is—and we weren't through driving around yet, so with me in full tourist mode, my head practically out the window, and while listening to Henry Mancini's "Moon River" on the car radio, we drove through the Hollywood Hills just when dawn was breaking.

Stefan and I joined up with local young guitar wizard Ry Cooder, and the three of us played the Ash Grove as the Gramercy Park Sheiks, a name that Stefan and I had already used back in New York when we were joined by Eric Kaz (later of the Blues Magoos and American Flyer). I added harmonica to my instrumental credits, courtesy of John Sebastian. The Ash Grove's owner, Ed Pearl, had an apartment that was available for us to stay in at no charge. We roomed with Mississippi John Hurt, who had been playing the club the week before us.

John was one of the gentlest, most down-to-earth people I've ever known. I thought I might have impregnated the girl that I had stayed with in Berkeley, and John would spend evenings assuring me that everything would come out all right. He made me feel good, just like his songs. When you see pictures of him, almost all with that patented playful smile, you know that's exactly what Mississippi John Hurt was like: a lovable and wise old man with the talent of a giant.

One day I volunteered to drive John to Union Station so he could catch a train to a gig. The only car available was a borrowed early-'50s

Chevy with a stick shift. I didn't know how to drive a stick, so was relieved when, like a bucking bronco, we finally made it to the top of an embankment adjacent to the station. I panicked and almost drove over the cliff and headlong into the station's parking lot. Had I not braked in time, I would have probably gone down in music history as the man who killed Mississippi John Hurt.

I wasn't crazy about Los Angeles, certainly not after a magical visit to the Bay Area. LA was too spread out, too cosmopolitan, and Hollywood was populated by too many immigrants of the heartland who longed for stardom but were doomed to anonymity. I felt as if every person was a child of the Dust Bowl, a character out of Nathanael West's *The Day of the Locust*; nothing wrong with that, but aesthetically, politically, and intellectually, I had fallen in love with the Bay Area. I always felt that the beauty of any city was tested by rainy days. Both New York and Paris take on a certain beauty in the rain. San Francisco is one of those cities; Los Angeles is not. I took a TWA Constellation back to New York late that September and rejoined my classes, but not for long. I had given myself a taste of the road, and it was now official: I had to be a musician.

<hr>

The first of my three LSD trips happened at the Adelaar farmhouse in Wiccopee, New York, a rural community about two hours north of Manhattan. Karen Adelaar grew up with my sister-in-law Ann and was crazy, as was the rest of her dysfunctional family, a sort of early '60s version of *The Royal Tenenbaums*. Karen and her friends loved to experiment with drugs, especially pills and psychedelics, and they had access to some of the finest Sandoz LSD that ever was exported from Switzerland.

In those days, one had a "pilot" if one was tripping for the first time—someone who took you through the various stages of your "trip" and made sure you were okay. I was lying on the living room floor with two detachable speakers from a portable hi-fi attached to either ear, watching the ceiling turn into the Sistine Chapel, and listening to Dylan's *Bringing It All Back Home*, when my appointed pilot, a fellow traveler by the name of Bob Armel, asked if I wanted to take a hike up the mountain. He wanted to bring a couple of axes with us to chop down a tree. *Of course, Bob, why not? Better to chop down a tree than to throw up for the second time today from my LSD-induced anxiety while watching paramecia float around the bathroom wallpaper.*

So up the hill we went, Bob taking one side of a tree and me the other. After a couple of whacks, I heard Bob whispering to himself, but I couldn't immediately make out what he saying, until it grew louder and I heard *This is for you, Mom.* Whack! *This is for you, Dad.* Whack!

Whoa! This was the last thing I needed to hear, especially in my state. I ran like hell down the mountain—not an easy task, considering that I was turning into a lobster and swimming three feet off the ground.

July 25, 1965, was the day that Bob Dylan played the Seventh Annual Newport Folk Festival with an electric band, shocking everyone who had come to hear his earlier work. Never mind the myth of the outrage; it had now become permissible for the rest of us folkies to experiment with electric guitars and amps. We went from folk to folk-rock; from acoustic blues to the urban electric blues of mid-century Chicago. Bands like the Lovin' Spoonful, the Blues Magoos, the Magicians, the Flying Machine (with James Taylor), and Circus Maximus (with Jerry Jeff Walker) were popping up all over the Village at places like the Night Owl Cafe, the Cafe Bizarre, the Cafe Wha, and the Cafe au Go Go. The streets of the Village, especially Bleecker, MacDougal, and West Fourth, were congested with traffic and kids from the outer suburbs of Long Island, Westchester, and New Jersey.

In only a few years, the aromas of the Village had changed. In the summer of 1965, the streets smelled of incense, falafel, espresso, pot, urine, patchouli oil, and cigarette smoke. The coffeehouses were going stronger than ever, most substituting rock for Beat poetry, and some, like the Figaro, still entrenched in the more-traditional world of chess and cappuccino. Musicians passed baskets in the funkier clubs while some were actually paid a wage, or at least *promised* to be paid a wage.

Greenwich Village during the summer weekends of 1965 was a circus. Every club and cafe was a sideshow, every street and alley a midway of freaks. By Monday the locals took back their inherently Italian neighborhood until the next weekend, when the cycle of wannabe hippies, suburban teenagers, freaks, drug addicts, and musicians would once again converge. But on a Saturday night, you could have gone to the Bleecker Street Cinema or the Garrick Theatre to see some of the more-obscure foreign films, or you could have hung out with some of the locals like poet Ed Sanders of the Fugs, who, with his long scraggly hair, T-shirt, and bell-bottoms, would be out on Mac-Dougal Street between sets, rubbing his crotch, trying to impress high school girls from New Jersey who drove to Manhattan to see what all the fuss was about.

CHAPTER 2

Is This Any Way to Earn a Living?

I WAS BACK IN SCHOOL AT C. W. POST IN LONG ISLAND AND TEACH-ing guitar on Saturdays at Fretted Instruments. I had taken over the guitar-teaching job from David Bennett Cohen, who'd gone out to Berkeley and eventually joined Country Joe and the Fish. Danny Kalb, an acquaintance, and another one of Dave Van Ronk's "prized" pupils, had a reputation as one of the best acoustic guitar players in New York. Danny had already played on some seminal folk music albums by Phil Ochs and Judy Collins and was featured on Elektra's anthology LP of white-boy blues, *The Blues Project* (1964). He was also a member of Dave Van Ronk's jug band, the Ragtime Jug Stompers. Musically, Danny and I came from pretty much the same place, both with a deep appreciation for country blues and traditional folk music, but also with a festering love for rock and roll.

Originally from Mount Vernon, New York, just north of Manhattan in Westchester County, Danny Kalb and his brother Jonathan, also a blues guitarist, grew up within the context of their parents' stormy relationship and political influence. They were raised as "red diaper babies," a term attributed to the offspring of leftists and communists from the 1940s and '50s. Danny's own leftist proclivities and domestic upbringing would help to mold his personality. Danny felt that the "people's cause" manifested itself in music. As a musician and as a social advocate, Danny found direction for his life in the blues, and through the blues and his unadulterated but less than pragmatic view of politics, Danny has lived most of his life. As stubborn as a mule and as pigheaded as a rhinoceros, in the 1990s he made a complete about-face and embraced American conservatism without losing any of the eccentricities that had defined him to his often confused and frustrated friends. He even participated in one of the historic Freedom Rides of the early '60s civil rights movement. Ironically, his bus only got as far as Baltimore.

Years later Danny and I performed together at a benefit to raise money for Dave Van Ronk's medical bills when Dave was hospitalized with emphysema. Pete Seeger was also on the bill. Pete's lovely wife, Toshi, approached Danny toward the end of the evening and said, "Danny, how come you're not talking to Pete? He'd love to say hello to you." Danny replied, "I don't talk to Communists."

His new band, formed in March 1965, was called the Danny Kalb Quartet, with Danny on lead guitar and vocals, Andy Kulberg on bass, Roy Blumenfeld on drums, and Artie Traum on rhythm guitar. Danny and Roy had grown up together in Mount Vernon and were close friends from high school. Roy was tall and ruggedly handsome, a gentle giant, great mime, and, like the rest of us, totally out of his mind. Andy was from Buffalo and the only band member with formal musical training and some common sense. The band had been booked at the Gaslight and was about to play the Night Owl Cafe on West Third Street, where they would open for the Lovin' Spoonful.

The Quartet broke up in June, just after they had signed with the prestigious William Morris Agency. Danny had suddenly decided to take the summer off and travel to London and Paris, where he would perform at various folk clubs. Around the end of August, the William Morris Agency sent Danny a telegram, probably because there was the possibility of a record deal for the band. Danny returned from England and got together again with Roy and Andy, but Artie Traum had also gone to Europe that summer and showed no signs of returning. Danny needed a replacement, possibly permanently.

For me, this was when Danny Kalb's thought processes began to emerge. Through most of his life, Danny, as brilliant as he was, would make decisions based on his heart and not his brain. Although musicians are infamous for their lack of practical thought, Danny Kalb, through his own unique brand of abstract idealism, became a model of stubborn righteousness and warped logic. So, hanging out one afternoon in September 1965 at Fretted Instruments, and hardly ever hearing me play a note, Danny Kalb asked me to audition as Artie Traum's replacement.

I was playing my beloved Gibson J-200 at the time, the guitar that I had worked all summer for in the record department of Korvettes—the guitar that Bob Dylan had borrowed from me one night to play a song on the Bob Fass Show on WBAI; the guitar that Reverend Gary Davis one day told me had a lovely blond color when I was convinced that Gary was totally blind. I had never played an electric guitar, so I made some inquiries, borrowed a DeArmond pickup from a friend, stuck it in my guitar's sound hole, and, one Saturday afternoon at the beginning of fall, walked up the block to the Night Owl Cafe where on the marquee I saw "The Danny Kalb Quartet Featuring Tom Jones." Wow, I thought, from *What's New, Pussycat* to this dumpy old bar. What happened to *this* guy's career? As it turned out, this particular Tom Jones was actually the stage name of Tommy Flanders, the new vocalist Danny had hired, and who had previously performed on the Cambridge, Massachusetts, rock 'n' roll circuit as a member of Tom Jones and the Trolls with Lowell Levinger, later "Banana" of the Youngbloods. Tommy was a mystery and, unlike the rest of us, was not Jewish, which only added to his mystique. I never found out where Tommy ever lived or where he had come from; he would just show up at one of our apartments on any given day, take a shower, and leave (although he was always polite about it).

I was introduced to the band and then set up with a little help from Danny, who, unlike myself, knew how to plug a guitar into an amp and turn the dials. Only later did I realize that that was about *all* Danny knew about electric guitars. Unbeknownst to me, the volume knob on my pickup was already set at ten, as was the amp I was to plug into. I was almost blown into the back of the room.

Before I played my first note, I had discovered the first rule of electric music: You get something called "feedback" if you raise the volume without keeping your hand on the strings. If the volume is really high, however, keeping your hands on the strings won't make a bit of difference. For those who know their instrument well, the pros, there is something called "controlled feedback" where, by physically positioning yourself in front of the amp, you bend the feedback to your own will within a creative context. Jimi Hendrix was a master of controlled feedback. I was not.

I was scared to death. I had never played an electric guitar, nor had I ever sat in with musicians who played anything other than mandolins and kazoos, though I did know some of the basic electric blues riffs that all of us folkies were playing at the time, like "High Heel Sneakers." I turned my volume down a bit, but it made no difference. Even though I avoided the feedback, the very power of the sound coming out of the amp was so frightening and uncomfortable that I eventually turned my volume down to zero and pretended to play for the rest of the set. Danny came up to me at the end of rehearsal and told me how much he liked my playing. I got the job. I might as well have been stuffing falafels next door for all Danny actually had heard, but as in so many other circumstances, Danny fantasized what he wanted to hear, probably because he liked me. That's what was so frustrating about Danny Kalb: heart over brain. I've always liked him for it, but at the same time, and on many occasions since, I've wanted to wring his neck for that very reason.

When I auditioned for the band, the Night Owl marquee still had the old name of "The Danny Kalb Quartet Featuring Tom Jones," but Danny had already decided to change the name of the band. After

Tommy Flanders and I got the job, Danny expropriated the name of the Elektra album he had played on earlier, and we became the Blues Project. When we played together for the first time at the Night Owl in October of 1965, we were billed as "The Blues Project Featuring Danny Kalb and Tom Flanders." Opening for us were the Magicians, with Garry Bonner and Alan Gordon, who went on to write "Happy Together" for the Turtles.

I traded in my J-200 for a Guild solid-body electric, purchased from Henry at Manny's Music uptown on Forty-Eighth Street. Manny's was the place where musicians would spend hours trying out guitars, drums, amps, picks, keyboards, and whatever else made sounds. Mingled in were the straight union guys, direct from Roseland, getting reeds, mouthpieces, brushes, and whatever else the *professional* musician would need. It was a place where young musicians could meet in the daytime and not be verbally abused for their long hair and multicolored wardrobes. Our white pallor from smoking lots of cigarettes and dope and staying up late was accepted here, and we loved Henry for his tolerance and humor.

My new Guild electric had a novelty accessory built into it. Because I was so naive about electric guitars, I was very impressed with the "E" tone that the guitar emitted when you pushed a button, to tune along to, something that might come in handy when you needed to tune fast onstage. I brought my new Guild with the "E" tone to rehearsal, figuring that not only could I tune to it, but Danny and Andy could tune to it as well. I'd impress the bell-bottoms off of these guys. Problem was, the "E" tone wasn't even close to a real "E," so back it went to Manny's for a good old Les Paul. I returned downtown to where we rehearsed, in the grungy old basement of the Albert Hotel on University Place, between Tenth and Eleventh Streets, a space we shared with James Taylor, and where we jammed one afternoon with the great Mose Allison.

I was still living with my parents, commuting to school during the week, and driving into the city on weekends, when the moment of truth finally arrived. The Blues Project had a gig out of town, in a bar, somewhere north of Boston. I was to turn in a paper the following Monday on Yeats and his Byzantium poems. I had a new girlfriend who was exotically British. We had met during her fourth month of pregnancy. No problem; as long as she was female, I was happy. I loved smoking pot and playing with the band. Being onstage and creating music with other musicians was an absolutely intoxicating experience. My obsessive nerd persona was in remission, and like a pimple about to burst, I blindly began to follow my libido. My decision was a no-brainer. To hell with Yeats; I was having too good a time. To my parents' disappointment, I quit school and chose a career in rock and roll.

I still had short hair, but I knew that style had to change if I was going to be in a rock band. I let my hair grow, but there was a problem: One of my sideburns was longer than the other by at least half an inch. I decided to let the one sideburn go untrimmed and wait for the other one to catch up. I figured that people only look at one side of a head at a time anyway and wouldn't notice the difference. Plus, I could always pose for promotional photos from the side with the longer sideburn. I found that having mismatched sideburns was not a problem until one day I saw myself in the mirror and realized just how crazy this was and how stupid I looked, so I balanced the sideburns myself.

Not long afterward, I gave myself a haircut for the first time. First, I tried to balance the front. As I cut, I kept noticing that the balance was off and that I wasn't cutting a straight line, so I kept cutting until the line was finally straight. The result: bangs. But not just any bangs—really *short* bangs. I looked ridiculous, but this time there was nothing I could do if I wanted the rest of me to have long hair. In the end, I finally decided to give up self-barbering and stuck to playing the guitar.

As the band grew, so did my role in it. There were some songs that needed harmonica, and so I took advantage of what John Sebastian had taught me when we were together in the Even Dozen Jug Band.

I had already been playing harp with Stefan and Ry, so I purchased some new harmonicas at Manny's and played them on a number of songs. I also started writing, not so much for the band, but for myself. I loved experimenting with open tunings.

In most open tunings, the guitar is tuned to an open chord, such as G major or D major, and sounds good just by strumming it, without holding any notes or chords. There are exceptions, like the popular and very beautiful DADGAD tuning that you will frequently find in Celtic folk arrangements. Most country blues guitarists of the 1930s used open tunings as well as standard tunings. An open tuning affords a player more opportunity for experimentation and fretboard control, and more easily facilitated slide, or bottleneck, playing. Robert Johnson, Bukka White, Son House, and Skip James used open tunings often, as did many more guitarists in a later rock context. Joni Mitchell proved to be most adept at writing songs in open tunings. The feeling of her songs verges on free-floating, yet they are controlled, unlike some of the excellent and hypnotic open-tune ramblings of guitarists who became intoxicated by Indian sitar music.

The Blues Project turned out to be a perfect vehicle for our few original songs. We didn't want to cover other people's songs exclusively, and so we decided to take advantage of the cultural freedoms that were becoming more and more available to us. I sang a little, played blues harp, rhythm guitar, a little lead, and now I began to write. As rhythm guitarist, I was laying the foundation for Danny to play his leads and to vamp behind Tommy's vocals. We felt we were ready to record, and so we took the next steps toward that goal. The only thing missing was a keyboard player.

Tom Wilson, a staff producer at Columbia Records who was responsible for Simon & Garfunkel's hit "The Sound of Silence," liked the Blues Project and decided to put us in the studio for a demo in late October 1965. Although we called ourselves a "blues" band, the song of choice for our demo was Eric Andersen's folk-rock ballad "Violets of Dawn." Danny and I, fingerpickers at heart, came up with a two-guitar arpeggio line that worked nicely within the arrangement.

Since we were missing a keyboard player, Tom asked his friend Al Kooper to play on our session. In those days we had only so many tracks on which to record and very little time to do it. We decided that acoustic piano would be the best fit. The problem was that piano and guitar, especially the way we were playing them, are essentially percussive instruments. When you have three parts playing arpeggios at the same time, somebody's got to pare down, so the piano, not yet an integral part of the band, was chosen as the session's sacrificial lamb. Kooper pared his part down to a few chords, and it seemed to work, except for the fact that the guitars were out of tune with the piano. Kooper had to play the part again to a readjusted tape speed.

Al Kooper started his professional career as a member of the Royal Teens in 1959, but never recorded with the band. In 1965, Al and his writing partner, Irwin Levine, went on to write the Gary Lewis and the Playboys hit "This Diamond Ring." Tom Wilson invited Al, who was doing session work at the time, to attend Bob Dylan's *Highway 61* recording sessions. Although he was asked to come as a guest, Al wound up playing organ, which became an integral part of Dylan's "Like a Rolling Stone." A master of self-promotion, Al has received more mileage out of that one organ part than most rock groups get throughout their entire careers. I didn't know then that our destinies would be linked, but beyond self-promotion, I was soon to find out that Al was also a master of condescension, whose effect on my own vulnerability would follow me throughout my career like the ghost of Yom Kippur Past.

Ultimately, Columbia passed on our demo, Kooper joined the band full-time, and an executive at MGM Records, Jerry Schoenbaum, who bore an uncanny resemblance to the German conductor Herbert von Karajan, signed us to a new spin-off MGM label, Verve/Folkways. Tom Wilson moved over to MGM and began working with Eric Burdon and the Animals, and us, almost as an afterthought. Other artists who were eventually signed to the new label were Tim Hardin, Richie Havens, and Laura Nyro. With the exception of Laura, Verve/Folkways signed mainly folk- or folk-blues-oriented acts that were playing around Greenwich Village at the time. It was time to move on from the Night Owl Cafe to a club with more class, where people would come to see *us* and not just the Village freak show out on the street.

Lenny Bruce had played the Cafe au Go Go, a few blocks away on Bleecker Street, the year before we began our internship as "house band." Both Lenny Bruce and owner Howard Solomon were arrested for obscenity charges. All of New York's hip elite artists and writers were up in arms over what was an obvious case of harassment and attempted censorship by the New York City Police Department. Petitions were signed by Woody Allen, Bob Dylan, Allen Ginsberg, James Baldwin, and Norman Mailer, among others. Howard Solomon's conviction was eventually overturned, but Lenny Bruce never lived to see the day that he was finally exonerated. In the fall of 1965, the Cafe au Go Go was where the Blues Project set up its not too impressive gear and took up residence. Our first run there (also the first with Al Kooper in the band) was from November 9 to November 21. Our opening acts included a couple of young comedians, Richard Pryor and George Carlin.

The Cafe au Go Go was an amazing venue in an amazing time. There were so many legendary acts that played or jammed there that, in retrospect, it made Woodstock look like a Saturday-afternoon picnic in Wichita Falls. The Grateful Dead, Eric Clapton, Junior Wells, Otis Spann, B.B. King, Jefferson Airplane, Jimi Hendrix, Bill Evans, Stan Getz, Van Morrison, Tim Hardin, Tim Buckley, Joni Mitchell, Judy Collins, Howlin' Wolf, Muddy Waters, Fred Neil, Richie Havens, Bo Diddley, The Youngbloods, the Paul Butterfield Blues Band, Cream, the Chambers Brothers, Canned Heat, The Fugs, Odetta, Country Joe and the Fish, Lightnin' Hopkins—they all played at this one fairly small club on Bleecker Street within a one-year period, and I was there for most of it, either onstage, backstage, or on the sidelines, a cigarette in one hand and an ice-cream soda in the other.

The room we played in was actually just a basement. You walked downstairs and found yourself in the lobby and, a little further on, in a long room with tables, chairs, a single aisle, and, to the left, a stage right in front of a brick wall. The sound, oddly enough, was much better than one would have expected. None of that helped, however, when you were playing with Danny Kalb and Al Kooper, both of whom were simultaneously trying to hit notes that didn't exist. Sometimes it was like a prizefight onstage, or like a Punch and Judy show—Danny on guitar and Al on his shrill Farfisa organ, both hitting each other over the head with as many notes as possible, whether they were the right notes or not.

In their rush to be the fastest and the loudest musicians in Manhattan, Danny and Al would make some pretty hideous noises, mostly in the higher registers. I would look out into the seats and see people grinning and mouthing phrases like "Far out!," "Wow!," and "Incredible!" Andy and Roy and I would look at each other in utter disbelief and horror as this auditory clash of egos and wrong notes played out in front of our very ears. What was even scarier and more ironic was that the Cafe au Go Go didn't even have a liquor license, and you can be sure that the audiences in those days were not high on the excellent but overpriced ice-cream sodas and banana splits that Howard offered.

In an attempt to capture the feel of our live performance and to also save a bunch of money, Verve/Folkways and *Cavalier* magazine, a *Playboy* wannabe, sponsored a weeklong concert event at the Cafe au Go Go, advertised as "The Blues Bag," which they held during Thanksgiving week of 1965. The artists were the Blues Project, Big Joe Williams, Judy Roderick, David Blue, Son House, Bukka White, Skip James, Eric Andersen, John Hammond Jr., John Lee Hooker,

Geoff Muldaur, Buzzy Linhart, T. Bone Walker, Barbara Dane, and Fred Neil, with none other than Izzy Young as emcee. Unbelievably, we were the headliners. We were the ones that were going to bring in those suburban white kids who were just beginning to acquire an awareness of the blues but didn't know Muddy Waters from a black cat bone. Ironically, we hardly played traditional blues at all. Of the young bands, traditional blues was the domain of the Paul Butterfield Blues Band. When it came to playing in the style of the masters, no band did it better.

Verve/Folkways recorded the event, but due to contractual restrictions, it was never released as a Blues Bag album. Instead, the tapes of our performances were held in storage until we returned from Los Angeles, where we were to play at the annual MGM Records convention. MGM put us up at the Beverly Hilton Hotel, a luxury none of us were used to. They wined and dined us, gave us a private screening of *Dr. Zhivago* and a tour of the MGM lot. On this trip we taped our first television appearance, *The Lloyd Thaxton Show*. We did "Hoochie Coochie Man" and "Back Door Man," and shared the bill with Del Shannon of "Runaway" fame. I became friendly with Danny Hutton, later of Three Dog Night. Danny was a solo MGM artist at the time and made the charts with a song called "Roses and Rainbows."

There was trouble brewing, however. Tommy, our lead singer and potential teen idol, acquired a new girlfriend, a tiny blonde motormouth by the name of Maxine. Maxine liked to come to band meetings and represent Tommy's interests. Tommy wanted to be treated as a separate entity within the band. He wanted top billing, and did not want to contribute to band expenses. Tommy wanted to be a star, and it didn't help that we were in Hollywood when all of this went down. This must have been the birth of rock-star girlfriend interference, later to afflict everyone from the Beatles to Spinal Tap. They should have put up a statue.

I took it upon myself, with help from some of the other band members, to get rid of Maxine—not in the *Sopranos* sense, because that would have been too easy. The plan was to fix Tommy up with a gorgeous girl and have Maxine somehow find out. Where were we going to find the girl? There were plenty of groupies around, but we were from out of town. How would we know we had the right girl for the job? It was all terribly devious and perfectly sexist in a way most hippies would never ever cop to, but those were the times. Sex and love were a lot easier back then.

It was decided that I would have to audition her. And that was how I met Kathy Crane, a beautiful, blonde sixteen-year-old who was a roommate of one of Donovan's girlfriends, "the girl-child Linda," aka Linda Lawrence, ex-girlfriend of Brian Jones of the Rolling Stones. Kathy and I spent a night together and became good friends. I was smitten. No way was I going to give her to Tommy. So it was good-bye Maxine *and* good-bye Tommy Flanders.

We were getting to deadline time and MGM needed an album right away while we were trying to reinvent ourselves without Tommy. Kooper and I were going to have to do a lot more singing. It was decided to keep some of Tommy's tracks for a second side and record a whole new set of songs for the first side, but we had to record live. Verve/Folkways had already invested in the Blues Bag tapes, and so the album had to at least sound somewhat like the same band. They certainly didn't want to come up with the money to put us in the studio. Anyway, we didn't have enough material yet to fill out a whole second side, so we recorded the other half of the album on January 29–30, 1966, when the band opened for Oscar Brown Jr. We invited a bunch of kids in for our audience and played a set while a remote truck was upstairs on Bleecker Street, recording our show.

And there it was, our first album: *The Blues Project Live at the Cafe au Go Go* (featuring Tommy Flanders), released in April of 1966—one half with Tommy Flanders at the Blues Bag, and the other half with five confused young Jews who, without a great lead singer, and despite our parents' protestations, were desperately trying to eke out a living in rock and roll.

———

The Blues Project was like a brotherhood—a micro-minyan of five dysfunctional lunatics, but a brotherhood nonetheless. It was a snake pit of neuroses and pent-up frustration, five barely adult musicians who had nothing more in common than their Jewishness and their love of the blues.

We brought out the best and the worst in each other. Whether we liked each other or not, the five of us lived through bad gigs, poor pay, and some major disappointments, the result of which was a bonding of sorts, with music as our common denominator and public acceptance our common goal. Except for Tommy, we were all indeed Jewish, but none of us was religious or had even considered that we were bonding for that reason. Rehearsals and meetings had become family feuds, complete with much yelling and rending of garments, and at some point, whether it was because they went to see James Coburn in *The President's Analyst*, or because it was just the zeitgeist of hip psychotherapy, or some inbred Jewish need to lie on a couch and talk, we decided we needed professional help.

In my later band, Blood, Sweat & Tears, if someone left, we hired a sub. It was that simple. With a group that had such complex personalities as the Blues Project, all someone had to do was *threaten* to leave and we would enter group therapy, so that's exactly what we did. There, we would discuss our profound problems, such as who was taking overly long solos ("chronic masturbation"), who was playing louder than the others ("chronic attention deficit disorder"), who was getting laid and who wasn't ("chronic insecurity"), who was getting the better pot (ditto), and, most of all, what was the artistic and commercial future of the band (the age-old story of integrity versus selling out, although truth be told, after much protesting as to the purity of our blues mission, all of us would have turned 180 degrees on a dime for a hit single).

The problems between Al and me began manifesting themselves around this time, although I don't believe that Kooper was even aware of them. Al condescended to everyone in the band. At rehearsals his suggestions were not just suggestions, they were dictums. Danny fought back, and I accepted them by crawling into a shell. After all, Al was the experienced one and I was the neophyte. Who was I to argue? The problem, though, was that Al never approached his demands as a teacher. He would lash out like a hurt child who was not getting his way because of the "buffoons" that he had to work with—namely anyone, no matter their talent, who shared a stage or studio with him. Sadly, I let him get under my skin. It made me self-conscious and unsure of my own talent, and it would continue throughout our relationship.

Danny Kalb was already seeing Arthur Eaton, a proto-hippie psychologist with an office on Fifth Avenue—the apex of hipster headshrinkers. Arthur would hand out joints and we would get high. He even held some private sessions with Andy's wife, Phyllis. Word was that Phyllis and Arthur would hold hands during the sessions (and maybe more), but if it was true, I didn't really want to know. We had a couple of group sessions, but pretty soon we were becoming belligerent, although not at each other. We began to tell Arthur to mind his own business. We turned on him, stomped over him, and trundled out the door, cured. It turned out to be much more fun to take our problems out on each other.

In those days guitarists were thought of like gunslingers were in the Old West. Arguments developed over beers and bongs all over the Village as to who was the fastest, the most articulate, who had the best chops and the most sought-after riffs. We played one weekend at the au Go Go with the Paul Butterfield Blues Band, and half the wannabe blues-guitar players in New York came to see if Mike Bloomfield or Danny Kalb was going to win the shoot-out on Allen Street.

We all knew by then that where Danny may have been the fastest, it was certainly Mike Bloomfield who was the tastiest. July 3, 1966, the last night of our gig together, turned into a jam session between the two bands and anybody else in town who might want to sit in, but you had to have credentials. Everybody who was anybody would come down to the au Go Go or up to Steve Paul's Scene late at night for a jam session, but this night was special. Bloomfield and Kalb were up onstage trading solos, and who should come downtown and join them onstage in the middle of this jam, this Olympic guitar summit? *B.B. King!* The audience went wild, and after an orgy of twelve-bar blues-guitar solos, B.B. played *one note!* One high, beautifully phrased, perfectly placed note. Game over.

I used to spend my afternoons between rehearsals at either the Bleecker Street Cinema or the Garrick Theatre. Both theaters were practically adjoining the Cafe au Go Go, and so, since I was on friendly terms with management at both theaters, I was allowed to walk in and watch movies anytime I pleased. For a whole year I watched movies in spurts, one scene here and another scene there, and not necessarily in any kind of order. Whenever my movie trivia skills are tested, when it comes to European cinema of the early and mid-'60s, I consider myself a near expert, as long as I'm not asked about the plot.

Most of the time that year, before the Tin Angel opened above it, the Dugout, across the street, was where we would have dinner and then return for beers after the show. The Dugout had the best burgers and the biggest draft beers in town for the money, and it was there that I first fell in love with french fries with vinegar. The Dugout also had a great jukebox, although we could never figure out which employee was driving us all crazy by playing Barbra Streisand's "People" over and over again. To this day, whenever I hear "People," like Pavlov's dog, I rush out and get myself a hamburger, fries, a beer, and a bottle of vinegar. Whether you were playing or just hanging out at the Cafe au Go Go across the street, or the Bitter End next door, where you could see Woody Allen, Bill Cosby, or Joan Rivers—and where, one Sunday afternoon, the world stopped to listen to a poetry reading by Cassius Clay—eventually you made it to the Dugout. It was the place to be, unless you ventured crosstown and up to Max's Kansas City at Union Square, where Andy Warhol and the Velvet Underground would hold court in the back room.

One of my fondest memories of our time at the Cafe au Go Go came late one afternoon when I had arrived early for a gig after watching a few scenes of *Jules and Jim* at the Bleecker Street Cinema. I walked down the stairs and went directly to the men's room. Standing in front of the urinal doing my thing, I heard someone in a stall talking to himself. My God, it was Bobby Kennedy! What was Bobby Kennedy doing in a stall in the men's room of the Cafe au Go Go at four in the afternoon?

I rushed out and told Howard Solomon that Robert F. Kennedy was talking to himself in a stall in the men's room. "Oh no," Howard laughed, "it's David Frye, the impersonator. He's your opening act tonight." I felt relieved, especially because David Frye wasn't practicing his soon-to-be-famous impersonation of Richard Nixon at the same time. I couldn't bear the thought of Bobby Kennedy and Nixon in the same stall together, even if it *was* in Greenwich Village.

In the late winter of 1966, the Blues Project was booked for our first gigs beyond the Hudson River. The initial show was in Pittsburgh, where we were to open for Stan Getz. We came, uncomfortably, by train, schlepping all of our equipment with us. We got to the gig late, so instead of opening the show, Stan Getz opened for *us*. He was not a happy man, and I couldn't blame him.

We then had two college gigs, back to back—one at Swarthmore College in Philadelphia and the other at Antioch, a small college that we had never heard of, in a state that we barely knew existed. We piled into a rental car and Andy's Volkswagen station wagon with our manager, Jeff Chase, and drove all day without stopping. We spent the whole trip smoking dope, and as we arrived at the venue, the college looked more like a ghost town than a school. That it was a bleak and wintry day only added to the aura. We finally found someone who directed us to the school's auditorium, where we settled ourselves into the backstage area and its adjoining restrooms.

All five of us were gathered around the toilet bowl, passing a joint and laughing about how we were the hippest people in Yellow Springs—or so we thought. Our proximity to the toilet was no accident, and while we were only a flush away from avoiding the gulags of Ohio, we were happy to be out of New York, if only for a few days. We were to be onstage in less than an hour and we were tired from the trip, but we were never too tired to play. Being high only made us laugh even harder at the concept of us ultra-hip New Yorkers having to play our music for what we assumed would be a bunch of Midwestern hicks with pompadours and corsages. These kids were not going to understand our sound. We had long hair. We were from New York City. We had thoughts, ideas, politics. We had even been inside of *museums*. We were sitting around a toilet getting stoned and we were just too hip for the local populace, meaning, of course, the entire Midwestern United States.

After a brief sound check and some more dope, we politely tiptoed back onstage. The curtain in front of us was closed so we could not yet see out into the hall. It didn't matter. We would flatten the pompadours and astound the corsages right off of these kids. As we stood there, practically in the dark, still stoned, still chuckling condescendingly at the audience we were about to encounter, I noticed some funny sounds on the other side of the curtain. There was a restless kind of activity that seemed unfamiliar, strange, like the sound of boiling water before it reaches its peak, or a giant sperm whale just before it surfaces. Then it happened.

The curtain opened.

What I first saw were the kaleidoscopes, and beyond the kaleidoscopes, people, kids, naked, half-naked, long-haired, short-haired, clothed, painted, red-eyed and dancing, even though we hadn't yet played our first note. We were looking straight out into what seemed like a freak-out party scene in a bad hippie exploitation film. The entire audience was completely stoned on acid and happy as a group of twisted larks.

Our opening song was Muddy Waters's "Louisiana Blues." Danny played a four-bar intro on the guitar as the rest of us joined in. We were like a locomotive picking up steam. I played harmonica with my left hand while banging a tambourine against my thigh with my right. Danny Kalb sang and parried his trademark guitar solos with Al Kooper's manic Farfisa organ as we dissected and psychedelically interpreted one of Muddy's many monumental creations. The crazier our music, the happier these kids were.

We continued our set with a ballad that I had written and that our record company decided to call "Steve's Song." I had originally entitled it "September Fifth," but just as our second album, *Projections*, was submitted to the record company, our manager, Jeff Chase, received a phone call from someone in MGM's art department.

"Hi, Jeff. We have everything—the master tapes, the artwork—but we're missing one thing. What's the name of the second song on the first side?"

Jeff, who had forgotten the name of my song, replied in a low thoughtful whisper, almost off-phone, "Let's see—second song, first side, second song, first side." Then, louder: "Oh! You mean *Steve's* song!"

"Good enough. Thanks, Jeff," the person said and hung up.

Rule number one: Never let a friend or family member be your manager. Jeff Chase was a friend of Danny's, and his job was about a thousand miles over his head. So, for the rest of my life, I've had to bear the question, "Aren't you the guy who wrote 'Steve's Song'?" And my answer: "Right . . . I'm Steve."

Chase later went on to cash my royalty checks for "Steve's Song." It went on for years, until we were able to track him down in the early '90s with the threat of legal action. I never did get the money back.

By now the shock of what we were looking at from the stage was beginning to wear off as we launched into Blind Willie Johnson's "Lord, I Just Can't Keep from Crying." Our version was crazy and manic. It was fast and it was loud and the kids were getting wilder. I could have sworn that more clothes were coming off, more kaleidoscopes were coming out, and that these kids were just beginning to peak. We were not only right there with them, we were feeding the frenzy.

Our next song, "Caress Me, Baby," a slow blues tune by Jimmy Reed, had Danny singing "Let me lay you across my big brass bed." For me, as funny as the image was, these kids ate it up. Jimmy Reed was another one of the great Chicago blues musicians who simultaneously played guitar and bent high notes on his harmonica, his trademark. As with Muddy Waters, we had worked together often. In our version, I played a low mandolin-like tremolo rhythm guitar. It was slow-dancing time, and I remember that as I looked down, I was thinking it might be more fun to be in the audience than onstage, dancing with some of the cuter topless coeds.

After "Caress Me, Baby," we moved on to an Al Kooper instrumental, "Flute Thing." This was one of our more popular pieces, and one of the highest-rotated tracks on album-oriented radio in the '60s. Kooper wrote it around a jazz coda that most musicians would play at "straight" or jazz venues. The phrase was used to end songs, and Al was clever enough to use it as a song unto itself. Andy, our bass player, switched to flute and I played bass. Andy's flute went through a machine called an Echoplex, where he was able to program long tape loops and essentially accompany himself live, the equivalent of two or more flutes playing at a time. Andy's flute and Echoplex combination was one of the early milestones of what has come to be called New

Age music. The kids at Antioch had never heard anything like it. They put aside their kaleidoscopes for the eight minutes or so of "Flute Thing" and just grooved to the music.

Depending on the venue and the number of shows required, I would sing a song by my friend Patrick Sky, called "Love Will Endure," or a Bob Lind song, "Cheryl's Goin' Home," or Donovan's beautiful "Catch the Wind." I began singing "Catch the Wind" one night at the Cafe au Go Go when the pedal on Roy's bass drum broke and we desperately had to fill time. I loved the song and spontaneously started singing it. By the second verse, Roy's pedal was replaced, the whole band had joined in, and it became part of our repertoire.

Danny next sang Chuck Berry's great road song, "You Can't Catch Me."

We worked with Chuck a couple of times. The first time was in December 1965 at the Village Theatre on Second Avenue, between Sixth and Seventh Streets, before it became the Fillmore East. We were to open his show and then back him up, but true to his reputation, Chuck never made it to rehearsal. After our last song, Chuck came prancing out onstage playing his "Brown-Eyed Handsome Man" as we went into a panic, trying to figure out what key he was in. Chuck loved to humiliate his pickup bands in this manner, but it was great practice for a bunch of kids like us to learn within seconds how to play his repertoire, especially when the master himself was doing his patented duck walk no more than four feet in front of us.

Our last song at Antioch was a Kooper-adapted spiritual called "Wake Me, Shake Me." This was our trademark audience rouser, a loud, fast gospel tune that had the few kids who weren't on their feet up and dancing and singing along.

One of the interesting things about the Blues Project was that if we were having a good time with an up-tempo song, it would get faster as it went on, but, conversely, if we did a slow blues, depending on how far Danny got into it emotionally, it would get slower and slower. "Two Trains Running" was Danny's ultimate tribute to Muddy Waters. It was our Ninth Symphony, our Sistine Chapel. I had visions of Muddy carrying a cross up Calvary. It was Danny in his church of choice, solemn and intense, every verse rising like a tornado and landing as softly as a falcon on a glove—Danny's version of the blues and an homage to his idol. We started off quietly, intensely, and then built to a crescendo and repeated the process until both the band and the audience were exhausted. Although it never came close to sounding like Chicago blues, it all worked. Four encores later, the band and the audience were spent. We both needed a good night's sleep.

When we woke up early the next morning, Antioch once again looked like a wintry ghost town. (We found out later that Antioch was a progressive school, liberal and ahead of its time. Maybe that's why we were booked there, or maybe they just couldn't afford one of the San Francisco bands. Whatever the reason, our performance and the kids at Antioch foreshadowed the direction that this generation was beginning to take.) Except for Kooper, we all packed and got ready to leave. Al had to stay overnight and fly from Columbus to Nashville, where he would play on Bob Dylan's *Blond on Blond*, while our manager fell asleep at the wheel on the New Jersey Turnpike, ran off the road, and almost got us all killed (which would have happened, if not for a timely bit of vigilance by the rhythm guitarist).

Back in New York we managed to do some recording on the side. Merv Griffin found a singer who he had dubbed "The Covered Man." The Covered Man was actually a young actor by the name of David Soul, who later became one of the stars of TV's *Starsky and Hutch*. Merv's gimmick was to have poor David wear a ski mask whenever he was out in public. Along with us, The Covered Man also recorded for MGM. Merv was David's mentor and producer, and we were the backup band. It was David's first single—"The Covered Man" / "I Will Warm Your Heart," released in April 1966. I liked David and felt sorry for him; I kept imploring him to remove the mask, saying, "C'mon, man, it's just the six of us—take the damn thing off!"

"Merv won't let me" was his pitiful reply.

Four months later the band played at the Phone Booth. The dance floor was around an elevated stage, bringing the musicians into very close proximity with their audience. One night, in the middle of a song, a blond-haired young man tugged at my pants leg. As the song ended, he looked up at me and said, "Steve, it's me!" I said, "I'm sorry, man, I don't think I know you." "It's me—David! Merv said I could I take off the mask!"

Bob Dylan would come down to the Cafe au Go Go in his *Blond on Blond* jacket and heckle us from the audience. He wanted Al Kooper to be a permanent part of his band. He would be accompanied by Dylan wannabe David Blue, nee David Cohen. David Blue, Dylan's closest friend, Bob Neuwirth, and Al Kooper all went around talking like Dylan, even walking like him, mimicking the same facial expressions as Dylan and, God knows, trying to be funny and hip like Dylan. Of course, Dylan did it best and humiliated a lot of other people then because of it. I once slammed the door on him at the Dugout after one of his heckling sessions—I was that pissed-off. I went to a big party one night that was thrown either by or for Pernell Roberts from *Bonanza*. Dylan was walking around, looking stoned, dropping what looked like pills from his pockets while Albert Grossman, his manager, was politely asking people not to pick up any of Bob's little "deposits" off of the floor.

A little over a month after Antioch, we ventured out to the West Coast for the second time. We added a singer, a black woman named Emmaretta Marks. Along with the Tokens ("The Lion Sleeps Tonight"), Emmaretta sang backup on our single "Where There's Smoke, There's Fire," another failed hit with a poor lead vocal by Al. *Maybe Emmaretta could save us in the vocal department* was our thought, but it was not to be. She just bounced onstage halfway through the set to liven things up a bit. Every time Emmaretta didn't like something, she would run to Eric Burdon to complain. She told us that Burdon was her boyfriend at the time, but this was never verified.

For this West Coast trip, Emmaretta brought her own roadie with her, Gail Sloatman. According to Al Kooper, this caused a bit of friction in the band because everyone fell in love with Gail at the same time and didn't bother to tell the others (Gail later married Frank Zappa). Gail and I were an item for about three and a half hours back in New York, a record length of time for my love life back then. We were also accompanied by our photographer, Alice Ochs, Phil's ex-wife. I hadn't been back to the Bay Area since my cross-country road trip of two years earlier and was eagerly looking forward to returning.

Our first gig, where we were billed as the Blues Project Blues Band, was an outdoor afternoon performance at the Fifth Annual San Francisco State College Folk Festival, held at San Francisco State College. We were there along with Doc Watson, Dan Hicks, Richard and Mimi Fariña, Guy Carawan, Malvina Reynolds, and Mark Spoelstra, among others. Chet Helms, a local San Francisco hippie entrepreneur and promoter, was running concerts every other weekend at the Fillmore Ballroom, alternating with Bill Graham's own concert series. After a falling-out with Graham, Helms rented his own ballroom under his company name, Family Dog Productions. The Family Dog was a communal enterprise. Chet, who wore his blond hair down to his waist and wore a Jesse James–style topcoat, was somehow able to organize the underground music scene into a coherent reality, giving local and visiting musicians a forum by which they could express themselves. The new venue was located at Sutter Street and Van Ness and renamed the Avalon Ballroom. The Avalon Ballroom first opened on the weekend of April 22–23. We were the first headline act.

Our opening band that weekend was a local group that called itself the Great Society. The Great Society featured Grace Slick on vocals, guitar, and piano and styled themselves as improvisers, but were somewhat humiliated by the musical "sophistication" of the Blues Project. After these shows, according to Jerry Slick, Great Society's drummer, his then wife Grace went crazy and started to look more and more critically at her little homegrown band. She was riveted by us. She made a mental note and tucked it away in the back of her mind: If this thing didn't go someplace soon, she would either join the Blues Project or find another band as strong as they were.

She didn't join the Blues Project, unfortunately, but just six months later she *did* join Jefferson Airplane, and the Great Society broke up. Later, back in New York, Jefferson Airplane was playing at the Cafe au Go Go. Spencer Dryden, their drummer, and I were friends. Spencer called me one afternoon before his gig that night and asked if I wanted to join him and Grace for a movie matinee, specifically, *Marat/ Sade* with Glenda Jackson. I didn't know they were actually a "couple," and like everybody else in those days, I had a crush on Grace. So there we were in the theater, Spencer and I on either side of Grace, and I made one of my stupid moves—I tried to hold Grace Slick's hand. She looked at me with those dagger-blue eyes of hers, while my penis shrunk to the size of a pecan. I hope Spencer never found out (or anybody else, for that matter).

The Avalon Ballroom was not very different from our gig at Antioch. Except for the locale and the size of the room, the only difference was that the kids here were not in school. These were the kids who had run away from home and did not accept being bound by the restrictions of a socially conservative society. Everything else was the same—the dancing, the drugs, the fashions, and the utter freedom—added to which were some things like Owsley LSD, the multitude of new bands, and the light shows that permeated both the Avalon and the Fillmore.

The light shows were called "psychedelic" by the media, and indeed they were. As impressive as it must have been for the audience, for the musicians onstage, these light shows were hypnotic and fantastic. While almost begging you to take drugs, the light shows at both ballrooms inspired improvisation. You stood onstage staring at the variously huge paramecia, amoebas, and photos over your head and at the walls to your side, as large as an IMAX screen, and you just played and played without limits. Words like "booked" and "headlined" conjure up visions of show business in the Catskills, and are a far cry from describing what the ballroom scene was like during the height of the San Francisco hippie movement in the mid-1960s.

Then it was back down to Los Angeles where we were to perform at Doug Weston's Troubadour, on Santa Monica Boulevard in West Hollywood, and at the Los Angeles Memorial Coliseum on a very large bill, with headliners Sonny and Cher and Peter and Gordon. The other acts on the bill were Cannibal and the Headhunters of the original "Land of a Thousand Dances," the Premiers, the Little Ray Revue, the Beau-Jives, and the Ambertones.

Kooper took sick that day—not a rare occurrence for Al, who had, like the rest of us, his own set of Jewish hypochondriacal tendencies. We had no keyboards and I had to do Al's vocals. It didn't make too much difference that afternoon. Although the stadium held over a hundred thousand people, I don't think more than five hundred showed up. There were almost as many musicians backstage as there were people in the audience, although the audience was so far away that it was hard to tell. The stage was on one end of the field, but the audience wasn't in front of us; they were on each side, as if it were an Olympic event or a professional football game. I'm sure the sound system was adequate, but the audience was so distant that it probably would have made more sense to hire runners to carry our music to the seats, torches in hand. It took so much time for the sound to travel in that arena, you could have been watching Sonny and Cher while still listening to Peter and Gordon.

The field in front of us was reserved for the headliner's limos. When Peter and Gordon's limo first entered, the small teenybopper audience got excited, or at least they looked like they did from our vantage point, which was probably not unlike what an officer's view of a large battlefield must have looked like during the Napoleonic Wars. Peter Asher and Gordon Waller exited their vehicle like a couple of clowns at a circus, running full speed to their locker room so as not to be mobbed by their adoring audience of fourteen-year-old girls. Problem was, the kids were so far from them that if Peter and Gordon had decided to walk instead of run, it still would have taken the audience, about an acre away, at least another ten minutes to catch up.

Groupies were abundant in the "rock" hotels of Hollywood during the mid-'60s. LA groupies were different from Northern California or Midwestern groupies. In the Bay Area, the groupies were hip and blended into the scene. Unlike in Cleveland or LA, in San Francisco there were no central "rock" hotels. In fact, you would hardly call them groupies at all. In Cleveland, the Midwestern capital of rock and roll, the groupies were more the industrial, no-nonsense type, and usually hung out with the bands at the infamous Hotel Versailles, where the top floor was put aside by management for the bands that were playing the club La Cave or taping *Upbeat*, Cleveland's local rock TV show.

A couple of years later, Chicago spawned Cynthia Plaster Caster—a local groupie who made plaster molds from rock stars' penises and displayed the results in clay. One of the highest compliments I ever received was a request to become one of her subjects. I turned her down, fearing that she might display my results on a shelf next to Jimi Hendrix.

In LA most of the groupies looked like Cher. There were fat Chers, thin Chers, tall Chers, and short Chers. There were Chers all over the place—in the lobby, by the pool, in the restaurant. Sunset Boulevard was a festival of Chers, and I must have slept with at least half of them, foolishly thinking to myself over and over, *Eat your heart out, Sonny.*

Projections, our second and only studio album, was recorded mainly in New York, with Tom Wilson producing. Tom was also working with Eric Burdon and the Animals at the time and squeezed us in whenever he could get a few hours before or after the Animals' sessions. When we recorded "Steve's Song," I had five minutes to lay down the vocal track, with no time for overdubs in case I needed to fix anything. There are a couple of tuning problems in my vocal that I never had a chance to correct, so not only did Verve/Folkways refuse to give me that extra five minutes while Eric Burdon was waiting by the coffee machine outside, but then they also changed the name of the song itself. One of Danny's strings loosened on "Two Trains Running," but did we stop? No, we didn't have time. Thank God he was able to tune it up and it actually worked within the track. You can hear it clearly on the record.

We weren't given choices. We continued recording some of the tracks in LA, with Jack Nitzsche and Billy James producing. Jack Nitzsche, as shy as he was talented, had to sit on his briefcase while our manager sat in the producer's chair. Jeff Chase was definitely on his way out.

The cover of *Projections* was from a photo session with Jim Marshall, one of the great rock photographers. It was taken in the middle of Haight-Ashbury during the height of '60s craziness. You can't see it in the photo, but there were hippies all around us—white hippies, black hippies, Chinese hippies, teen runaway hippies—with flowers in their hair, joints in their mouths, patchouli oil in their clothes, and LSD on their brains. It was glorious. Despite all of this, I still had not moved out of my parents' apartment in Queens.

We were playing the Cafe au Go Go quite a bit, and were also invited to the Newport Folk Festival, where I ran into my friend Tim Hardin, one of the great songwriters of the era ("If I Were a Carpenter"). Tim was a heroin addict and could be quite difficult to be with. We were alone in the dressing room at Newport and Tim was about to go on, but he was nodding out and turning green. There was no way he was getting onstage, much less performing. I ran out to get some help and to look for a doctor, but by the time I found someone, Tim was announced. *Uh-oh*, I thought. But Tim came out and did one of his most memorable sets. I once saw Bill Evans in the same shape at the Top of the Gate in the Village in the '70s. I didn't think he'd make it over to the piano, but when he did, playing those magnificent chords and voicings, that's when I said to myself, "Boy, I have to try some of that shit," so I tried it once, but my thumping nausea overrode whatever curiosity I might have had. I never tried it again.

We went uptown to play for a "non-Village" audience. The audiences at the uptown clubs—Ondine, the Peppermint Lounge, Ungano's, the Phone Booth—were very different. We loved our West Village audiences, but they were hipsters and stoners. Uptown audiences were drunks, an entirely different dynamic. If an audience is drunk, you'd better hope they like you. If they're stoned, just give them a light show and a drum solo and they'll be happy. The Young Rascals, who were about to do away with their silly outfits to become "the Rascals," were playing at the Phone Booth on East Fifty-Fifth Street. After the Jeff Chase experience, we hired Sid Bernstein, of "Beatles at Shea Stadium" fame, to manage us. Sid also managed the Rascals and was able to get us booked there for a week in July and a week in August. It was our first uptown show. They hated us. There was a reason the Village bands didn't play uptown. Audiences up there wanted to hear hits, and we didn't have any. Nor did we have songs that sounded like hits. They wanted songs that lasted no longer than two and a half minutes, and we didn't have those either. We had songs that sounded like us. I remember that, as we came offstage from our "audition," the house DJ played "Help" by the Beatles. That's how much they hated us. But we still got the gig.

One night I went up to Harlow, on the East Side, to see the Vagrants with the guitarist Leslie West, who later went on to form

Mountain. I was introduced to Jim Morrison. He was polite, somewhat shy, and probably sober. Later on, Morrison and I had more in
common than just a friendly handshake.

In June, just one month before our own date there, the Phone
Booth hosted the Bobby Fuller Four, and I went up to see them. "I
Fought the Law" was one of my favorite songs from those days, and
Bobby and I talked for a while. Coming from the Texas rockabilly
school, he was a really sweet kid. It broke my heart when he died on
July 18, only one week before our own gig. He was found dead in a
car from toxic fumes. According to the Los Angeles County coroner's
office, Bobby's death was ruled a "suicide with a question mark."

Our first week at the Phone Booth, Kooper became sick again.
Toward the end of the first show, Al was rushed to the hospital with
what turned out to be mononucleosis. He was there for a few weeks,
and for the remaining shows was replaced by his old friend Paul Harris. There I was, doing lead vocals again, with Danny and Paul Harris
subbing for Al on keyboards. Paul Harris later arranged "Touch Me"
by The Doors, after Morrison had heard Blood, Sweat & Tears at The
Troubadour. Jim wanted a horn section and hired Paul to write the
parts. Funny how despite everything our sound kept percolating up
into the ether, no matter how dysfunctional we really were.

⌒⌒

It wasn't so much that I was against the war in Vietnam as I was expe-
riencing something extraordinary for the first time in my young life.
I was free—free from the confines of school, free from academics and
disciplinarians, free from my parents, free to choose who my friends
would be, free to stay up late, free to have my own panic attacks, free to
experiment with sex, and free to choose if and how I would get high.
Most of all, I was free to make music, fearlessly prepared for the reality
that there might be little or no reward or compensation for the path
I'd chosen, except to have the freedom to enjoy myself.

Despite the clichés of the free-wheeling '60s, the truth is that I was of a generation that grew up in the '50s, one that respected authority and did its bidding. There was a day in my first year of high school where we had one of the many air-raid drills that were performed regularly in public institutions during the Cold War. We questioned nothing, and so, when we were asked to march outside to the football field, sit down, bend forward, and put our hands behind our necks, it took at least ten minutes for one of the more free-thinking kids among us to say, and say it out loud during an enforced silence, "Wait a minute. If this is an air-raid drill, then what the hell are we doing out *here*?" Finally, one of us was exercising some common sense. The drill turned out to be a bomb scare, but, lemmings that we were, our marching to orders was indicative of the blind trust that we had put in the "authorities," or, as I saw them, the generation of adults that was supposed to have known better. And just as I thought that my peers were rid of that authoritative nonsense, and just as I had started to lose respect for the establishment who had suffered through the Depression, World War II, and Korea, along came Vietnam.

My draft board was in Great Neck, on Long Island. I was classified 1-A, which meant that I was eligible for the draft. It was 1966. There was no lottery yet. You went for a physical, and if you passed, you were whisked away to basic training and then, most likely, because of the very high draft calls that year, you would wind up in Vietnam, where I most emphatically did not want to be.

I knew I had to get out of the draft, and to do that I had to give an Academy Award performance. I had to be a rebel, and fool the authorities; however, these guys weren't the suburban teachers, parents, or school principals that you could pretty much get around with a little bit of wit. These were guys in uniform, dead fucking serious, and I had to convince them that I was just too far-out to join their ranks.

If you were assigned to the Great Neck draft board, your physical took place in Brooklyn, at Fort Hamilton, right by the

Verrazano–Narrows Bridge, the bridge that links Brooklyn with Staten Island. My notice said that I was supposed to report to the Great Neck draft board for the bus ride over, but I knew that would be a mistake, and so I was prepared to travel separately from the bus. I called up the draft board days before and and was able to receive permission to get to Fort Hamilton on my own. It was absolutely imperative that I got there earlier than the bus from Great Neck, or the next stop was Vietnam.

I spent the two weeks prior to my physical drinking beer with lots of salt to raise my blood pressure, and I also took a wild assortment of drugs of every imaginable color, shape, and psychotropic effect. I hardly slept. I was a disaster, definitely a liability to the armed forces. A Vietcong victory waiting to happen.

The night before the physical was spent at Andy Kulberg's apartment. No sleep, and my friends were coming in and out for support and guidance. I had taken some speed and some downs, drank more salt beers, and smoked a lot of hashish, essentially preparing myself to have what would look like—or perhaps actually be—a nervous breakdown.

I arrived at the appointed building at the same time as the kids from Jamaica High School in Queens, mostly poor black kids who were ready to fight, whether it be in Southeast Asia or back in their own neighborhood. We were all sitting in what could have passed for a classroom. A tough-looking sergeant at the "teacher's" desk up front informed us that we were now legally in the army, and that if we were missing a leg or an arm or were blind, there might be a *chance* of getting deferred, *if* you were lucky.

He then requested that everybody in the room bring whatever weapons they were carrying up to the front desk, no questions asked, and that they would get them back at the end of the day. Just as these kids brought up their knives, zip guns, brass knuckles, chains, etc., I looked out the window and noticed the Great Neck bus pulling up, the bus I *should* have been on. I knew it was the Great Neck bus because out poured a bunch of kids, all stoned and looking like they hadn't slept for weeks, all looking to fail their physical. One even threw up as soon as his feet touched the ground. These were the rich kids, the Jewish intellectual kids, the nerds. I would not have stood a chance if I'd ridden in with them, just one of the thundering herd, waiting to be deferred. With the Jamaica kids, I stood out like a sore thumb.

We had to fill out forms, including our medical histories. First trick was to write as *few* negative things in your medical history as possible, make them go straight to the one that's going to get you out, or get you sent to the psychiatrist. That was the goal, that was Home, Go, Bingo all in one—the army psychiatrist. The only box I checked was the one that asked if I was suicidal. I also wrote that my vocation was "musician." After the forms, we had to go to another room and fill a cup with urine. I peed all over my hand. That was easy, everybody did that, but at least it was a way of getting attention, of letting them know that something was wrong here. After a few more tests, I wound up with the proctologist, who stuck his finger up my ass and asked if I'd ever thought about joining the army band. *Oh God*, I thought to myself, *please don't make me laugh!*

I was beginning to feel the drugs wearing off, pulling this way and that until I really *did* feel like I was coming apart. The timing couldn't have been better. It peaked at the hearing test. I put on headphones and was supposed to signal when I heard a beep. I just sat there—not because I was unwilling to go through the test, or because I was faking it. It was real. I just froze. I became a zombie and could hardly move, much less hear any beeps. That was it; off to the psychiatrist. *Bingo!*

I was escorted to a chair in front of the psychiatrist's office, completely out of it, still able to function, but barely. There were a couple of other guys waiting, and it wasn't until a few minutes later when I realized that one of them was a classmate of mine at Mineola High. *Oh God, please don't let him recognize me.* The last thing I needed to hear was: "Katz, what the hell are you doing here? How's the band? You guys putting out another album soon? I saw you guys at the au Go Go last week. You were great! What happened to you? You don't look too good."

I tried to hide my face, but luckily, at that moment, I was summoned into the doctor's office. It didn't occur to me until later that this guy was probably thinking the same thing about *me*.

Psychiatrist—"Says here you tried to kill yourself at the age of ten. Tell me about it."

It's sort of like method acting; you take an incident in your past (see next chapter), like a temper tantrum, blow it a bit out of proportion, and relive it as psychodrama. I couldn't tell him the truth, but I was able to twist the story around a little: "I was depressed and didn't want to live anymore—still don't."

"Well, son," he said, "I'm afraid you're not army material just now. Maybe if you join a program that our health nurse can recommend for you, and you stick to it, maybe then the army will have you."

I knew what that meant: a temporary deferment, a 1-Y. Outwardly, I expressed sadness. Inwardly, I was having multiple orgasms. I'd done it! After seeing the health nurse and not listening to a word she was saying, I left the building for home and my first good night's sleep in weeks. I was so blissed out, I could have even jammed with David Crosby.

Back in New York, my 1-Y deferment, which had come in the mail a week after my first army physical, was rearing its anxiety-producing head. I knew that a 1-Y was the best I was going to get without a note from a doctor. I was going to be called up again, and in order to get out the next time, I'd have to have a note.

Enter Arthur Eaton, our old Fifth Avenue hippie psychologist. Danny Kalb was still seeing Arthur, who shared Danny's strong antiwar sentiments. I would go to Arthur for a note, but only on the condition that I see him as a patient. Arthur and I composed the note together. My favorite sentence:

Frankly, psychotic imagery has begun to emerge as he pictures what he believes to be a plot by the Military and the Selective Service to literally abduct him and use him for experimental reasons as a sexual object.

The note went on to say that I actually *wanted* this to happen. Having my note meant that there was going to be no problem getting a 4-F this time around, except that I still had to look like a wreck and get somebody to read it and discharge me.

I reached a doctor relatively early. He looked at me with sympathetic eyes and then opened the envelope. Disgusted by what he read, the doctor practically threw me out of the office. I bid farewell to the army and to Vietnam.

CHAPTER 3

Mimi

IT WAS NOVEMBER OF 1966. RONALD REAGAN HAD JUST BEEN ELECTED governor of California, and the Beatles had begun recording *Sgt. Pepper's Lonely Hearts Club Band*. I tiptoed into my apartment, not wanting to wake Mimi, but the moment I opened the door, I knew instantly that she was gone.

The Blues Project had just returned from a gig in upstate New York, where we'd opened for Jay and the Americans, and it was late. The bed was made and her suitcase was missing, but her scent lingered. I was blindsided. My cockiness and stage swagger from just a few hours before felt foolish and trivial. Shock changed to panic, but at three a.m. there was no one I could call. I looked around my little Eighth Avenue walk-up and thought of waking up Larry, my junkie friend from upstairs, but the last time I had seen him, he was on his way to the Tombs, and I didn't know if he had made bail yet. Then I noticed Mimi's note. She'd left for San Francisco. That was all; no good-bye, no reason, just "I've gone home."

I was devastated. After all, Mimi—the widow of author and hipster Richard Fariña and sister of Joan Baez—was my first love.

A couple of days later, days I can't recall, nor, like a bad acid trip, will I ever care to, Al Kooper suggested that I come up to the Elektra Records' offices and hang out. I thought it would be a good idea. I needed to be with people, and in those days Elektra was one of the places to which the folk-rock elite gravitated before the bars and clubs opened at night. I walked out of the elevator and through the Elektra lobby. It was after five p.m., and the secretaries had all gone home. As I turned into the corridor, I almost fainted at the sight of Mimi on her way to the ladies' room. My legs weakened and my voice became hoarse. I asked what she was doing there; she was supposed to have gone home. Just as surprised to see me, but ever the sweet and graceful California flower child, Mimi smiled and condescended to a hug and a kiss on the cheek.

She told me that when she had left my apartment that night, she'd gone to stay with Judy Collins at Judy's apartment on the Upper West Side. She had thought it best not to let me know that she was still in New York. She then suggested that we spend one last night together, to which, of course, in my jellyfish-like state, I agreed. Certainly not a rational choice, but I didn't give a damn. I didn't suspect until much later that there was something very wrong with this situation.

We took a taxi up to Judy's, and while I remained on the verge of a breakdown, Mimi was all smiles, like nothing had happened. Bruce Langhorne, the legendary guitarist, was visiting Judy and Mimi, and so, after a bite to eat, the four of us jammed. We sang folk songs. I mean, I'm dying, and we're having a fucking *hootenanny*. We made love that night, Mimi as warm and caring as ever, and me, with a broken heart and hard-on, trying to make the evening last as long as possible.

The next morning, the Blues Project had a photo session scheduled with Linda Eastman (McCartney). In the photo, I'm off to one side wearing my old peacoat. I looked like I swallowed a lemon when, in fact, I had been hit over the head with a very heavy dose of what I mistook for real life.

It wasn't until a long time had passed that I could look back on the first few weeks of my first real love affair; how beautiful those days were, and how crippling the consequences.

❧

Richard Fariña had died in a motorcycle accident on April 30, 1966. His book, *Been Down So Long It Looks Like Up to Me*, had just been published two days earlier, and Richard, through his writings and his musical partnership with his wife Mimi, was about to become a posthumous counterculture folk hero.

I had met Richard a couple of times and liked him. Like Mimi, he was of Spanish-Irish descent. Brooklyn born and raised, Richard was bright and every bit the cool and affable hustler. We had played the Fifth Annual San Francisco State College Folk Festival together back in April, but I had not yet met Mimi.

Four months after Richard died, the Blues Project was booked back in San Francisco at a converted pizza parlor called the Matrix, on Fillmore Street in the Marina District. The Matrix became one of the classic rock venues of the era. Our list of San Francisco friends was growing, sometimes through our newfound reputation among the Bay Area culturally hip elite, and sometimes through word of mouth from friends like comedian Larry Hankin, who used to open our show at the Cafe au Go Go in New York. Larry was a founding member of The Committee, San Francisco's prolific improvisational comedy group. At the time, The Committee also included Don Sturdy, who, as Howard Hesseman, went on to become "Johnny Fever" on the hit TV show *WKRP in Cincinnati*, and Carl Gottlieb, who went on to act in and cowrite the screenplay to *Jaws* with its author, Peter Benchley.

Among The Committee's circle of friends were two of the three Baez sisters, Joan and Mimi. Joan Baez's first album was one of the reasons I became enamored with folk music. Even before I was introduced to country blues, hers was the album that weaned me off The Kingston Trio. It was 1960. *Joan Baez* took me right to the heart of the eighteenth and nineteenth centuries and introduced me to the art of "balladry." I idolized Joan Baez and, like so many kids of my generation, fell madly in love with her.

When I heard that Mimi Fariña was coming to the Matrix to see us, I was overjoyed. The small house was packed, and as was my custom at a few of the more informal and intimate gigs, I announced onstage that some of us could use a place to stay for the night and asked if there were any volunteers to put us up. And that's how I met Mimi. She was more beautiful up close and in person than in any of her pictures or album covers. Her green eyes were positively hypnotic, but I maintained enough composure to be able to hear her say that she could put two of us up. Our bass player, Andy Kulberg, and I were the chosen two.

Mimi lived in what was then a modest house on Telegraph Hill, only a short walk down from Coit Tower. We arrived late, Mimi, Andy, and I. Her apartment was small, appointed with the typical accoutrements of the period—Indian tapestries, a few antiques, flowers, candles, and incense. After playing a couple of sets, the only thing that interested me was the sight of a bed, but there was only one bed in Mimi's living room, and Andy and I began arguing over who was to get it. One of the many things I had learned in my short time on the road was that no matter if you slept in the shabbiest no-star hotel or in Buckingham Palace, a floor was a floor, and I couldn't sleep on a floor. I told Andy that my back was acting up, but my smile gave me away and Andy wasn't buying.

We needed a third party to officiate, and as if on cue, Mimi walked in, having heard the noise, and said, "What are you guys arguing about?"

We told her, and she said that Andy should get the bed.

I was shocked. "Does that mean I sleep on the floor?"

"No," Mimi said, "you can sleep with me."

I had been out of college two years, honing my skills as a seducer of women with varying degrees of success. Suddenly I had become the seduced. Unbeknownst to my naive self, Mimi had planned this all evening. Things like this did not happen in real life, did they? But there I was, totally in love, seized, and arrested, even before I had my pants down.

The next morning was one of those beautiful San Francisco mornings that had me feeling like I was in an animated film, with the birds singing and the flowers as radiant as a dozen rainbows. We spent the next days waking up late, playing guitar, and singing together. Sometimes we walked down the long steps of Telegraph Hill to North Beach where we would enjoy brunch at Enrico's, the local Italian eatery and hangout. We then strolled over to City Lights Bookstore to peruse the Beat and the obscure, to scan the New Directions paperbacks, and possibly to spy poet Lawrence Ferlinghetti behind the cash register. Back up the long stairway to home, we still had a few days to get to know each other, to talk and play before I had to go back to New York and the dingy world of rock and roll.

Curiously, during our late-afternoon conversations, Mimi didn't have very nice things to say about Richard. Maybe she was trying to tell me that it was okay, that she wasn't using me as a foil for her grief, but I never felt that she was grieving very much at all. Richard had been close to author Thomas Pynchon, and Mimi had implied that Richard might have lifted some of Pynchon's work for his own. I felt that she was angry with Richard for leaving the duo, and that needing someone to take Richard's place in a musical partnership was more important to her than the mundane world of matrimony. For me, our days were like heaven, and I was falling deeper and deeper into something that would take many more months for me to comprehend.

Mimi had arranged a field trip to Big Sur. We were to meet her sister Joan for dinner at Esalen Institute and stay for an overnight. A couple of members of The Committee joined us, as did our drummer, Roy Blumenfeld. While smoking monumental amounts of hashish along the way, we witnessed, as anybody knows who has ever made the trip, one of the most spectacular views in the world, that of the Pacific Ocean and the Northern California coastline. We arrived late that afternoon, Mimi and I settling into our little bungalow before meeting Joan in the dining room. I don't remember if Joan Baez and I shook hands or politely kissed, but I'll never forget the first thing she said to me. "So you're going to be my next brother-in-law?" I tried to come up with some kind of hip New York musician response, but instead probably said something stupid like "I am?" I was too spaced and awed to be charming.

After dinner our whole party undressed and got into the hot baths that were embedded in the cliffs of Big Sur and looked out on the stars over the glittering Pacific. It was only a couple of hours earlier that I had met one of my idols, Joan Baez, and now here we were, immersed, naked, side by side in a hot tub and looking out at a scene that rivaled van Gogh's *Starry Night*.

Hanging around in the West Village with Dylan and Phil Ochs had been great, but sitting in a hot tub with a naked Joan Baez was definitely in a different category altogether. After the bath, we all converged on Joan's bungalow where Joan handed out sleeping pills to the assembled crew. We all listened and softly sang along as she serenaded us with that perfect and perfectly familiar voice. Mimi and I then went back to our little bungalow, stoned, satiated, and, so I believed, thoroughly in love.

It was just before Martin Luther King's march on Grenada, Mississippi, where Joan would join Dr. King, that we had made our little trip to Big Sur. We stopped at Joan's house in Carmel on our way back to Telegraph Hill. Joan planned to follow us in her gray Mark II Jaguar and stay at Mimi's for a few days.

Late one afternoon, while Joan and Mimi were out getting supplies for a spaghetti dinner, and while I was contemplating a new song and noodling on my guitar, the phone rang, breaking my shaky concentration. It was Dr. King, and he asked me to leave a message for Joan about the coming march. It was the first time I had become involved in a historic moment, albeit in a totally ephemeral context. Boy, was I having fun.

But then it was time to return to New York. We had gigs coming up, and I had to figure out a way to prepare for Mimi's visit in November. First I had to move out of my parents' place and find an apartment in Manhattan, preferably in Greenwich Village, and I had to do it fast. I set up an appointment with a real estate agent to see a second-floor walk-up that I could barely afford, over Garber's Hardware on Eighth Avenue and Twelfth Street in the West Village. Our appointment was set for eight p.m. I had no idea how to look for an apartment, so when I saw the place, I took it, no questions asked.

A week later I recruited some friends for an evening to help me move. I fell asleep in my new place around midnight and woke up the next morning to find that it was still nighttime. I went to my only window and saw a brick wall not more than three feet from me. I had rented a cave. I sat before the window next to my cartons and my guitars, about to burst into tears. I unpacked the first box, left a tennis ball on the floor, and watched helplessly as it rolled to the other end of the room along the slanted floor. Not only had I rented a cave, I had moved into Davy Jones's Locker. It did have a fireplace—just right for romantic November nights with Mimi, staring into the fire while sitting on the rug that I was about to steal from my parents.

I phoned Mimi regularly. Those were the days when telephones were attached to walls by wires and you had to pay exorbitantly for each long-distance call—and there were many long-distance calls. It was a busy period for me, but I found time to check in with Mimi frequently, usually at night. We made plans for her New York trip. She wanted to come to some of our gigs, and I even planned a day for us to take a train out to Queens and have dinner with my parents. No matter how hip and independent I was, there was no denying I missed my mother's food, as atrocious as it could sometimes be.

During this time, I received a strange and upsetting call from Mimi. She had spent a weekend in Novato, north of San Francisco. She called me afterwards and said that she had slept with another man and hoped I wouldn't mind.

Mind? Of course not. Why would I mind? Oh, let me call you back—I have to run downstairs to the hardware store for some single-edge razor blades.

My oven hasn't been working properly, so I'll need to keep the gas on for a day or so to see if I can detect what's wrong. I would jump out my window but there's a brick wall right in front of me, and I doubt if I would cause more damage than a broken leg when all I really want is a quick death.

I decided to just ignore the red flag that had been waving desperately over my head since September, be reasonable and act like nothing had happened. I can't remember who paid for Mimi's trip to New York, but in retrospect, I hope it wasn't me.

Mimi came to New York and the first thing she tried to do was to get me to come back to San Francisco, move in with her, and become second banana in our musical duo. It was either common sense or fear that prompted me to turn down this kind offer, most likely the latter. I couldn't see leaving New York, the band, my friends and family. Though close to being the starving artist, I was loving my life in New York and wouldn't have given it up for anything, including a one-way trip to Eden.

She didn't say anything, but I could tell she hated the apartment. I couldn't blame her, coming from where she did, so there was no way at this point that I could possibly turn the tables and get her to live with me in New York. We were in limbo and it was getting uncomfortable. One night I thought we'd sit in front of the fireplace and chill with a bottle or two of red wine, talk things over, and try to figure out the logistics of our affair. The logs were in place, prepared weeks before. I lit the fire and smoke came streaming out of the flames, backing up into my little flat and permeating through the higher floors of my unsuspecting tenement as I cursed myself for not opening the flue.

Out on Eighth Avenue waiting for the fire engines, I thought this was as good a place as any to talk about our relationship, but Mimi thought it best that we wait. And besides, tomorrow we were due at my parents' for dinner. There was some consolation in the fact that, according to the New York City Fire Department, it wasn't the flue. It was concrete that had sealed the fireplace, most likely right around the Teddy Roosevelt administration.

The next afternoon we took a train to Douglaston, Queens. Douglaston was known for being the home of Arthur Treacher of Arthur Treacher's Fish and Chips. It was also the home of Ann and Leo Katz—Ann of Ann Katz's Overdone Pot Roast with Much Too Much Oil and Way Too Much Paprika. Mimi would not be trading any recipes with Mom that day.

My parents' main mode of entertaining guests was to leave the TV on and let it fill spaces in the conversation. Every now and then, my father would look at the TV, see a personality he recognized, look back at Mimi and me, and say, "You know, he's Jewish," or "You know, she's Jewish." Mimi would politely reply, "No, I didn't know that," as I contemplated crawling under the couch that I used to easily negotiate when I was four years old.

By the end of the day, Mimi looked as if she had just spent three hours on another planet. I tried to console her but the shock was too much. The visit to Queens certainly wasn't going to help my cause. I could no more imagine Mimi wanting to visit my parents again than spending a few days taking in the giant landfill in Canarsie or going to Secaucus for a breath of fresh air. But she was polite and understanding, and didn't at all give away the fact that she was dying to get the hell out of there.

Her visit was coming to an end and we still had not worked out our future plans, but, for now, I had to be upstate with the band. We were to open a show for Jay and the Americans in Ithaca. I thought it odd that Mimi did not want to join me that night.

<hr />

Each of my songs on the first two Blood, Sweat & Tears albums were about Mimi. Both songs are bitter and resentful. Sometimes, I wish I hadn't written "Megan's Gypsy Eyes"—I certainly shouldn't have recorded it the way it was. "Sometimes in Winter" was a different story, but no less bitter. I was blindsided, true, but in some ways I must have seen it coming. I didn't allow myself to believe that this small affair, this cross-country tryst, had ended as swiftly as it had begun. I later came to understand that ours was not a true relationship in any classic sense. Nor, as long as I refused to move to California and partner with Mimi, could it ever have been lasting. Mimi's world revolved around Joan and her family, homogeneous and matriarchal. I was a temporary substitute for Richard, but Richard was the prototype and, in the end, I was still a child, naive and in way over my head.

I'm sure that Mimi had her own problems and her own agenda. I don't know how much she was actually committed to our relationship, but in retrospect, I'm also sure that Mimi wasn't aware of how painful this breakup was to a nerdy little kid from Queens who was usually able to get his way. I spent the next few years comparing every girl I met to Mimi, writing songs about Mimi, and feeling sorry for myself, the loser who had somehow lost Mimi. If I had been aware enough at the time to realize that she was never mine to begin with, I could have avoided much of the pain.

—◆—

Mimi and I met again briefly on September 25, 1971, at the Eighth Annual (and final) Big Sur Folk Festival, a gala thrown every year for Joan's birthday. Blood, Sweat & Tears was booked there, along with Kris Kristofferson, Lily Tomlin, and Taj Mahal. Mimi asked if I would meet her in the dining room with the implication that I might like to spend the night. By now I was married, so instead, I got on a plane to New York and went home to my wife. The last time Mimi and I made contact was in 2001, just before she died of a neuroendocrine tumor. I sent her a card and she responded with a very sad letter in which it was obvious that she was going through a lot of pain, but at least, and at last, we got to say good-bye.

Mimi had founded a nonprofit organization called Bread & Roses, which puts on free concerts for institutionalized people in the Bay Area. It is still going strong and doing great work. If for nothing else, this alone will ensure Mimi's place in Heaven.

CHAPTER 4

Blues Implosion

THROUGH THE EYES OF A FOUR-YEAR-OLD, OUR APARTMENT BUILDING in Brooklyn was a massive brick fortress. My parents, Ann and Leo, and my older brother, Dennis, and I lived on the third floor of the walk-up. The smells of the old world, namely blintzes and gefilte fish, potato kugel, matzo brei and chicken soup, permeated the dimly lit lobby.

Most of our relatives lived in our building, as was the custom of the day. My maternal grandmother's brother, Uncle Benny, gave my brother and me a penny whenever he saw us, usually as he bounded down the stairs on his way to work, happy to be out of the shtetl and grateful to be living in postwar America.

I remember my mother's lullaby as she rocked me in my carriage—"Lavender Blue." And I remember the people next door who liked to throw boiling water out the window at kids who would gather on their stoop and make too much noise. I remember sleeping out on the fire escape on hot summer nights, and being dragged to Rockaway Beach with the masses, like in that famous Weegee photograph of Coney Island. But most of all, I remember Martin Block's show on the radio. That was how I first fell in love with music—Martin Block and his *Make Believe Ballroom*, WNEW. I can still sing you the theme song.

In 1950, when I turned five, my parents decided to move from Brooklyn to a "garden apartment" in Bayside, Queens, called Windsor Oaks, near the corner of Springfield Boulevard and Seventy-Third Avenue. My father was working for Witty Brothers clothiers at the time, mostly on the road as a traveling salesman. When my paternal grandmother, Bertha, found out we were moving to the adjacent borough, she said to me, with a hint of sadness in her thick Yiddish accent, "So, you're moving to the *country!*"

Bertha had come to America in 1910 when she was in her late twenties. She grew up in Bialystok, Russia, and joined the great turn-of-the-century migration of Jews who were escaping Russian persecution. She traveled to Bremen, Germany, and caught a boat to New York where, like so many immigrants of her day, she disembarked at Ellis Island. Bertha had made the trip to America alone, barely able to speak the native language. I'm not sure if my grandfather joined her later, but my guess is that he was already in New York, making preparations for their future in the New World.

Despite Bertha's geographical assessment, life in Queens wasn't that much different than life in Brooklyn had been. Instead of burrowing in the sand with the masses at Rockaway, we now burrowed at Jones Beach, and spent most Sundays visiting my grandparents back in Brooklyn. With every visit I was treated to a shot of schnapps by Bertha's husband, my "little grandpa," Sam. We would then drive over to Schenectady Avenue where my "big grandma and grandpa," Gussie and Jake, owned a luncheonette, and where I developed my sweet tooth and lifelong obsession for egg creams, that Brooklyn-invented concoction of chocolate syrup, milk, and seltzer. The luncheonette had its own host of smells: candy, malt, tobacco, a multitude of syrups, baseball cards and gum, racks of fresh magazines and newspapers. For a kid it was nothing less than paradise, but for my grandparents it was nothing more than a way to survive.

One day, while playing in the luncheonette, I had to use the bathroom. A woman already occupied it, but she'd forgotten to lock the door. I opened the door. She screamed; I screamed. My grandparents panicked. It was the first time I'd ever seen something close to a vagina. Later that month my father asked me whether he should vote for Eisenhower or Stevenson. It was the 1952 presidential election, and my father did not have a preference. I said, "Eisenhower." I was seven years old. He voted for Eisenhower. So it was that within only one month's time I saw my first vagina and voted for my last Republican.

We had a Dumont TV back then, or maybe it was a Philco. I watched the news bulletins about the death of Stalin, the coronation of Queen Elizabeth II, the Army/McCarthy hearings, and Sugar Ray Robinson on *Friday Night Fights*, brought to you by Gillette—*Hey, mister, how are you fixed for blades?* The Million Dollar Movie would broadcast one film over and over again for an entire week, and all you had were three TV stations to choose from.

The Hamburger Express was in our little shopping strip a few blocks away, along with a grocery, a toy store, and a record store. A walk out the front door of my apartment brought me to Seventy-Third Avenue, where I turned left toward Bell Boulevard, passing the antiaircraft guns that were spaced at intervals throughout the boroughs in case of attack. The Korean War was full-blown at the time, but neither North Korea nor China had the delivery systems to bomb the United States. We believed the Russians did, however, and so I walked past these symbols of the Cold War and Red Scare and sat down at the counter of my favorite restaurant, feet dangling, as Lionel trains customized with plates to carry burgers and fries rounded the corner and steamed directly toward me through the haze of pre-nonsmoking New York. I couldn't care less about air raids and I cared less about Joe McCarthy. Hamburgers and music were my life. Not much has changed.

My next stop was the bakery, where customers took tickets and waited for their number to be called. The acquisition of baked goods is a matter of Jewish pride, a desperate attempt to seek out the freshest bagels, the tastiest rugelach, and the most sought-after bialys in the store. A bullfight in Spain doesn't hold a candle to the violence and excitement of a Jewish bakery in New York on a Sunday morning.

But my favorite pastime of all was to listen to music.

We all have our prized childhood possessions. For some it was a pet or a blanket, or for those of us who grew up in the 1950s, maybe a Captain Video Flying Saucer Ring or a Howdy Doody doll. For me it was the RCA 45 rpm record player, a relatively small but heavy box that had its own speaker and an automatic changer, where you could stack the wonderful little discs of plastic known as "45s" or "singles," still my favorite delivery system for rock 'n' roll and pop music.

My parents let me buy the latest hits of the day. I imagined myself as Perry Como, Tony Bennett, or Frankie Laine, and sometimes sang their songs out in the street in front of our garden apartment.

In the summertime I used to sing Eddie Fisher songs in my underwear while the neighbors threw change at me. I gathered the change, put on my pants, and ran straight to the record store. Like I said, some things never change.

I was getting spoiled by all the attention and money that was being tossed at me, but that soon ended when I was recruited to sing for Rosh Hashanah services at the local Jewish Center. It was the autumn of 1954, and I was nine years old. There were four of us. I was the soprano. Our cantor coached me and I had to sing phonetically, as I would also recite my bar mitzvah speech a few years later. The cantor had the annoying habit of injecting "I mean, I say" either before or in the middle of every sentence, like a Jewish Foghorn Leghorn, and although his habit drove me up a wall, I started to mimic him unconsciously. "Hey, Mom, when is, I mean, I say, when is dinner gonna be ready?"

As Rosh Hashanah approached, I began to get terrible headaches. Somehow I made it through the service and sang my songs, but the headaches kept coming for fifty more years. *Migraines*, the doctors called it. I called it *stage fright*.

My parents believed I had talent and tried to support me, albeit with their limited knowledge of how to go about it, neither one coming from a musical background. With the best of intentions, in the spring of 1955, they signed me up for accordion and clarinet lessons, but the wooden clarinet reed gave me the chills, the same chills I suffered from those little wooden spoons that were given with Dixie cups by the Good Humor Man and the Bungalow Bar guy. I just couldn't stand the way the wood felt whenever it touched my teeth. The accordion was way too heavy for me and my arms weren't long enough to negotiate the bellows. You had to be from a race of giants to play it. Neither instrument was for me. I wanted to sing.

My mother brought me into Manhattan to see Al Greiner, a vocal coach who had also worked with Connie Francis and Frances Gumm (who later became Judy Garland). Al worked out of a funky little room somewhere in what is now known as the Ed Sullivan Building. The Ed Sullivan Building never achieved the legendary status of the Brill Building down the street, but its credibility in the world of Tin Pan Alley was just as real.

At each floor that the anciently reverberant elevator stopped, you heard live music in a multitude of keys. There were doo-wop singers roaming the halls, practicing their scales while combing their hair and bathing in the echo of the high ceilings and marble floors. There were old veterans from Broadway past who now coached and cajoled young people like me into show-business serfdom amid promises of stardom. There were dancers, singers, instrumentalists of every sort. There were agents, managers, hustlers, freeloaders, and stage mothers. The old building was a beehive of popular music, a carnival of tunes.

Al's room was furnished with a couple of chairs and an old upright piano. Although he taught me how to breathe and use my diaphragm, I lasted only a few lessons. I don't remember why I quit, except that I must have thought that you shouldn't have to actually *work* to be a singer, you just sang.

At my mother's behest, I was to audition for one of those "make-a-wish" TV shows that were prevalent on local stations at the time. One day, as we waited in the lobby of NBC's New York TV studios, I heard a man galloping down the stairs. Basil Rathbone came into view, tapped me on my head, and complimented my mother on my cuteness.

Meanwhile, at home, we had a black woman come in to clean every week. Her name was Josephine. We were pretty close, Josephine and I. She and her boyfriend took me into Manhattan for a matinee one day during the summer of 1955. It was at the Palace Theatre that we saw *Blackboard Jungle*. I was mesmerized and ran out the next day to buy the movie's theme song, "Rock Around the Clock" by Bill Haley & His Comets. We strolled through Times Square, past Jack Dempsey's Restaurant where Jack himself was holding court. We went in and I was able to shake Jack's humongous hand, a hand that was responsible for fifty-one knockouts in his distinguished boxing career. Eventually Josephine stopped coming. My mother said it had something to do with Josephine and her boyfriend breaking up, whatever that meant, but my mother wouldn't elaborate, so I had to use my imagination. I missed Josephine and the exotic R&B and jazz she would listen to on the radio while cleaning.

I hadn't yet reached the age of eleven, but my live celebrity count already included Jack Dempsey, Junior Gilliam, the great Dodger infielder who worked off-season for my uncle, and Basil Rathbone. I thought of inviting all three together some evening for dinner. What conversations we could have! My mother could make her renowned spaghetti with ketchup while my father mixed us egg creams with a dollop of fragrantly aged Fox's U-Bet chocolate syrup. We could sit outside in the court fronting our little garden apartment while Jack delighted us with tales of his fight with Gene Tunney. Basil could regale us with gossip of Errol Flynn's dalliances while on the set of *The Adventures of Robin Hood*. All this as we listened to young Jewish mothers gathering up their children in voices that sounded not unlike the giant macaws of Costa Rica.

In early 1956 we moved upstate to the Schenectady suburb of Niskayuna. Our house was a tiny ranch on Fairlawn Parkway, just off of

Balltown Road, then the main route north to Saratoga Springs. Our little community was the quintessential '50s neighborhood, right out of *Leave It to Beaver* and *The Adventures of Ozzie & Harriet.* The main industry in Schenectady at the time was General Electric. Many of the white-collar engineers and scientists who worked for GE lived in Niskayuna. My father was a car salesman now, general manager of King Cadillac and Oldsmobile on State Street. He used the name Leo King at work, probably for two reasons: so people would think he owned the dealership, and because many of the Jews in Schenectady then, like in most small American towns, used Christian pseudonyms—Katz became King, Levine became LaVine. It was necessary to change one's name if one played golf and wanted to join the local gentile country club, and it was certainly easier to "pass for white" if one were Jewish than if one were black or Hispanic.

Nonetheless, Niskayuna was a wonderful place for a kid to grow up, especially if you didn't have a driver's license and could hardly leave the neighborhood. My friends and I would take a bus downtown to the Proctor's Theatre to see a movie, and usually stayed to see it twice if we were playing hooky.

I got my big break in show business in 1957 when I was in sixth grade. Craig Elementary School was not more than two miles from where I lived. For most of the school season, we were accompanied out to the bus stop by a parent where, in the predawn darkness, the pervasive smells of preteen children affected me in much the same way as the buzzer affected Skinner's mouse. To break the monotony of our little commute, I'd sometimes sing.

One day my sixth-grade class had a talent show and I decided that I wanted to perform. This time, though, I would have to sing in front of the class instead of from the backseat, where all I could see were the backs of a bunch of greasy little heads. I had to sing a cappella. The song I chose was "Singin' the Blues" by Guy Mitchell, a big hit of the day. Nervous as I was, I got up in front of the class and sang, and to my total and very pleasant surprise, my audience loved it. Girls that I had unrequited crushes on were swooning. I was in heaven. It was nothing less than massive ego satisfaction, and at only twelve years of age, I had to have more. So I auditioned for *Teenage Barn*.

Teenage Barn was a weekly show on WRGB-TV, the local NBC affiliate. It was broadcasting out of a weather-beaten studio located on the banks of the Mohawk River in Scotia, New York. It was live television and could be seen in the Tri-City area (Albany, Schenectady, and Troy) every Friday night. It was 1957—I had passed my audition and become a regular. The kids danced, sang, and generally did whatever their parents told them to, but these were the most talented kids in the area, and I was one of them. Every week I could choose the song I was to sing. Earl Pudney, pianist, local wedding minstrel, and TV personality, was my accompanist when he wan't spending time trying to get his toupee to stay on his head.

One week I would be singing "April Love" by Pat Boone as I wandered across a set of faux gray withered trees and plants (in those days, since most shows weren't in color, gray sets were commonly used). Another week I would sing Debbie Reynolds's "Tammy" while standing in a gray barn surrounded by artistically challenged two-dimensional models of goats and cows. Or I would sing Frank Sinatra's "All the Way" while standing on a little bridge that crossed over a gray stream, abutted by, again, the same phony gray withered trees and plants. This last performance was particularly scary, since the bridge that was hauled out from the scenery department was gathering mold from the basement where it was stored, getting soft, and was, at best, precarious to stand on, much less to walk across.

WRGB had decided to build new offices and studios in Niska-yuna, close to my house. By mid-1957 the building was ready and everything was moved. Our opening show was to be a celebration of the new venue, and so, for the first time, I would not be allowed to pick my own song. The producers wanted something more appropriate to the occasion and told me I had to sing "It's a Grand Night for Singing" from *State Fair*.

When I look back now at the patterns of my life, one that particularly stands out is that if I had to learn something that someone told me to learn, rather than to learn something of my own choice, I waited until the last minute. I would repeat this pattern later on when I had to write a term paper or study for a test. It was always at the last moment. I believe it started that week with my role on *Teenage Barn*. I didn't like the song they'd chosen for me and waited until the afternoon of the show to try to learn it. It was no use. Mr. Mental Block was sitting on my shoulder and would not budge.

At dress rehearsal I requested that I be able to read the lyrics for my performance. Showtime was at eight p.m., and it was to be a live broadcast, the first from the new studios. The director didn't need this, the crew didn't need this, and the producers didn't need this. But the director came up with a solution: I would be broadcast from the album room, a room that held all kinds of LPs used for sound effects and background music. I would hold an LP in my hands with typed lyrics taped to the back. I would hear a live feed of Earl's piano through a speaker that was set up in the room, and I would get my cue from Earl as I normally would. Excellent! Problem solved.

Wrong.

Eight o'clock arrived, the show was introduced, and the *good* kids went through their performances until it was my turn. I was about half a muscle twitch away from peeing in my pants when the red light on the camera went on and I heard Earl's intro. *This is not going to be that hard*, I thought, as I sang the first couple of lines. I looked down for the next line. Wait a second; *they had single-spaced the lyrics, and I couldn't find my next line*! Earl repeated his part and waited for me . . . and waited. What was meant to be a half-hour show that ended at 8:30 became a thirty-five-minute show that ended at 8:35. I didn't have time to find out what I was responsible for preempting for those five minutes. I was fired on the spot.

Life was good, though. The economy was on a roll, cars were huge, and we were at peace. The only rumbling of discontent we heard was about something called rock and roll. My favorite hangout those days was Apex Records, located downtown on State Street about a half block from Proctor's Theatre.

By the time I was fourteen, my love for records had eclipsed my sense of morality. Downtown Schenectady was only a hitchhike away from our little hamlet of Niskayuna, but my mother would have none of it. She insisted on driving me. Record stores were my playground. In those days you could sample records by taking them into your own private booth where you would have your own private turntable (and ashtray, if you were so inclined) and your own set of very uncomfortable headphones. Most records were in mono, so the ones that were in stereo were, to my mind, magical. I especial loved stereo demonstration records where you could listen to things like bowling balls rolling from one ear to another. Now that I look back on it, I wish I'd had one of those records years later, when I smoked my first joint.

Since my mother had volunteered to drive, and she had the cash, I asked her one day if she would buy me a record. I was totally dependent on my parents for the money I needed to feed my teenage shopping habits. The LP that I absolutely *had* to have was Stan Freberg's crazy comedy album, *A Child's Garden of Freberg*. She refused. I nonchalantly picked up my Daisy Red Ryder BB Gun, strolled into the bathroom, locked the door behind me, and threatened to blow my brains out. She caved.

———

Learning about the birds and the bees was a particularly sensitive topic in the 1950s because everyone then was trying to deny the very *existence* of "the birds and the bees," with the exception, of course, of the actual birds and bees. In our family my mother was the designated messenger. I came home from school one day, daydreaming as usual, when my mother told me she wanted to have a serious talk. She then asked me what the word or words were that described a man and a woman physically coupling to have a baby. She never learned the word *copulate*, and unfortunately, neither did I, so when I very hesitantly whispered the word *fuck*, my mother slapped me from one end of the room to the other, told me never to use that word again, and left me there without uttering another sound. I would imagine that pioneer children in the nineteenth century might have had things as rough, but certainly never as weird. I was stunned, caught totally off guard.

My brother, Dennis, was the next designated messenger. The following afternoon, while I was still suffering from a bruised cheek, he asked me if I knew the "facts of life." My first thought, *What the hell is going on here?*, became *I better get this over with*, and so I answered, "Sure, you're born, you're bar mitzvah'd, you marry, you have children, and you die." Frustrated and confused as to his role in all of this, he walked away without leaving me a clue as to why he had asked me such a stupid question in the first place. In retrospect, my answer was a pretty good one, and would have simplified many things for me if I'd just followed that path myself. As it happened, I finally learned about the birds and the bees much later in life, way after I copulated my way through the '60s.

While Dennis was attending the University of Buffalo, I was home in Niskayuna, rifling under his bed for the nudist magazines he so poorly hid from my parents. I can't say that my brother and I were very close. In retrospect, I can see that our divergent values began to exhibit themselves at around this time. Dennis began writing letters home to my poor beleaguered parents about how his undertaking in life was to make money and gain prestige among his peers. No doubt influenced by his friends at school and my father's lack of success in business, Dennis started smoking a pipe, wore Brooks Brothers sport jackets, and had his picture taken with some of the classiest small foreign sports cars that his richer friends at Buffalo would make available to him. After Buffalo he moved back home (we were then on Long Island), attended and graduated NYU, and then went on to Fordham Law School. Although living in the bedroom across from me, I still had little contact with my brother except for the times that he'd yell at me to keep my music down, especially while he was studying or smoking his pipe while listening to Telemann and all of the other effete baroque composers that were his contribution to the college milieu of the 1950s.

As time went on, I saw that Dennis and I were heading in opposite directions. His values remained firmly entrenched in the raising of his own social and financial place in life. He only cared about politics in the ways that it affected him directly, and had no proclivities toward charity or the human spirit. But he was my brother and we worked in parallel patterns for years. While I was happily contemplating becoming a musician in New York's favorite psychedelic blues band, my brother was climbing up the ladder of New York's middle-class Jewish elite. He married the daughter of an Upper East Side Harlem pawnbroker. They were married, of course, at The Plaza. (Somebody forgot to invite the groom's brother to the reception, but that was okay; I never liked those functions anyway.)

It was September of 1957, and Van Antwerp Junior High School was the next stop in what I loosely refer to as my education. It was here that classes were separated, as they are today, into different time periods in what we Americans call a "liberal education"; *liberal*, meaning, here's a bunch of things you should know and we'll guide you onto the path we think you should take. In my case they could have saved a lot of time. For instance, I hated math. I spent my entire time in seventh-grade math with a transistor radio in my briefcase attached to a wire that went up my shirt and ended at a tiny headphone in the palm of my hand that I would lean my head on. I heard a lot of music and listened to a lot of ball games, but learned nothing about math for a whole year, and I haven't caught up since. I don't know what I would have done if Texas Instruments hadn't invented the calculator.

In a perfect world I never would have had to dissect a crayfish or solve an equation. It would have been a world where I was allowed to daydream. English class was perfect because daydreaming was encouraged. I wanted to live in a world of literature and music, a world of the imagination. There existed a paperback book on the stands of the local luncheonette that for many a day I would covertly read after school. It was a book of cartoons about beatniks. It was written and illustrated from a straight person's point of view. The beatnik with the beard and beret was always the foil, the Maynard Krebs character from *The Many Loves of Dobie Gillis*. I related to the beatnik. I loved his poetry, his rebelliousness, his exotic women, and his cool jazz.

But my teenage daydream was disrupted when my maternal grandmother took her life. Gussie's Jake, my grandfather, had died a year earlier and Gussie was inconsolable. She could not live without Jake. They had made the trip together from Poland earlier in the century and built a life for themselves in America, but their children, my mother included, could not match the love that they shared for each other. Grandma was whisked off to live with her daughter, my aunt Betty, and her husband, Ted, at their home in Roslyn. Gussie slowly became incommunicative and one day walked down to the basement and hung herself.

It was the first death in the family that I had experienced. The closest I had come until then was when I asked my mother if my father's brother, Uncle Charlie, was still alive. She didn't know, and so she decided to call Uncle Charlie's wife, my aunt Frida, to find out. Frida answered the phone and the two exchanged pleasantries, at which point my mother, as tactfully as possible, asked: "So Frida, how's Charlie?"

Frida—"Charlie? How *should* Charlie be?"

My mother—"Well, how's he doing?"

Frida—"You know Charlie. How did he ever do? How are you?"
My mother—"How's his health?"
Frida—"How do you think?"
This went on for a few more minutes until my mother finally gave up. In the great Jewish tradition of answering questions with questions, my mother got off the phone still not knowing whether my uncle Charlie was dead or alive.

My father was the Willy Loman of our family. He lived in a dream world of hope—not far from reality, but not close enough to fulfill any dreams of success in the dog-eat-dog world of commerce. When we moved back to Long Island in 1960, my father began working with my uncle Teddy in Teddy's various business ventures. My uncle was a gambler, a hustler who would, without a glimmer of conscience, borrow from Peter to pay Paul. He built businesses with questionable foundations and brought my father into his schemes. My father was in over his head and did not have the wherewithal to deal in Teddy's somewhat sordid business world. They built a stable of racehorses that ran at Aqueduct, Belmont, Bowie, and Narragansett—the East Coast circuit. I don't think horse racing on the level that my uncle was involved was very profitable; their box at Aqueduct was too close to the betting windows. We had a few winners, but I don't imagine that they came close to paying expenses.

Uncle Ted and Aunt Betty eventually moved to Roslyn Harbor, an upper-middle-class town on the North Shore of Long Island. One of their neighbors, Peter Tripp, was a famous disc jockey in New York City. Tripp, known as "The Curly Headed Kid in the Third Row," broadcast for WMGM, a rival station to WABC and WINS, where Murray the K held his "submarine race watches." All three were Top 40 AM stations. Peter Tripp first gained notoriety during a stunt called a "Wake-a-Thon," where he broadcast from a glass booth in

Times Square for 201 hours without any sleep. He started to hallucinate after a few days, and doctors kept reviving him with what the more informed of us would later call "speed."

I babysat a couple of times for Peter Tripp. I watched his color TV, most likely part of the $38,000 in payola that he was later indicted for accepting. But the best part of my relationship with him was the stacks of promotional 45s he gave me. Although these records weren't in the Top 40, to me they represented an encyclopedic cross section of the independent music that was being produced in America at the time—R&B, electric and acoustic country blues, New Orleans funk, early Allen Toussaint and Ernie K-Doe, Minit, Jubilee, and King Records, the Chicago R&B that Chess and Checker would release and not get airplay on "white" stations, country, western swing, and gospel. Each artist, each label, told a story and described places that I'd never known existed. This wasn't always great music—some of it was not great at all—but as I listened, new worlds, way beyond the Top 40, began to open up for me. I sat on my bedroom floor and, like an explorer, went through each record, studying the labels, examining the B-sides, and finding new things that I had never heard before.

My uncle built the Plainview Country Club (later, the Americana Country Club), more precisely, a pool club located in Plainview, also on Long Island. I don't know whether the contractors were paid in cash (or were ever paid at all), but the place was built and functioned fairly well as an alternative to the Long Island beaches. Husbands would drop off their families for the day and join them on weekends where they'd be treated to performances by some of the top talent in show business.

I had two jobs at the club during the summers of 1960 and 1961. I swept out the place during the day, and for the weekend shows, I was lighting "director." I worked the lights for Della Reese, Jackie Mason, and others. Every now and then I got to sing with the band, the Hal Lynn Orchestra, a bunch of older union guys who probably couldn't wait for me to leave the stage. I'd sing my usual standards, only now I wore a white sports jacket, combed my hair in a pompadour, and struggled with a voice that was just reaching its postpubescent maturation.

My opening number was "The Gypsy in My Soul" by Moe Jaffe and Clay Boland. The song is about feeling free and wandering the world without a care, most likely in a baby blue '59 Cadillac while wearing a white sports jacket and combing back a four-inch pompadour—pretty ironic, coming from a kid who hadn't even learned how to drive yet. And I wasn't as adored as much as I was in elementary school; my audience was too busy with their roast beef and chicken cordon bleu dinners to pay any attention. A real tough crowd. But so what? I was paying my dues and building my credentials.

By February of 1967 the Blues Project had returned to San Francisco after our extended club gigs in New York. I had technically been in show business for ten years. We were still on the cusp of homelessness, but not for long. Although we never made any money, we were becoming well-known, and I was even getting recognized on the streets of Manhattan. How did I cope with success? I loved it. I was having a great time. It was fun to have this happening to me, and especially to have it happen when the whole of the country, and especially my generation, was changing so rapidly. I never was fully able to separate our own limited success with what was encompassing the rest of America at the time. I never saw what was happening as anything unique to the times, and that made it feel like I was a part of something—that I finally "belonged" somewhere. Aside from an inconvenience or two, like the odd venereal disease or the war in Vietnam, I was having the time of my life. After all, my job was to play and create music; how much better can it get than winding up doing what you love the most?

We moved on from the Avalon Ballroom to the Fillmore Auditorium. As Chet Helms did with the Avalon, so Bill Graham did with the Fillmore, although Graham was a totally different kind of person than Helms. A Korean War veteran, Graham was the Berlin-born orphaned son of Russian Jewish immigrants. His father died two days after Bill was born, and his mother died at Auschwitz. Graham worked for a time in the Catskills, then moved out to San Francisco and started working as the impresario for a radical theater group, the San Francisco Mime Troupe. He eventually opened the Fillmore Ballroom in partnership with Chet Helms, until the two had a dispute over who could book the Paul Butterfield Blues Band.

Bill Graham could be impossible to work for, his temper was infamous, and he could at times be loud and belligerent, but he treated musicians well and with respect. The first time the Blues Project played at the Fillmore was with Jimmy Reed and John Lee Hooker as our opening acts. Bill gave each of us bonuses. This was unheard of for a musician in those days, and I never forgot him for it. He could be gruff and impossible, but he was a good man and had integrity, something rare both then and now in the music business.

Graham always added little touches to his promotions, little things like the barrel of free apples that was always in the lobby of the Fillmore. It was the small but meaningful touches that helped foster Graham's legend. We played the Fillmore again on February 17–19, with Canned Heat and the Mothers of Invention opening. The Fillmore Auditorium, like the Avalon Ballroom, was just that—a ballroom about twice the size of a high school gymnasium, maybe a little bigger. Half the audience was stoned on LSD or pot, and the Joshua Light Show embraced you with its visual barrage of dancing amoebas and tie-dyed paramecia projected from liquid slides.

At one of our Fillmore gigs, I had pneumonia. Although I was very sick, I got up and played—not an easy thing to do when you're playing harmonica for a good part of your set. But once I got onstage, I felt fine. It's amazing how the adrenaline of performing can kill the symptoms and detonate any pain. As soon as the show was over, however, I fainted—just fell over—and had to be carried upstairs to the dressing room.

We were staying out by the sea at the Seal Rock Inn, southwest of the city, the place we normally stayed when we were in San Francisco and not begging for lodging from our fans. I awoke the next morning with what must have been a very high fever. I turned the radio on to try to find some healing music, soul or rock, anything to help my cause, and that was the first time I heard "Strawberry Fields" by the Beatles. I didn't know it was the Beatles—in fact, it sounded like nothing I had *ever* heard before. I honestly thought I might have been hallucinating. I was convinced that I had died and gone to heaven—until I had to get out of bed and pee.

Al Kooper visited my room a couple of days later and insisted that I take a hit from the joint he was smoking and, stupidly, I did. The pain in my lungs was excruciating. I had *pneumonia*, for chrissake! This may have marked the beginning of many problems I would have with Al over the years. A more delusional, paranoid version of myself might conclude, in retrospect, that this was the first of many attempts by Al Kooper to do me in.

CHAPTER 5

Submarine Race Watching

I FIRST MET MURRAY KAUFMAN IN 1961 AT MY UNCLE'S COUNTRY club on Long Island. Murray, better known as Murray the K, was in Plainview to host a pre-Beatles rock extravaganza starring Frankie Avalon. I was sweeping up around the pool for less than minimum wage, but I was able to peek in at rehearsals and watch Murray and Frankie as they schmoozed each other half to death.

This kind of schmoozing was a new concept for me, one that I was not quite comfortable with until years later when I was in Blood, Sweat & Tears and was forced to be friendly with folks who worked in "radio." Before then, during the mid-'60s, the Art of the Schmooze was just not cool for hip young musicians—was not too different from "kissing ass." It was the first step toward selling out.

Murray the K was the most popular DJ in New York in the early '60s. His show on WINS (which later became a famous all-news station) was called *The Swingin' Soiree*. Murray played songs for "submarine race watching," and invented a new language, "Me-a-Surray," more or less Murray's version of Pig Latin. In the mid-'60s, Murray made the move to WOR-FM radio, helping to create a revolutionary format sometimes referred to as "underground radio," where there were no time restrictions on airplay. The growth of FM rock radio inspired a new kind of creative energy for musicians, as bands were no longer confined to the two-and-a-half-minute single. Murray and people like him were playing album cuts and sometimes even whole albums.

Murray the K would invite bands to come up to the WOR studio to do interviews or to hang out and "guest-DJ." Years after first seeing him at my uncle's country club, this was how Murray and I became friends. The Blues Project was New York's hip underground rock band, and Murray's show was New York's hippest radio program. I would sometimes go uptown to WOR and listen to new American music and the latest imports coming out of England. It was how I first heard The Who and Jimi Hendrix. Sometime during the summer of 1967, a friend lent me a copy of Jimi's first album before its stateside release, and the second after I heard Hendrix's solo on "The Wind Cries Mary," I immediately called Murray and told him he had to play it. Murray did, and didn't stop playing it. Murray was small in stature, but he was a giant in radio. He was brave and took chances and had as much energy as a small rocket ship.

Murray augmented his radio shows with rock 'n' roll extravaganzas that he produced and in which he starred with a bevy of dancers and a roster of famous pop acts, mainly at the Brooklyn Fox Theater. He would put on these shows three or four times a year, brilliantly coordinating the timing with school vacations to make sure the teenage madness was at its peak when he came to town. The last of Murray's "spectaculars" was a 1967 Easter offering, now moved from Brooklyn to Manhattan's RKO 58th Street Theatre on the East Side, a stone's throw from Bloomingdale's and Alexander's World of Tomorrow Shop, where one could buy overpriced Tom Jones shirts and paisley bell-bottoms. Not only was Murray's show during Easter school vacation, but it was during its run that the very first Easter Be-In, also known as the Easter Sunday Love-In, was held in Central Park, not far from the RKO 58th Street Theatre. The times, they were a changin', indeed.

"Murray the K Presents Live in Person Music in the Fifth Dimension" ran for nine days in 1967, from March 25 to April 2—five shows per day, from ten a.m. to past midnight. One thing that I will never understand about the history of the music scene in the '60s is how underplayed and forgotten Murray's last show has become; it was ahead of its time, a few months before Monterey Pop, and was the American debut of The Who and Cream. Later I would play Monterey and Woodstock, and many more festivals, with both the Blues Project and Blood, Sweat & Tears, and in my mind, the most unforgettable was Murray's RKO 58th Street Theatre show. Here was the lineup:

Mitch Ryder with the Mitch Ryder Show (headliner)
Wilson Pickett (headliner)
Cream (first American performance)
The Who (first American performance)
The Blues Project
Jim & Jean
Mandala
The Hardly Worthit Players
Jackie & The "K" Girls
The Chicago Loop (with my friend Stefan Grossman)
Phil Ochs (special guest)
The Blues Magoos (special guest)
The Young Rascals (special guest)

Simon & Garfunkel (as special guest) and Smokey Robinson and the Miracles were scheduled to appear as well, but Smokey dropped out at the last minute, possibly because Murray was under pressure to name Mitch Ryder as the headline act, but more likely because Smokey wisely wanted cash and half up front, which was something that Murray couldn't afford (or most likely didn't even have).

The lineup was amazing, but the stories that came out of the show were even more amazing. The jam sessions backstage were legend.

Imagine Eric Clapton jamming with Wilson Pickett, or Buddy Miles with Pete Townshend. Mandala from Toronto was one of the best blue-eyed soul bands to emerge from the era, with the wonderful Domenic Troiano on guitar. Buddy Miles, playing drums for Wilson Pickett, was being courted by Mike Bloomfield during the show and wound up working with Mike in the Electric Flag. Wilson Pickett's band must have had fifteen musicians, most of whom were screwing teenage groupies under the stage in between sets.

We were all allowed three songs per show. At first, Cream played "I Feel Free," "I'm So Glad," and "Toad." As their jams got longer, they were down to two songs, and finally just one, usually "I'm So Glad," which they performed five times a day. For The Who, the show put an amazing amount of pressure on Keith Moon's drum set, which had to be cobbled together five times a day. By the last day of the show, Keith's kit was hardly recognizable anymore. The same could be said for Pete Townshend's guitars. Roger Daltrey destroyed no less than eighteen of Murray's precious microphones.

But the truth, as strange as it seems, is that aside from the weekend shows, there were very few people in the audience. The show was basically a bomb, and we all knew that we probably weren't going to get paid our full fees, if we'd get paid at all. Mitch Ryder would get mobbed by a few audience members every show, an obvious setup that most of the rest of us musicians thought was funny and pathetic at the same time, ten kids rushing the stage out of an audience of fifty. Mitch would go back to his dressing room and literally cry after some shows. We were told that he was crying because he couldn't sing as well as Otis Redding, but I had a suspicion that there was something more to it than that.

We shared a dressing room with Cream. I had arrived at the theater early on the first day and was still trying to digest my breakfast when a tall, thin, red-headed, red-eyed apparition of a man-child flung open the door and tossed a bottle of vodka at me. Ginger Baker then asked—well, sort of insisted—that I take a swig.

We got to be good friends with Ginger, Eric, and Jack, and wound up hanging out together between and after shows, sometimes at my apartment, and then later, if we were in any condition to hail a cab, at Steve Paul's The Scene on West Forty-Sixth Street. One Saturday night a few of us took a cab downtown from Fifty-Eighth Street to MacDougal Street. Eric Clapton was the first one out of the cab, and I was right behind him. He still had his hand resting on the door frame when I closed the door, right on his hand.

Eric Clapton was the god of the guitar, even then. And as he was standing there doubled over, howling in pain in the middle of Mac-Dougal Street, my mind was racing. By the time he stopped screaming, I had already come up with eight different ways of committing suicide. Luckily, I hadn't broken any of his fingers. In fact, he was actually able to play the show that night.

There was also one evening when some of us came from Murray's uptown show to the Dugout on Bleecker Street. At my table were Pete Townshend and Ginger Baker. Townshend was telling us about an idea he had for something called a "rock opera," all the while gallantly trying to be heard over the strains of the ubiquitous Barbra Streisand emanating from the Dugout jukebox. We then all left for Gerdes Folk City; on our way, in a field that was to house future NYU buildings, an inebriated Ginger Baker stopped suddenly, bent over, and threw up. Totally ignorant of this quaint old British custom, I ran to Ginger's side and asked if he was okay, to which he looked up at me quizzically and said, "Aren't we going to another bar?"

On the day of the first big Easter Be-In, Al Kooper, Jack Bruce, and I decided to walk over to Central Park. Al and Jack made the mistake of eating some popcorn and jelly beans that people were handing out. Pretty soon they were tripping. I didn't take Al seriously; in fact, I thought he was faking it. All he wanted to do for the rest of the day was play with a toy duck that he'd found somewhere. It was too ridiculous to be real. I suggested to Jack that we go down to my apartment where someone had kindly left me a tranquilizer a couple of weeks before. Jack declined, and Kooper held that duck in his hands for the rest of the day.

Everyone hated Murray. He could be crass and egotistical, and most people didn't see the other, generous and very genuinely hip side of him. All that schmoozing made him look like a cheap hustler.

Things came to a head during the show when Murray got wind that we were planning to do some crazy shit on the last day. The first incident involved Murray's wife, Jackie the K, who was the leader of Murray's dance girls. It was hard to tell who did it because we were all pretty wasted during the show, but someone took a fire ax and chopped down the door to Jackie the K's dressing room. Murray was finally incensed enough to call a meeting of all the musicians. We decided that a couple of us would head on over to Times Square and buy a bunch of rubber Halloween masks that all of us would wear when he confronted us. We were there, with Cream and The Who, and I don't know how we were able to keep a "straight face" under all that rubber. When Murray entered the room and looked out on at least twenty monster masks, he conducted his meeting like it was business as usual, reprimanding us and our plans to sabotage his show, all without a single acknowledgment of the ridiculous sight before him. For me, this was one of the great moments in rock and roll.

Because we had doubts about getting paid, and because we were essentially kids who had no respect for Murray or any other adult over thirty, no matter that they had actually helped us to whatever degree, we decided to put into effect our plans for the last night. This time, aside from blowing up Keith's drums, The Who's roadies were going to place explosives around the audience to make it look like the whole place was getting blown up. Al Kooper elected, for some idiotic reason, to throw a tambourine. Voilà! Fifteen stitches required in the arm of a very frightened and unsuspecting attendee. Kooper couldn't be found for days.

Murray never did pay anybody. A few days after the show, I ran into Wilson Pickett's bass player at The Scene. Pickett would fine his musicians five dollars for every mistake they made onstage. This wouldn't be so bad if you were getting paid. I asked how he had made out, and he told me that, by the end of the show, he owed Pickett thirty-five dollars.

At the same time the Murray the K shows were happening uptown, Frank Zappa and the Mothers of Invention took up residence downtown at the Garrick Theatre, above the Cafe au Go Go. Some of the best music I ever heard and some of the funniest moments I ever spent were at Frank's shows. I was there when Frank got three marines up onstage to sing at a time when the Vietnam War was in full swing, and military personnel did not look very kindly on long-haired, antiwar, hippie-musician, draft-dodging freaks. I was there when Louie the Turkey was in the audience, which was for almost every performance. Louie laughed loudly and sounded like a turkey, so Zappa dubbed him "Louie the Turkey." Zappa would often spend time at Andy Kulberg's apartment, playing music and talking. Frank and Andy both came from formal musical backgrounds and enjoyed each other's company; I would join them whenever I could.

There's a story in Al Kooper's autobiography about a very difficult gig we had in Montreal around the same time. It was just a few weeks after the Murray the K shows, and on the eve of Expo '67's official VIP-only opening. Designer Francois Dallegret threw what he called "The Super Party" at the main exhibition hall of the recently opened Place Bonaventure. Also on the bill were Lothar and the Hand People and Tiny Tim.

This was Expo's supremely unofficial opening party. The stage was, somewhat appropriately, a boxing ring. The sound system was horrible, *we* sounded horrible, and there were people in the audience throwing beer bottles at us. There was a lot of tension backstage, which culminated in a fistfight between Al and me. What Al doesn't mention, though, is that the argument began when Al accused me of stealing his ham sandwich. He started the fight by pushing me, so I pounded him, and I couldn't help but think to myself, *Here we are, two Jews, fighting over ham.*

We were flown to Montreal from New York in a de Havilland Twin Otter, a small ten-seater plane. On the way back to New York, Danny Kalb had horrible pressure problems in his ears. Every time the pilot tried to fly lower, Danny would scream in pain and demand that the pilot go back up. This went on for quite a while until we finally explained to Danny the consequences of staying in the air indefinitely.

That spring I moved from my little firetrap on Eighth Avenue to a new studio apartment just around the corner, at 39 Jane Street, a four-story building in the far West Village. The little kitchenette was new and the floor was level. There was even an elevator. The Jane Street apartment became a popular hangout. I hung an old fiddle and banjo on my wall and played my Gibson B-25 acoustic guitar while sitting either on my couch or on the edge of my fold-out bed, across the room and next to the desk on which I had written my newspaper column when I was in high school. Rock star or not, I was still carrying around furniture from my youth.

That guitar can be heard on "You've Made Me So Very Happy" from the second Blood, Sweat & Tears album. It's played through a Leslie speaker at the end and sounds like an organ, although I've never actually heard an organ do a "hammer-on." Eric Clapton once spent an afternoon at my Jane Street apartment playing my B-25, along with my Albert and Freddie King records, while I went out to do some grocery shopping. Don Everly, from the Everly Brothers, played it, too. He came up one evening for a jam session with myself and John Sebastian. I asked Don if he would play "Wake Up, Little Susie." Don then proceeded to tune the guitar to an open G tuning.

This was a revelation for me; I had been playing it for years in regular tuning, but when I tried it myself in G, it worked. It just sounded right. Everly magic.

Probably the most memorable evening for me at my Jane Street apartment was when Canadian guitarist Lenny Breau came up after a gig at the Bitter End. There were about eight other people there. Lenny played my little B-25, which at this point needed a setup badly. The action was high and the frets were coming up. That didn't stop Lenny, who played like Chet Atkins and Bill Evans combined. I put headphones on him as he played into my mic and, luckily, I recorded it. Lenny Breau was murdered on August 12, 1984. He was one of the greats, a musician so good that the only way to describe him would be to say he was a freak of nature. When I listen to that tape today, I remember Lenny, small and compact, a stutterer, a great guy and a genius. Whether he's playing "Autumn Leaves" or "The Claw" by Jerry Reed, you can't help but be in awe and at the same time feel so sad for someone who died that young, and whose music was so powerfully human and transcendent. It puts music and musicians into a whole other place, a whole other world, and at times I wonder how some people can go through life and not play an instrument or love music with a passion.

The only bad time I had at Jane Street was a few years later when I brought home a pre-release test pressing of the Blood, Sweat & Tears second album and played it for some friends. Everyone was polite; a bit *too* polite. This was also the album that was practically ignored by Clive Davis and Jann Wenner when I played a test pressing for them in Clive's office up in Black Rock, the CBS building on Fifty-Second Street and Sixth Avenue. I was depressed for days, ready for unemployment compensation. But then it turned out to be the album that spawned three top-ten singles, was number one on the charts for weeks, went on to win an Album of the Year Grammy in 1970, and sold over six million units in America alone, more or less, depending on who was on duty at any given time in the Columbia Records Royalty Department.

In early May of 1967, Al Kooper went on to have another breakdown. This time he wanted out of the band and wanted to do more of his own music. He had a point. Danny was rigid in his taste for blues, and Al was still steeped in Tin Pan Alley. Al wanted to add horns, and Danny was against it. The two had to clash at some point, and so Al left the band, and not on the best of terms. Al has also cited his ulcer and drug problems as a cause for leaving, but after working with him in two bands, my feeling has always been that Al and his ego need total control over whoever he works with, and at the expense of some pretty good people. He probably would have wound up with a lot more friends if he had never joined any bands in the first place; his biggest mistake has always been to think of himself as a better singer than he was a writer.

One of the last gigs with Al in the band was at the Town Hall on West Forty-Third Street, just east of Times Square. It was on Friday, May 5, 1967, and the show was sold out. The concert was later released as the band's third album, *The Blues Project Live at Town Hall*. Some of the tracks were actually recorded in the studio and dumped onto the album with canned applause and no particular aesthetic consideration as to feel or flow. My contribution was a Patrick Sky song, "Love Will Endure," a track that some drunk at MGM must have mixed. Sadly, and thanks to MGM, that was the legacy of the Blues Project—a great live band who, thanks to an uncaring record company, made some pretty poor-sounding records that never went further than FM radio.

Danny Kortchmar, from the Flying Machine with James Taylor, a group we had played with often at the Night Owl, knew of a talented black kid by the name of John McDuffy. He was Kortchmar's former bandmate in the King Bees. Danny thought that John-John, as he was known to friends, might make a good replacement for Kooper, and we agreed.

John-John's first gig with us was on Friday, June 9, 1967, at the Action House, Long Beach, New York, and then a gig that Sunday at the Village Theatre with The Doors for a "WOR-FM Birthday Party." John-John joined us just in time to fly out to San Francisco and drive to Monterey for the Monterey Pop Festival. We had an invitation from Lou Adler and John Phillips of the Mamas and the Papas to play there prior to Al's departure. It was a very big deal; the only New York acts that were invited to perform there were us, Laura Nyro, and Simon & Garfunkel. But when Adler and Phillips found out that Al had left the Blues Project, our invitation was rescinded. We were furious and insisted on coming.

I flew out to Monterey, not feeling great about doing a festival where we weren't wanted, and with a band that was on the verge of collapse. Once there, I was won over by the beauty of the venue and the hipness of the festival. Al Kooper was there as well, as assistant stage manager for the promoters. Based on Adler and Phillips's invitation to the Blues Project, Al also performed. I guess they figured *The guy is out here; we might as well get him up onstage.*

So Kooper donned his new clothes, borrowed wholesale from the emperor, and turned in a typically cocky, nonchalant set. We couldn't afford to rent a car, so I spent the three days bumming rides from Art Garfunkel. Art and I were both New Yorkers, but he had the hits, so he could afford the car. The rest of us New Yorkers had to fend for ourselves amid a herd of West Coast celebrities, entrepreneurs, and record company moguls looking for the Next Big Thing.

Backstage at Monterey was an amazing scene. There was something akin to a rustic chophouse where the cafeteria was located. Wandering around were Brian Jones, Janis Joplin, Hendrix—on and on. There was a hot dog stand where one night I had dinner with Jimi Hendrix. Jimi was in the middle of eating his hot dog when his road manager came to tell him to get ready for the stage. The next thing I knew, he was setting his guitar on fire.

It was a crazy time: I met Otis Redding before he went on, just months before he was to die in a plane crash. I was backstage when Big Brother and the Holding Company came on, and I ran to the wings to watch Janis Joplin's performance of "Ball and Chain." It was raining when Ravi Shankar was brought to the stage, and when he started playing, the sun came out. I turned to our drummer, Roy, and said, "Wouldn't you know it," typical East Coast cynicism. I saw Laura Nyro perform her wonderful song "Poverty Train," which later was unfairly blasted by West Coast rock critics.

It was our turn to perform, on the last of the three days, Sunday, June 18. Tommy Smothers of the Smothers Brothers introduced Paul Simon, who introduced us. We were the first act of the evening set. Only Ravi Shankar played before us that afternoon. The acts that played after us, in order of appearance, were: The Group with No Name, Buffalo Springfield, Grateful Dead, The Who, the Jimi Hendrix Experience, the Mamas and the Papas, and Scott McKenzie. We were purposely put into the schedule while people were returning to their seats from an intermission, and it was a disaster. John-John's microphone wasn't working, either for his keyboard or his vocal.

The live recordings of us at Monterey were without vocal or organ! The excellent video of outtakes from D. A. Pennebaker's film contains "Flute Thing," which did not have a vocal anyway, but lacks keyboard. I didn't mind the negative part about being at Monterey, since all the magic made up for it. My heart was not in the band anymore either, and, like Al, I also wanted to move on. I just never even imagined that I'd be moving on *with* Al.

⌐∾⌐

Back home after the Monterey Pop Festival, we found that we had a very busy month coming up in July. We played at the Fourteenth

Annual Newport Jazz Festival and did two gigs with The Who—the first at the Malibu Shore Club on Long Island and, the next night, at the Village Theatre, where, believe it or not, The Who and Richie Havens both opened for us.

Steve Paul got himself a TV program called, of all things, *The Steve Paul Scene*. In July we went into a TV studio and taped the first and only edition of the show. The guests were Aretha Franklin, Moby Grape, the Staple Singers, the Rascals, the Chambers Brothers, and us. Mavis Staples kept coming into our dressing to have a smoke. Pops Staples led his own family antismoking campaign, so Mavis had to sneak one every now and then. Imagine—Mavis Staples and Aretha Franklin on the same TV show as the Blues Project. They must have been *thrilled*.

We did "Wake Me, Shake Me," "Steve's Song," and "Flute Thing." The show was broadcast on Monday, September 4, 1967, on WNEW-TV in New York and also syndicated across the country.

That July we did our last recording, yet another abbreviated three-hour session. The record company assigned us producer Shadow Morton, who had produced "Leader of the Pack" by the Shangri-Las. I can't remember Morton adding anything or even *doing* anything. The session was for a single, two songs: the A-side, a medium-tempo shuffle called, ironically, "Lost in the Shuffle," by John-John and Joel "Bishop" O'Brien of the King Bees, and the B-side, a song of mine called "Gentle Dreams." Andy Kulberg wrote a little flute piece to go into the track, so Andy and I shared the writing credit.

It was during that summer of 1967 that the danger of being drafted and my heartbreak over Mimi were fading comfortably into my past. I felt I could concentrate on my music and have a better time hanging out with my friends without any shadows hanging over my head. During the day I would write or rehearse. I would spend time at Manny's Music, trying out guitars, or I would visit sessions in town, like the afternoon I spent at Atlantic Studios with Cream while they were recording *Disraeli Gears*. When not playing with the band, I'd spend my nights either uptown at Steve Paul's The Scene in the heart of the theater district, at the Dugout, or at the new restaurant upstairs from the Dugout called the Tin Angel, which is where I first met Joni Mitchell.

Joni was introduced to me by Dave Van Ronk, who had befriended her and recorded a very beautiful version of Joni's "Both Sides Now" (Dave renamed it "Clouds"). One evening a few of us decided to go back to Joni's Chelsea apartment to jam and trade songs. Somehow I talked Joni into coming back to my place, and by the next morning we were a couple. At least for the moment.

Joni had some dates in the South and had to leave the next day. After carefully thinking about any commitments and having yet another panic attack over it, I decided I was having too much fun to settle down. It didn't help that Joni wrote a short letter to me while she was away and used someone else's first name in the salutation. So when Joni came back and called to say she was coming over, I called our drummer, Roy, and asked him over as well.

I introduced her to Roy and left the building on some silly excuse. When I came back, Joni and Roy were a couple and spent most of the summer together. Problem was, Roy already had a girlfriend, Marie, whom he could not leave. Joni was distraught for weeks.

I saw her once after that, when she opened for Blood, Sweat & Tears at Hunter College. She was so nice and polite that it wasn't until later that I questioned whether or not she even remembered me. Our short tryst is well documented in Sheila Weller's wonderful book, *Girls like Us: Carole King, Joni Mitchell, Carly Simon—and the Journey of a Generation*.

Around the same time, I met Bobby Colomby, the drummer for Odetta, while hanging out in the Village. His brother Harry managed Thelonious Monk, and so Bobby, who had a degree in psychology, was brought up in a musical home surrounded by some of the jazz legends of the 1950s and early '60s. Bobby still lived at home with his mother,

Elsie, in the Bronx, just off of the Grand Concourse. Bobby and I became good friends and wound up hanging out a lot together.

I was club-hopping almost every night—at Steve Paul's The Scene, Ondine, the Electric Circus. I didn't enjoy being alone. If I didn't have a date or a friend over, I would panic and go out until I was either too tired or too stoned to stay up any longer. If I hadn't "scored" a girl by two a.m., I would be on the lookout for a waitress who was just getting off. Sometimes it was the only reason I had to choose whatever restaurant, bar, or club I would visit. I couldn't sustain a relationship, but I couldn't be alone. If I still hadn't scored by about three or four a.m., I would go to my apartment, depressed, frustrated, and in a panic. I would turn on the TV, but in those pre-cable days, after a certain time at night, there *was* no TV. So I just sat there, waiting until morning, when I could play guitar without waking my neighbors, and hoping we would have a rehearsal that afternoon until the entire cycle started over.

By mid-July we had gone our separate ways. A week of gigs at the Fillmore had to be canceled. Roy and Andy went off to the Virgin Islands, John-John and I stayed in New York, and Danny went back to San Francisco and fell in with Stanley Owsley, the Bay Area's leading LSD manufacturer and Grateful Dead adjunct. Danny, who was already in a fragile state—not only from the band breakup, but because of his own psychological history—was given a large dose of acid by Stanley and flipped out. According to Roy, he went to a park and "communed" with nature, then went to the Avalon Ballroom and "communed" again for hours with a streetlight outside the venue. He couldn't come down from the acid and subsequently had a major psychotic paranoid panic attack, which landed him in a jail cell, screaming all night long.

In the following days, he was placed on a flight back to New York. Roy and Andy cut their vacation short when they received word that

Danny, back in New York, had attempted suicide by jumping out of the window of a six-story office building. He escaped death by bouncing off of a landing on the floor below, falling onto a storefront awning (breaking his fall), crashing through a plate-glass storefront window, and narrowly missing a sharp wrought-iron fence. As he got up, he began walking around in a daze. A bystander told him to lie down while an ambulance was hailed from St. Vincent's Hospital.

After Danny had been released from the hospital, he was temporarily taken in by a friend, an ex-nun by the name of Fran. When Roy and Andy got back to the Village, they visited Danny and found him standing in an empty hallway in Fran's apartment building, banging his head against a wall and crying. Someone arranged for Danny to stay at a retreat called "The Country Place," a facility in a beautiful rural setting in Connecticut that was run by a team of psychiatrists. Danny would never fully recuperate.

We played the Cafe au Go Go one last time, for a week, and this time with Al back in the band for a hot second, along with John-John. There exists video footage of the gig, of us doing "I Can't Keep from Crying," one of the very few videos of the Blues Project that exist today. In September 1967 the band broke up again and a last gig at Carnegie Hall was canceled.

Roy ran into John-John years later, in Ithaca, New York. At that time he was "Professor of Soul Music" at a local university. Sadly, he died in 2005 at the age of fifty-nine in a fire at his Queens, New York, apartment.

Andy and Roy decided to move to San Francisco and get a house in Marin County. They would wait for Danny to join them when he was well enough. The plan was to start a new version of the Blues Project (which later became Sea Train), but it became obvious that Danny still wasn't fit enough to play, and so he returned to New York to rebuild his psyche and his guitar-playing abilities by teaching and playing as much as he could.

I went into a period of creative woodshedding, writing, and learning new songs in preparation for whatever was to come next. This was a good opportunity for my friend Bobby Colomby and I to put something together.

One day, however, as I was in the middle of writing a new song, the phone rang . . .

CHAPTER 6

"What Do I Do with All This Money?"

Al Kooper, who had just returned from his California sojourn, gave me a call. It was a July day in 1967. He wanted to put together a band for a benefit he was organizing for himself at the Cafe au Go Go. He wanted to purchase a one-way ticket to London to start a solo career.

Al wanted to bring in Jim Fielder from LA to play bass. Jimmy had started out playing rhythm guitar for the Mothers of Invention, and then spent some time filling in on bass with Buffalo Springfield when Bruce Palmer was arrested on a drug charge. I'm not sure what I was thinking when I agreed to join, except that I was eager to play in front of a crowd again. I recommended my friend Bobby on drums and inserted myself on guitar.

We played three nights in a row, July 27–29, 1967. Al had invited some special guests to play, including Judy Collins and Eric Andersen. I remember Judy and Eric being advertised, but I don't remember them actually showing up and playing. Unfortunately, Al only raised enough money to take a cab to the airport. He insists to this day that Howard Solomon underpaid him for the gig, but according to my memory, very few people came to contribute to Al's getaway after the first "star-studded night." Ironically, we did "I Can't Quit Her" that night, which Al dedicated to the Statue of Liberty—quite appropriate, since he never got around to leaving America.

Kooper was writing some terrific songs then, probably the best of his career. Bobby, Jimmy, and I persuaded Al to continue with us in a band where we would add horns, like Al had wanted to do with the Blues Project, and work up some really good material. Al liked the idea, and so in August of 1967, our search for the horn section began, beginning with one of the people Bobby knew from the Bronx, alto sax player, pianist, and arranger Fred Lipsius. Freddie did most of the horn charts, mainly with Al.

I had written a song called "Megan's Gypsy Eyes." I had gone from pain to bitterness since Mimi Fariña had left, and wrote this nasty little song about her. To this day, I wish I could take some of it back. That's the problem with releasing records. You bare yourself and sometimes regret the mistakes when it's too late and it's released for posterity. I named "Megan's Gypsy Eyes" after Phil and Alice Ochs's daughter, a beautiful blonde child who can be seen in a classic photo that Alice took of Reverend Gary Davis. Freddie and I wrote the chart together. The horn part on the bridge sounds like the Tijuana Brass— mea culpa, but it worked.

I had remained close friends with Keith Moon since the Murray the K show. Some nights Bobby Colomby and I would hang out with The Who at Chris Huston's studio while they were recording *The Who Sell Out*. We had done a demo there earlier of "Megan's Gypsy Eyes."

Our new band needed a name. I thought of a couple that were rejected—Fish Flesh was one, and Herpes Simplex was the other. (Imagine the DJs on classic radio today if we had named the band Herpes Simplex—*And here's that great hit, "Spinning Wheel" by David Clayton-Thomas and his Herpes Simplex!*) So, one afternoon as I was lying in bed with a new female friend, the phone rang. Kooper says, "I've got it—Blood, Sweat and Tears!" I was in a rush to get off the phone and get back to business so I just said, "Okay," and hung up. According to Al, he got the idea from looking at the Johnny Cash album of the same name in his apartment earlier that afternoon. Typically, Al's story has changed a few times over the years.

In September 1967, Al Kooper took Bobby Colomby and Jimmy Fielder into Regent Sound in New York to cut three song demos that would also be used to shop the band. Al hired two studio trumpet players and overdubbed them to sound like four. They recorded "I Can't Quit Her," "My Days Are Numbered," and a song called "I Need to Fly," which I don't remember at all.

One month later, in October 1967, we held open auditions to recruit the horn section. We added Dick Halligan on trombone, keyboards, vocals, and flute; Jerry Weiss on trumpet and flugelhorn; and a genius from Philadelphia by the name of Randy Brecker, also on trumpet and flugelhorn. These guys were schooled musicians, pros, and, except for Freddie, young and hip. Freddie was young but not very hip, but his music was. In fact, you could say that Freddie had a one-track mind—all he thought about was music—and he ignored the rest of life around him, especially such frippery as fashion and style. The rest of us had a limited musical education, if any at all, but were plenty hip by now, and wore the decade on our sleeves. It was a perfect combination, rock players meet jazz players. But the rock part had to be dominant, or, as later proven, the concept wouldn't work.

Kooper and I had both been listening to the Buckinghams' album, *Time & Charges*, produced by a young guitarist who had played with England's Chad and Jeremy, James William Guercio. Guercio, originally from Chicago, used some of the Chicago Symphony horns on the Buckinghams' album, and it sounded like nothing we had ever heard before. The charts were fresh, exciting, intelligent, and masterfully played. We wanted to do something like this, but wanted to choose or write better material and be able to take it on the road.

Howard Solomon let us rehearse afternoons at the Cafe au Go Go. In retrospect, Al must have forgiven Howard for stealing money from him, but then again, Al has made the same accusations about others over the years. I will never forget our first rehearsal with the new horn section. We had worked up Tim Buckley's "Morning Glory" and I was the singer. When the horns entered on the second verse for the first time, I almost couldn't sing. I hate to describe the feeling with an overused word like "orgasm," but that's the only thing I can think of that comes even remotely close to the realm of pleasure and transcendence I experienced. The sound, the feel of the building verse into the chorus, it was at that moment that I said to myself, *So this is why I wanted to be a musician.* It was an ethereal moment. Forget the music business and the dues one has to pay to survive in it. That one moment made it all worthwhile. That's something you can carry with you for the rest of your life.

The Monterey Pop Festival produced a race among record companies to sign "alternative" bands. Record executives were everywhere, signing and crediting themselves with "discovering" the great bands of the '60s. According to the "What Goes On" column in *Crawdaddy* magazine, we were expected to sign to the Blues Project's old label, Verve/Folkways Records. If they ever did actually offer us a contract, Al and I would have had a good laugh over it. MGM, the parent company, never allowed the Blues Project any decent studio time. They mixed tracks without our permission, screwed up our album covers without any input from the band, and God knows whatever else they did with our royalties, which we never saw anyway. We would look at our Verve/Folkways experience as a cautionary sign on how to avoid situations like this in the future. But then again, it was only a rumor.

The word was out on the street about Blood, Sweat & Tears, and soon we had offers from Mo Ostin at Warner Brothers, Jac Holzman at Elektra Records, and Clive Davis from Columbia Records. Mo Ostin dropped out when he heard what we were asking, which today wouldn't even have covered a week's salary for Lady Gaga's hair stylist, so we had to choose between Elektra and Columbia. Both companies offered the same except for one deciding factor: Columbia Records had just purchased Fender Instruments, and they threw some free Fender amps into the deal. We went for it. My only personal stipulation was that Columbia Records would have to forgive the debt that I owed to the Columbia Record Club—an outstanding liability that had been open since 1958. The total due was around $20 plus interest, but I did not want to carry this burden to my credit standing for the rest of my life. They went for it.

On Friday, November 11, 1967, the new lineup entered Columbia Studios in New York for the first recording session, a six-song demo, which included an instrumental of Kooper's, "Refugee from Yuhu-pitz," "Morning Glory," "So Much Love," "Just One Smile," and "My Days Are Numbered." Columbia signed the band five days later on November 16, 1967.

How my brother became a rock band manager is still somewhat of a mystery to me. After graduating law school, he worked at a law firm for a time, and then went into partnership with one of the other attorneys at the firm, a short, balding, mole-like human by the name of Bennett Glotzer. Glotzer and Katz, figuring they had enough experience to make a go of it, opened an office on Fifth Avenue and Fifty-Seventh Street, in the old offices of fashion designer Anne Klein. They were to be entertainment lawyers and managers, and from what I gather through the dim telephoto lenses of time and nepotism, their first client was Blood, Sweat & Tears. They also represented Procol Harum in America, Dave Van Ronk, Rhinocerous, the semitalented Bob Dylan clone David Blue, and a little-known Canadian band called The Churls.

After six weeks of rehearsals, our new lineup debuted live at the Cafe au Go Go on the weekend of November 17, 1967, with Moby Grape and comedian-friend Larry Hankin also on the bill. One of my most enduring memories of our debut night at the Cafe au Go Go involves Randy Brecker, who later, with his brother Michael, was to deservedly become one of jazz's all-time greats. I remember Randy coming to the gig, and as he walked toward the dressing room, I heard an assortment of pocket change hitting the floor. "Randy," I said, "you have a hole in your pocket. Your change is falling out." Randy, who was stoned virtually all the time then, looked down at the spinning coins and said, "Thanks, man." He then proceeded to carefully pick up the coins and carefully put them back, in the same pocket. And down they would go again. It was to be repeated all night.

Our next gig was uptown at Steve Paul's The Scene. The band was booked from November 19–27 for a series of shows billed as the "Thanksgiving Blues Jam," where Tiny Tim emceed and the Chambers Brothers opened. Also on the bill was my old bandmate, John-John McDuffy and The Soul Purpose. On a "boxing" poster that I own, Sam Lay (the first drummer of the Paul Butterfield Blues Band) and his band, the Mojo Men, were supposed to be on the bill, but they canceled, so the final advertisement read *Al Kooper and Steve Katz's Blood, Sweat & Tears*, and below were the names of the Chambers Brothers, John-John McDuffy, The Soul Purpose, and, below that, "Guest Stars: Steve Katz, Al Kooper, Bobby Colomby, Jim Fielder, Fred Lipsius"— but not the rest of the horns. We had not yet given Randy, Jerry, and Dick equal membership in the band, as we thought of them as salaried sidemen. But that didn't last long. We finally gave them an equal share so that they would be able to suffer like the rest of us. Al and I got top billing because we had come out of the Blues Project and were well-known around the New York area.

I used to go up to The Scene early just to hang out with Tiny Tim, who I loved dearly. We once spent a day together with Bobby Colomby at Bobby's mom's apartment in the Bronx, watching the World Series. Tiny was a baseball fanatic, a huge Red Sox fan. Born Herbert Khoury in 1932, Tiny Tim, as Larry Love, played odd clubs in Manhattan in the 1950s, and could sometimes be seen on Forty-Second Street at Hubert's Flea Circus, a freak show that I would visit myself, and where the great photographer Diane Arbus gathered much of her of inspiration. How sad, I thought, when Tiny Tim was co-opted by Hollywood and humiliated on national TV, along with a woman who obviously had limited interest in him. Tiny Tim was real and a good person, and didn't deserve the Hollywood treatment that was accorded him.

Meanwhile, Al asked John Simon, who produced Simon & Garfunkel's *Bookends*, and then went on to produce The Band's *Music from Big Pink*, if he would be interested in working with us. John agreed, and so the album concept started taking shape. The album would have an overture, played by a string section, that would show up again at several points, including on Harry Nilsson's "Without Her" and Al's "The Modern Adventures of Plato, Diogenes, and Freud," a narcissistic exercise that would later be a point of contention between Al and what Kooper later referred to as the "Katz-Colomby faction."

We went into Columbia Records Studios on East Fifty-Second Street in December of 1967, and in two weeks, from December 7 to 22, we had completed our first album. I sang "Megan's Gypsy Eyes" and "Morning Glory." Al sang the rest. We dared Bobby to laugh all through the "Underture," which he bravely did, and then he threw up right after. If you try doing what Bobby did, chances are you would wind up with the same result.

There are two stories about the recording of *Child Is Father to the Man* that Al and I have disagreed with over the years. The first concerns "House in the Country," which Al wrote after he heard of the acid trip that Roy, Andy, and I had taken at a farm in upstate New York's rural Dutchess County. Years later, Al insisted that it was written about something else, but who am I to argue? He wrote the song. The other story is that when I was doing my vocal on "Megan's Gypsy Eyes," he ran into the main room and jumped me, naked. This is not true; I have never seen Al Kooper naked (thank God).

Our engineer was Fred Catero and our assistant engineer, who also doubled as a pimp for the Carnegie Deli, taking kickbacks from all of our take-out orders, was Lou Waxman. One night he accidentally hit the "erase" button on what was to be the final mix of "House in the Country." It had to be remixed. We felt sorry for Lou, who, after a profusion of apologies and tears over the incident, quietly asked if anybody wanted to order in some corned-beef sandwiches.

The song that ended up closing side one was Randy Newman's "Just One Smile." Our arrangement was considerably different from the original publisher's demo, but when we recorded it, the brass ensemble coda at the end sounded like it needed something. Someone suggested that Randy Brecker put a little tag on it, a solo flugelhorn as the last chord petered out. Randy went into the studio carrying his horn, the engineer played back the end of the track, and in one take he improvised that amazing little sequence you hear at the end of the song. We were all sitting there with our mouths hanging open, and Randy said, with no false modesty, "Was that okay?" Randy's short but prolific overdub was the perfect example of how well a jazz part could work within a rock context. I've come to see it as a milestone in the merging of the two genres. And Randy didn't even have to try; it just came naturally.

I recorded a backwards guitar solo on "I Can't Quit Her" and received credit on the liner notes as "Ztak Evets." The solo wasn't bad, but I still haven't heard it frontwards to this day. Probably best to let sleeping dogs lie. The background vocals were provided by Melba Moore (credited as "Melba Moorman" on the liner notes) and Valerie Simpson, who, with her husband, Nicky Ashford, wrote, among other things, "Ain't No Mountain High Enough" for Marvin Gaye and Tammi Terrell. The album cover photo was taken at Columbia's photo studio by Don Hunstein, where we scuffed up the black floor with our muddy shoes and were each given a child to sit on our laps. The children's heads would eventually be replaced by our own, and voilà—*Child Is Father to the Man*, the first and possibly the best of the Blood, Sweat & Tears albums. Our heads may have been replaced, but the scuff marks are still visible.

Our first gig was at the Village Theatre on Saturday, September 16, 1967. We were to open for the James Cotton Blues Band. The theater was located on Second Avenue, between Sixth and Seventh Streets, in New York's East Village. The building had a long show-business history. It had opened in 1926 as the Commodore Theatre, a 2,700-seat Yiddish vaudeville house, and was part of the strip known then as "The Jewish Rialto." The Loew's organization bought it at some point and operated it as a movie theater, and finally as a concert hall called the Village Theatre. Bill Graham bought it in June 1968 and reimagined it as the Fillmore East. It was where the Blues Project had opened for and backed up Chuck Berry, and it was now to be Blood, Sweat & Tears' first major theatrical gig.

The day of the show, drummer Bobby Colomby and I were hanging out, not doing much of anything. We were at Gem Spa, the legendary luncheonette down the street, me with my egg cream and Bobby with his chocolate malted. I had an idea. I said, "Let's go over to the theater and have a look at the marquee, and then we'll have lunch." This was a big deal for us, our first hometown show in an actual theater. Seeing our name on the marquee would be a thrill. We wandered over, and as the theater came into view, we saw on its magnificently ornate 1920s marquee:

AL KOOPER'S BLOOD, SWEAT AND TEARS

I think it was Bobby, but it might have been me who broke the silence: "Al must have gotten up earlier than us today." After the initial shock wore off, I ran upstairs and into the theater's offices, completely livid, shouting, "That marquee needs to be changed, and changed now! Blood, Sweat and Tears is a democracy! We're not Al Kooper's *anything!*" It didn't occur to me that I was probably speaking to some bewildered employee who had no idea what I was talking about and couldn't have cared less. It was a huge overreaction on my part, but things like that used to upset me tremendously. When I was young, I had a bad temper, which never mixed well with Al's ego. My seismic display of anger—for which I'll now apologize to the poor hapless theater employee, whoever you are, wherever you are—had the desired effect. "I'm so sorry, I'll have that changed for you," the employee said. "Why don't you come back in a couple of hours?" I ran back down to Bobby's little tan VW Beetle, still in a rage, and said, "They're gonna change it. Let's go have lunch, then we'll come back and make sure it's done." We drove away, had a bite to eat, walked around, and came back to Second Avenue and East Sixth Street and looked up at the marquee:

AL KOOPER AND STEVE KATZ'S BLOOD,
SWEAT AND TEARS

We just stared at it for a while, and then I said to Bobby, "I can live with that."

The night of Tuesday, February 1, 1968, Al and I decided to visit Moby Grape up at Columbia Studios. When we got off the elevator, something didn't feel right. Each member of the band was in a different place, a different corner of the studio, and not talking to each other. I told Al that it might be best under the circumstances to leave, but when it comes to putting together a jam session, especially if it's in a recording studio where Al can play, nobody has ever had the balls that Al Kooper had. Somehow he gathered the band together, got them to their instruments, sat down at the piano, and played on what later became *Grape Jam*, the second disc of Moby Grape's *Wow* album. I had to leave before the jam started. The vibe was just too uncomfortable. It was four months later, in early June of 1968, that Skip Spence, in that same studio, took a fire ax to their producer, David Rubinson. Rubinson survived, but Skip Spence became a sad victim of schizophrenia, wound up on the streets, and died from lung cancer in 1999.

Our only tour as what has since been called "the first Blood, Sweat & Tears" (as opposed to the multitude of BS&T's that came afterward) occurred during February of 1968. It started in Boston at the Psychedelic Supermarket, where we opened for Big Brother and the Holding Company.

Big Brother and BS&T were label mates at the time. The last time I had seen Janis was from the wings of the stage at the Monterey Pop Festival. Now, in Boston, we all got to hang out backstage and I got to know Janis a little better, and even share some of her Southern Comfort.

The next day, we were at Boston's Logan Airport to catch a plane to Cleveland. Al decided to wear a bulbous, pink, faux fur contraption that made him look like a Hostess Sno Ball. The rest of us dropped our carry-on bags for Al to look after. I will never forget the sight of Al Kooper, looking a lot more like something that had a cream filling than an actual human, sitting all alone amid trumpet cases, guitar cases, and a very confused group of travelers who probably thought that we were with the Barnum & Bailey Circus.

It turned out to be a pretty good tour. One of our first gigs was at La Cave in Cleveland, sort of the Cafe au Go Go of the Midwest. We had to wake very early one morning to tape a couple of episodes of *Upbeat*, a TV show hosted by the local weatherman, Don Webster. For that taping, and just for a laugh, since it was lip-synced, we traded instruments. At one point, Jerry Weiss was holding Jim Fielder's bass and Jimmy was holding Jerry's trumpet. Al was still wearing his Sno Ball suit, another casualty of the times.

The rock bands in Cleveland in those days stayed at the Versailles, a '60s-style dive that put aside a whole floor for musicians. The top floor of the Versailles was a monument to hedonism. I don't know how many TVs were thrown out the window late at night by stoned rock 'n' roll band members who were passing through, but I'm sure the TVs were soon replaced and paid for by the deposits on all of the empty beer cans that flooded the rooms. The cacophony of guitars and various kinds of percussion filled the halls, and the ashtrays were piled high with roaches by morning. You could not get any actual sleep at the Versailles. The problem was that *Upbeat* had to be taped so early that none of the musicians wound up going to sleep at all, and that's when all kinds of mayhem broke loose. The Versailles was classic rock and roll.

While in Cleveland, we all went to Leo's Casino, a large, mainly African-American venue, to see the Temptations and Gladys Knight and the Pips. A few of the guys wound up with a hooker named Angel, but I was too naive and scared to partake, so my memories of that wonderful show were based on the fact that not only were the Temptations, with their original members, amazing, as was Gladys Knight, but the big Motown band behind them were most of the original guys on those great Motown records from the '60s.

The Grande Ballroom in Detroit (March 3) came after Cleveland. Our opening act was a new local band—the Psychedelic Stooges with Iggy Pop. In San Francisco we played the Fillmore Auditorium on March 7 and opened for Cream at Winterland on March 8–10. The Fillmore Auditorium hadn't yet changed its name to Fillmore West— Fillmore East had yet to open. Randy Brecker, who evidently had dropped some LSD the day of the Fillmore gig, lifted his trumpet just as we were about to count off the first song, Little Milton's "More and More." The trumpets were supposed to play the intro. Randy had his horn up to his face with his mouthpiece leaning on his nose and a broad grin stretching across his lips. He didn't start playing until halfway through the song, as soon as he realized where he was, and that the Joshua Light Show was not designed specifically for him. I could not stop laughing. The hell with professionalism; we were having a good time.

While still in San Francisco, Kooper got word that Randy was going to bring a large quantity of pot with him to LA. Al decided to call a band meeting where he informed us that the LAPD was on very high alert, and anyone with long hair would do well to stay as clean as possible.

Al—"For the good of the band, none of you guys should carry any drugs to LA."

Jerry Weiss raised his hand.

Jerry—"Al?"

Al—"Yeah?"

Jerry—"I'll carry it."

End of meeting.

We made it to LA without incident. Colomby and I would later spend a night at my apartment with Jerry Weiss, coaching him on his army physical that he was to take, only hours away at Whitehall Street in downtown Manhattan. Four a.m., we were stoned and exhausted. Jerry read his draft notice, probably for the first time. "Hey, it says here that you're not eligible to be drafted if you have a felony conviction. Is car theft a felony?" We wanted to kill him.

Randy Brecker and I were rooming together at the Chateau Marmont. Randy must have had, literally, a pound of marijuana. We just kept it right out on the table with the door open. The LAPD may have been a bit uptight about weed, but once you were in an environment like the Chateau Marmont, everything seemed safe and easy, and, in retrospect, astoundingly stupid.

After LA our next stop was back to San Francisco, where we played the last gigs of the tour at the Avalon Ballroom. We finished the promotional tour, which went quite well. None of us had a clue that it was going to be our only tour with that configuration of band members. I remember a few of us were in a car together, and Kooper mentioned that he was very disappointed with the way the album was selling (it had been released just three weeks earlier, on February 21), and therefore, he didn't know how much longer he was going to stay with the band.

Really? This came as a shock. I don't know if Al had been plotting this, or if his speech was some sort of trial balloon. I certainly didn't know what plans he might have had for what would come next, but Bobby and I both realized that this gave us an opportunity. We both considered Al's singing to be the weak link in the band. We decided then and there that he had a point. If he insisted on being the band's lead singer, then yes, he should leave.

There had been friction already, as Kooper has noted in his own book. He and Bobby had an argument when Al presented his song "The Modern Adventures of Plato, Diogenes, and Freud" to the band, a song that consisted of nothing other than Al's vocal over a string ensemble. Bobby was annoyed and said that the song did not represent the band. He was right, of course. It was a nice little song, a great arrangement, but it wasn't the band. And there was Kooper's voice again, right out front.

Al never liked my guitar playing and I never liked his voice, even though we were in two bands together. I never thought of myself as a guitar hero. I was never as comfortable playing electric guitar as I have been with acoustic. I always considered myself to be a singer/songwriter/harmonica-playing guitarist who happened to also play washboard. I never thought of myself as a lead guitarist, and never really wanted to be one. I had just come from a band in which I'd stood onstage next to Danny Kalb, a seminal lead player. Al Kooper has a myriad of talents, as keyboard player, songwriter, and guitarist, but he was not a singer. No matter how hard he'd try—and God knows, Al tried—Mother Nature had not given him a good voice.

But it wasn't just the voice. Al Kooper wanted to be considered a genius by the pop music world, a la Brian Wilson. The thing about Brian, though, was that he was able to stand back and create while the other Beach Boys did most of the singing. Al mistakenly thought he could do it all.

Al considered Blood, Sweat & Tears to be his own band with his own musicians, literally there to back him up and to expedite *his* ideas. Personally, however, this is not what I had signed on for. In his autobiography, Al asserts that we all agreed up front that his vision would be the band's vision, but that was just not true. In fact, I don't remember agreeing to anything like that at all. Why would I want to be part of Al's "vision" when I needed to find one of my own? True, Al was going through a profoundly creative period, as writer and, with Freddy's help, arranger, but so were the other band members, especially Randy, Freddy, and Dick. And I also needed room to be creative. Unfortunately, Al sucked all the air out of that particular room. The *last* thing I would have wanted was to be part of Al's backup band. This was not *meant* to be an Al Kooper solo album. It could only have succeeded with a singer who could interpret the songs in the best way possible. There were some great songs on that album. It would have benefited Al to understand that, but his ego couldn't see the forest for the trees, and that's probably why he was so flabbergasted when Bobby confronted him and said that "Plato, Diogenes, and Freud" should not go on this album. And Bobby was right. We could have used that space for another track, maybe an instrumental of Randy's or Freddy's, maybe another song of mine, but that wasn't part of Al's "vision."

We played the Garrick Theatre, next to the Cafe au Go Go, April 11–14. After the very last set of the last night, Bobby and I approached Al backstage and told him that we thought he should stay with the band, that his ideas were valuable and important, and that we could have hit records, but only with a different singer. Be the writer, be the arranger, take a leadership role if you like. Al answered by quitting the band, but before he did, he asked everyone but Bobby and me to call him at home if they still wanted to work with him, thereby pulling a power play that would essentially have fired Bobby and myself. Nobody called him. Randy was the only one to split right away; he got an offer to play with Horace Silver that he couldn't turn down. It was a once-in-a-lifetime opportunity, and we were all thrilled for him.

I spoke earlier about how Kooper thought of the Blues Project as a jumping-off point for his own career. Now he did the same with Blood, Sweat & Tears. Al stayed with the band for about ten months, from July 1967 to April 1968. Like the Blues Project, we just weren't selling as many records as he would have liked. For Bobby and me, Al's singing was the issue.

He's stated that he left the band when we all turned against him. The fact is, we didn't want him to leave the band; we just wanted another singer—a good one.

BS&T finally did get a great singer after Kooper left. But it turned into a very dark case of "Be careful what you wish for . . ."

CHAPTER 7

"You've Made Me So Very Happy"

There were two decisions that Blood, Sweat & Tears had to make after Al Kooper was gone. The first was how to ensure that the record company would still support the band. The second, a personal decision that I had to make, was whether I should prepare for the worst and do something else entirely in order to earn a living. I made contact with Paul Shalmy, editor of a new magazine, a *Cosmopolitan* spin-off called *Eye*.

Eye was intended to lure a younger, hipper, and more worldly, affluent reader than *Cosmopolitan*. The offices were conveniently located on LaGuardia Place, around the corner and north of Bleecker Street. *Eye* was doing an article on up-and-coming New Yorkers in the arts. I was included, as was Woody Allen, Richie Havens, Michael Pollard, and Janis Ian. As an English major in college and a quasi-successful rock musician, I suggested to Paul that I might write album reviews for the magazine. Paul liked the idea, and so I became an album reviewer for *Eye*.

My new career lasted only two issues. I could not write a bad review. As a musician, I knew what it felt like to be on the receiving end of a bad review, and it wasn't fun. For me, a bad review meant anxiety attacks and depression. I would even consider walking around my neighborhood with a paper bag over my head so as not to be recognized by anyone who had read the latest issue of *Rolling Stone*. Three of the albums I reviewed were *The Papas and the Mamas* by the Mamas and the Papas, *Gris-Gris* by Dr. John, and Quicksilver Messenger Service's self-titled first album. The Mamas and Papas album was not for me. It wasn't my kind of music, but I gave it a good review anyway. I loved Dr. John's first album, a voodoo excursion into the New Orleans netherworld. I gave it a rave review and couldn't take it off my turntable.

Later that year I was in the waiting room of a studio in Los Angeles, and the same issue of *Eye* was on a coffee table. I picked it up and noticed my review had been cut from the pages. I was informed by the receptionist that Dr. John himself saw it and clipped it out. That was a nice feeling.

I worked with Quicksilver Messenger Service when I was with the Blues Project and liked the guys in the band but didn't like their album. I kept thinking to myself how horrible I would feel if I was one of them and read a bad review from a nationally syndicated magazine. I gave it a good review and quit being a rock critic.

The main reason for leaving the world of rock 'n' roll criticism, however, was BS&T. We were about to hold auditions for a new lead singer and we needed to restructure. Most of my time had to be devoted to that, and on the off chance that Columbia Records didn't drop us, I needed to have everything lined up to be a full-time musician again. The "chairs" that needed to be filled were for two trumpets and a lead singer. Dick Halligan was moved to keyboards (along with trombone and flute), and so we needed a trombone player to replace Dick. Through Fred Lipsius we added Lew Soloff and Chuck Winfield on trumpets and Jerry Hyman on trombone. Hiring Jerry proved a convenient bonus, as he was also selling pot at the time.

The difficult part was getting a new lead singer.

I first met Laura Nyro at the Matrix, in San Francisco, when I was with the Blues Project. Laura was one of the most talented people I knew, as well as one of the sweetest, a magical person with a positively ghostly presence. She was Goth before Goth was cool. We called David Geffen, who had left his job at the William Morris Agency to manage Laura. We wanted to see if she might fit in as Kooper's replacement. After one afternoon rehearsal at the Cafe au Go Go, we saw that it wasn't going to work. Laura had too strong a personality to fit in with what we foolishly thought of as our little "democracy." Geffen agreed. But Laura and I got to be good friends.

Laura was very much a New Yorker. She was droll, incredibly gifted, and, in a way, very sad. Having a conversation always included a few notes of abstract impressionism. Here's a typical example of one of my many phone conversations with Laura Nyro. It must have been seven a.m., and I had just come home after making my nightly rounds of some of New York's least-elegant rock venues:

"Steve, it's Laura."

"Hi, Laura."

"It's raining."

"I know."

"I'm in bed."

"Oh?"

"There's a leak in my roof. And it's raining on me. In bed."

"Well, here's what I think you should do. I think you should get out of bed."

That same night, Laura rented a limo and picked me up. We went for hamburgers at White Castle—something Laura loved to do every now and then.

I own a copy of a *Cash Box* Top 100 chart from 1969. It was the week when our version of "And When I Die" went to number one. Also in the top ten that week were "Eli's Coming" by Three Dog Night and "Stoned Soul Picnic" by the 5th Dimension. All three were written, amazingly, by Laura.

But if Laura wasn't going to work out as our lead singer, we needed to keep looking. Jimmy Fielder and I had dinner with Stephen Stills one night at the Tin Angel. Jimmy had worked with Stills in Buffalo Springfield, and we wanted to feel him out about the possibility of joining BS&T; luckily for Stills, nothing ever came of it.

I was also scouting around the New York clubs and saw a Canadian band uptown at Steve Paul's The Scene. The band belonged to frontman David Clayton-Thomas, a Toronto native who was a Ronnie Hawkins protégé, a Bobby "Blue" Bland–inspired R&B singer with a powerful voice and a great feel for the blues. He was also a pretty good guitarist, although his style was too rough for BS&T. I told Bobby about him and we both went to take a listen. We asked David to come down to our Bleecker Street loft and audition.

David Clayton-Thomas had the perfect voice. Of course, like most things in life, nothing is really perfect. Although David was a great singer, he never scored any points in the human being department, something we didn't know at the time, but would later find out, and would have to live with for the next few years.

When we first heard David sing Billie Holiday's "God Bless the Child" with the band at our loft, we were amazed. It was the first time we had heard him sing something that wasn't pure R&B. This was a singer who could interpret anything, especially within the BS&T repertoire. Whether it was Kooper's "I Can't Quit Her" or Brenda Holloway's "You've Made Me So Very Happy," everything David sang sounded right—and even better, sounded like a hit. It was a perfect combination of band and singer. Our vision was about to be achieved. That was the good news. In retrospect, the perfect situation would have been to surgically remove David's vocal cords, set them up on a stool with a microphone for recording sessions and concerts, have them perform, put them back in a box at night, and give the box to the roadies to stick with the rest of the equipment until the next gig.

Now we had to convince Columbia Records that not only were we a viable "commodity," but we were actually better and certainly more commercial than ever. Making matters more difficult was a newly developing problem. All of the acts that were managed by Glotzer & Katz were getting paid through an escrow account set up by management. Unfortunately, there was not enough money coming in to support all of the acts *and* their Fifth Avenue office. When our second album was going up the charts and the money started rolling in, BS&T was essentially paying most of Glotzer and Katz's bills. To his credit, my brother blew the whistle on Glotzer, but only after several months had gone by. We left Bennett Glotzer, as did my brother, who then went to work in the legal department of Columbia Records.

Clive Davis and a few other people from the label came up to the loft, liked what they heard, and decided to go ahead with the band. Our first gig with the "new" band was again at the Cafe au Go Go. We then played with The Who in Rhode Island and the Blues Image in Miami. By the end of July, we were back at Cafe au Go Go, but not before Clive had unveiled us at the Columbia Records Convention in San Juan, Puerto Rico, where we were showcased with Big Brother and the Holding Company. The night before the show, some of us—along with some members of Big Brother, including Janis—were hanging out and getting somewhat loaded. David Geffen had joined us, and we all decided to run over to the main hotel where the functions were being held. In doing so, we had to climb over a high wire fence. Geffen was the last to climb over, and the struggle had him on the verge of tears, so I helped him, all while trying to nudge that famous wallet of his into my waiting hands.

Janis and David Clayton-Thomas got along so well that they hopped into bed with each other that night. The next morning, Janis came down to the pool wearing a two-piece bathing suit with a hand-shaped appliqué on each breast. DCT was hitting on a waitress, and when Janis saw this, she almost took his head off. Lew Soloff, acting as our reconnaissance man, saw their room before it was made up and compared it to scenes from the London Blitz.

We were a success at the convention and managed to get the whole CBS promotion staff excited, a necessity if you wanted to "make it" at that time in the music business. These were the guys that had to hustle your records on to the radio, and our job was to make it easy for them. We were now officially schmoozers.

In October we were back at CBS studios on Fifty-Second Street to record our second album and, apparently, to share an elevator with Arthur Godfrey, who broadcast his syndicated radio show from one of the studios upstairs. Our brushes with celebrity never ceased.

Our engineer, Roy Halee, decided to try something new: drums in stereo. Roy loved playing with percussion at CBS studios, exemplified by Hal Blaine's snare drum on Simon & Garfunkel's "The Boxer." Roy had Hal Blaine hit the snare in the elevator shaft for an amazing natural echo. The sound of our album was to be fairly flat and right in your face, with no extraneous sounds or noise, as we'd had in the first album. There was no reason not to record it this way; the band and the singer were terrific, and there was nothing to hide or gloss over. But this was a more serious, polished affair. Guercio was a serious producer, and you might even say that he lacked a sense of humor. We didn't need strings, although they were overdubbed originally for "Spinning Wheel." We had our own brass section, and again, we had some great songs.

The album was to open and close with Dick Halligan's arrangement of Erik Satie's "Third Gymnopédie," a short classical piece where I played two chords in open-G tuning and Dick played the melody and harmonies on flute. By opening and closing the album with this piece, it gave the album a "concept" feel, like the beginning and ending of a book. It made the album feel as though you had just taken a journey. Three of the songs were from the *Child Is Father to the Man* band, but not yet recorded with Kooper—Steve Winwood's "Smiling Phases," Little Milton's "More and More," and Brenda Holloway's "You've Made Me So Very Happy." And along with the newer material, David made these songs his own. It's not an easy task to take on Billie Holiday's "God Bless the Child," but he did it, and it worked.

I had written "Sometimes in Winter" after Kooper left. I broke the first rule of composition for any dedicated folk-blues musician by using a couple of forbidden major-seventh chords, and the song didn't really have an obvious "hook," but that didn't bother me. Halligan did the arrangement, and luckily for me (and my royalty statements), it wound up on the album, later to be covered by a few people, including Sergio Mendes and Brazil '66. The Coen Brothers would also use it in their classic 1996 film, *Fargo*. In the scene where Marge is having lunch with her Asian-American friend from high school, a piano is playing "Sometimes in Winter" in the background. I didn't even know about this until I got an unusually high royalty check. Unusual for *me*, that is.

I e-mailed Carter Burwell, who does most of the music for the Coen Brothers, thanked him, and asked him why he used my song when he could have written his own and kept the royalties for himself; after all, the song is almost buried in the background. He replied that Ethan Coen was a fan of the song and felt it fit in with the winter ambience of the film. This very generous act raised my sadly pessimistic view of humanity, and the music and entertainment business in general. It was a really nice thing for the Coens to do. And to have a song in one of the great American films of all time? Be still, my beating heart! I was a fan before *Fargo*. For me, the Coen Brothers can do little wrong, although they definitely made a few historical errors in *Inside Llewyn Davis*.

The album was released in December of 1968. And like I said before, I played the test pressing for some friends at my apartment, and for Clive Davis and Jann Wenner at Clive's office. The response was underwhelming and disheartening. And then the album was released. The first single was "You've Made Me So Very Happy." It went to number two on both charts. My parents, who were still grieving over my lack of a law degree or an MD shingle on my door, called me and said with knowing delight, "We *knew* it, Steven. We *knew* how talented you are and how you were going to make it big someday! We *knew* it! Your father would come to the phone, but he's announcing the chart positions to the neighborhood from our balcony and will have to call you later. Do you need anything? Food, linens? A haircut? By the way, we need twenty tickets for your Fillmore concert."

By the time our second single was climbing up the charts, we were still doing gigs that were previously booked. We again played the Troubadour in Los Angeles. Wanting to record some of our shows, Lew Soloff put a tape deck up in the balcony. At one show, Jim Morrison came to see us, obviously ripped. He watched from the balcony near Lew's tape recorder and started screaming "Fuck!" at the top of his lungs and at various intervals. Lew probably still has the tape.

When The Doors were in New York next, I received a surprise phone call from Jim's girlfriend, Pam, who I had met one night at the Troubadour. We got along well enough to exchange phone numbers and addresses and promised to stay in touch.

She was with Jim at their hotel, and Jim had taken too many drugs and was drinking heavily. He became belligerent, as he normally did under those circumstances, and lashed out at Pam. She called me and I told her to get out of there and take a cab down to my place, where we began a small affair.

Pam was a beautiful redhead and impressed me as being somewhat straight and very "LA." I never really saw her being with Jim, especially after learning that their relationship was stormy and sometimes even violent. But he did have the mojo. Women found him irresistible.

I must have had a little something, too, because Pam and I were to meet on a few more occasions, sadly under the same circumstances. I came to understand that that was the nature of their relationship, and that I didn't seem to be the only person she had turned to. It was fine with me. Pam was a lovely girl and a good friend. The only strings attached were the ones that she couldn't break with Jim.

Pam was living with Morrison in Paris when he died. I later learned that she became addicted to heroin and that her life took some nasty turns, until she herself passed away from an overdose in 1974. I was saddened, of course, but I'd seen it coming, and there was certainly nothing anyone could have done. I didn't like Morrison because of the way he treated Pam, but in retrospect, he was just a talented kid who had an enormous amount of problems.

—⁓—

In those days you called *Cash Box* or *Billboard* on Wednesdays when they would have the chart positions for the following week. I had become friendly with one of the secretaries at *Cash Box* and would call in to find out where music ranked, mostly interested in our album, which one week had actually made it to number sixteen on the LP chart. Not bad, but a top-ten album would have had me doing cartwheels down Jane Street.

"Hi, it's Steve Katz from Blood, Sweat and Tears. How are we doing next week?"

"Uh, let me see," said the secretary. She put me on hold for a minute or so and, when she came back, said, "I can't find it."

My heart sank. Well, sixteen isn't bad, I thought, but why would it drop off the charts so fast when our single was still climbing? Oh, well.

Five minutes later my phone rang.

"It's me again. I couldn't find your album because I didn't even think to look at number one. It's number *one* next week! Congratulations!"

I immediately called my mother to ask if their balcony was free that afternoon. I had an announcement to make, and, "Oh, I'll be able to afford my own blintzes from now on, Mom."

The gigs and our fees started to reflect our success.

Our first major network TV appearance was on *The Ed Sullivan Show*, February 16, 1969. We did "Smiling Phases." David had decided to add a large Chinese gong to the song after the instrumental break, and then a triangle. He hit the gong and missed the triangle. It was live TV, but it was cute and didn't really matter. We played well and David sang well, despite looking like a bull in a china shop—awkward, clumsy, and sometimes grotesque. Unfortunately, the gong stayed in our live show. I hated that fucking gong.

I had an acquaintance at the time, a press agent by the name of Billy Smith, who must have somehow known Sullivan. Sullivan, probably a little out of it from his morphine habit, referred to David as "Billy Smith," despite David's protestations and attempts at correcting him. It's sad, but my favorite part of the show was the STP commercial that preceded us, an arm-wrestling match between former world heavyweight champion Rocky Marciano and Andy Granatelli, race-car legend and owner of STP.

It may seem counterintuitive, but one of the differences between being on the road when you're paying your dues and being on the road when you have hit records is that when you have hits, you have to work twice as hard. If you once played Chicago on a Saturday night and Detroit the next Saturday night, you now had to play every college in between on the weekdays, and the best way to do that was to travel by bus. But these weren't the Pullman-style buses of today. These buses had no beds, and sometimes you'd be traveling long distances to get from one gig to the next. You'd get into town, check into a hotel, maybe nap for an hour if you were lucky, then bus over to the gig for a sound check, back for a bite to eat, back to the gig, and then you'd have to hang out with the local record promotion people and whoever they wanted you to meet, like press, disc jockeys, their families, the radio stations' sponsors and *their* families. It would be an interminable cycle. And somewhere in between, you had to create and rehearse new material. Of course, you might just find time to do that after all the meetings with the band, and with management and accountants and lawyers who flew out to meet you—meetings that were also interminable, and so boring that I think they did it on purpose to lull us to sleep during the bad news, like the fact that they were probably pocketing half of our profits.

We put ourselves on salary, one of our biggest mistakes, because the rest of our money was put into investments like apartment buildings in Maryland that were never maintained, or cattle in Texas that were probably suffering from mad cow disease. Chuck Winfield, our second trumpet player, was smart; at some point, Chuck, a devoted Jehovah's Witness, decided to take his share while the rest of us partook in those less-than-rewarding investments. Add to that some pretty corrupt practices on the part of those who were supposed to be working on our behalf and representing us, practices that we sometimes didn't find out about until years later, and you wake up and say to yourself one day, if you're not too stoned, "Wow, I worked my ass off. Where the hell did it all go?" Well, chances are it never got there in the first place.

Chuck Winfield and I did a lot of traveling together, but that was before Chuck found religion. We did a gig in Phoenix and had to be in San Diego the next day. Chuck and I decided to drive overnight. We had a large chunk of hashish in the car and were listening to *Bill Evans with Symphony Orchestra* on the tape deck while the sun was rising from behind. It was one of those magical moments—that is, until we reached the California border and saw that there was a border patrol station just ahead. No time to think, we had no choice but to throw the hashish out the window. As we pulled up to the booth, we noticed that it was only a vegetable checkpoint manned by one old dude who welcomed us to California.

Visions of Chuck and I slowly walking around on the Arizona side of this isolated little "toll" booth for the rest of the day convinced us to just accept the loss and move on, but at least we left with the knowledge that some lucky iguana was going to have one hell of a fun week while the two of us cried over our loss. Chuck and his wife, Sandy, would later move into a house in southern Connecticut that they claimed was haunted, so they moved right back out. Chuck Winfield today teaches at a college in Maine and refuses to stay in touch with any of his old bandmates.

Mort Lewis was one of the good guys. Mort became our manager and was also managing Simon & Garfunkel, The Brothers Four, and Stan Kenton. Mort was a big no-nonsense guy, honest and well-connected. Sadly he didn't last long with us because he didn't trust Bobby and didn't want to deal with band politics. Mort used to take me for lunch at the Friars Club, and we remained friends over the years.

Our lawyer was a West Coast attorney by the name of Lee Colton. Colton recommended that we hire someone to manage us—someone who would be on salary instead of commission, who would essentially take orders from us, "us" meaning mainly Bobby and I. We hired someone from LA on Colton's recommendation by the name of Larry Goldblatt, who had the experience. When we later learned that Larry also had a prison record for embezzlement, we still stuck by him and gave him a vote of confidence, until he inevitably embezzled thousands from us. Duh!

I loved our roadies because they had what this band lacked—a good and somewhat twisted sense of humor. I would hang out with roadies Jon Chesler and Bob Lampert as much as I could. They both had hair almost down to their waists; Jon was a recovering heroin addict, now on methadone, and Lampert was a stutterer. My favorite Lampert story was when we were in Warsaw, Poland, at a party at the American Embassy. There were all kinds of dignitaries present, including Russian brass and Polish officers. The American ambassador's wife walked up to Lampert and, thinking he was one of the band, asked him how he liked Warsaw. Lampert replied, "I r-r-r-really l-l-l-like it. I've been here only an hour and I've been l-l-l-laid *already.*"

During one of our West Coast trips, where we had first been to San Francisco, the roadies and our soundman, Bill Motzing, couldn't stop talking about the crab cakes they had eaten at a restaurant in North Beach. We were in LA and had a couple of days off. Jon, Bob, and Bill had nothing to do and were still talking about their North Beach crab cakes, so they decided, on the band's American Express card, to fly back up to San Francisco for dinner and fly right back the next day. One day I asked Chesler how much he had embezzled from the band so far. He replied, "I'd say about $30,000, and you got away lucky." If it was our accountant or lawyer, I would have had a conniption, but when I heard this from Jon, I just thought it was funny. I loved these guys, and sometimes wished that I had their balls.

Back home, I was still living the carefree promiscuous life, yet also suffering the consequences. I got crabs so many times, I started giving them individual nicknames. My friend and trumpet player Alan Rubin (who played on "Spinning Wheel" when Chuck Winfield couldn't make the session) and his girlfriend, Kay Oslin, decided to fix me up with one of the chorus girls that Kay had been working with in *Promises, Promises* on Broadway. Kay was later to become K. T. Oslin, a huge country music star of the '80s. Alan was the maître d' named "Mr. Fabulous" in *The Blues Brothers* movie, one of the most beloved musicians in New York, and a great trumpet player.

The woman they fixed me up with, Melissa Stoneburn, was raised in Kansas City, which made her somewhat exotic to a Jew from Queens. Her mother, Tilda, had been a chorus girl in the 1940s, and later became Richard Rodgers's personal secretary. Melissa had studied with Balanchine a few years earlier and spent some time in the New York City Ballet before dropping out and entering the world of musical comedy. Melissa accused Tilda of being a "stage mother," a "Mommy Dearest," but I liked Tilda and suspected that Melissa's unhappiness was more deeply rooted. I didn't understand just how deep it was until much later in our relationship. And, naive as I was, I felt that I could fix whatever was wrong, that there were no mental aberrations that Steve couldn't cure with just a little understanding and a lot of lovin'.

We began seeing each other. Melissa eventually moved in, becoming the first girl I ever lived with—actually, the first roommate I ever had.

The problems began almost immediately. Melissa was a slob. Her clothes were strewn all over the apartment so haphazardly that by the time the winter of '69 rolled around, I couldn't find the heater. Clothes were piled up so high that I felt it would be easier just to move than to attempt to clean the place. We found an apartment on the Upper East Side, on the twenty-fourth floor of a high-rise on Seventy-Fourth Street and York, with a balcony and a view of the East River. The first thing I purchased was a large hamper for my future wife.

We were married up at Bobby Colomby's house in New City, New York, with half the staff of Columbia Records present.

I decided to hire a decorator for the new apartment, since Melissa was going to be on the road with me often, and we wouldn't have time to do it ourselves. I informed the decorator to make sure we could take everything with us if we decided to move, but the decorator had other plans, like having a photo layout of my apartment in one of those *Architectural Digest*–type magazines. Wallpaper was glued everywhere, and nonremovable. The walls, the ceilings—all became permanent "fixtures." She even had wallpaper glued to the lamps and tables that she had purchased at Bloomingdale's, on my tab. When she gave me the bill, I contested it and she sued me; we eventually settled, and I learned yet another lesson: If you can, always do it yourself!

The records kept selling and the bigger bookings kept coming in. "And When I Die" turned out to be our biggest hit, with DCT's "Spinning Wheel" right on its heels. Artie Kornfeld and his partner Michael Lang booked us at an upcoming festival that they were planning many months in advance. The festival was to take place in the as-yet-not-world-famous arts community of Woodstock, New York, in the Catskill Mountains, not far from the Hudson River. We were to be paid $10,000, which amounted to us headlining. As 1969 wore on, and Jimi Hendrix was becoming a superstar, Jimi was booked as headliner for $15,000. I didn't feel so bad when I found out that Santana was to be paid $750.

We played the Fillmore East a couple of times with some interesting opening acts—Jethro Tull on one bill, and the Allman Brothers on the other, the latter show providing a somewhat embarrassing
moment when Leonard Bernstein opened our dressing-room door
with kids in tow, catching me in the act of changing my pants. I wasn't
wearing underwear in those days, as it was all about going commando.
Speaking of surreal, even Salvador Dali came to see us one night at
the Fillmore.

We played the Newport Jazz Festival, the Atlanta Pop Festival, and did an amazing tour of Texas with B.B. King, Miles Davis,
Hugh Masekela, and Nina Simone, who hated the fact that we were
doing "God Bless the Child," a song she considered to be an African-
American anthem, even though Billie Holiday's cowriter was a Jewish
guy from Detroit by the name of Arthur Herzog Jr.

We then made the mistake of playing at Caesars Palace in Las
Vegas, the gig that was probably responsible for us losing a good part
of our audience and our credibility. Las Vegas was like the Antichrist
of the counterculture. It stood for everything wrong that epitomized
America at the time, and we jumped right in, insulting many of the
fans who had originally supported our first album. In those days, even
though you could still see tumbleweed rolling down the streets, Vegas
already had the reputation of being plastic, bourgeois, and decidedly
not hippie-friendly. BS&T was not the Rat Pack, and playing Las
Vegas was seen as us "selling out to the man." No matter how cool it
was for Duke Ellington to be playing in the lounge at Caesars Palace,
you didn't see Jimi or Janis or The Dead playing in casinos, and we felt
the brunt of that feedback for years. It's funny, but in those days people
really cared about those things; one gig in Sinatra's backyard, and we
may as well have been criminals, the way our stoned and idealistic fans
looked at us. It was actually all pretty silly.

But it was fun, I'll admit, and hanging out with all the stars that
came to see us was a treat. Harry James, Sidney Poitier, Joe Louis, and

Sammy Davis Jr. all latched on to us like Velcro. We had carte blanche in the restaurants and stores. We were stars, and treated as such. David was given a credit line at the tables, and when he got up to a loss of around $5,000, we were subtly told to keep him off the tables and out of the casino. But the most fun was that Duke Ellington and his band really *were* in the lounge, so that was where I hung out.

CHAPTER 8

Spinning Our Wheels

BLOOD, SWEAT & TEARS APPEALED TO A HUGE DEMOGRAPHIC. WE
were loved by kids and by older people who could relate to the jazz, by
audiophiles, Democrats, right-wingers; everyone seemed to love our
music. After the Caesars gig cost us some street cred, I was looking
for some "good" publicity from the underground press, and said to a
police officer at some concert out in the boondocks, "Officer, what if I
told you I had an ounce of marijuana back at my hotel room?" And he
answered, "Oh, come on now, my wife *loves* you guys." It was then that
I first learned the real meaning of the phrase, "I couldn't get arrested."

We were on the radio constantly and playing live almost as often.
Sometimes our audiences were polite, especially in the more rural
Republican areas of the country. It didn't mean they liked us less; they
were just polite. But if David felt the first song, "More and More,"
didn't go over well, he would condescend to the audience, "Maybe the
next one'll wake you up!"

Bobby and I would look at each other, totally embarrassed, wanting to kill David. If you're going to insult an audience at all, do it at
the *end* of the show, not at the *beginning*. It was horrifying, but it didn't
just happen once. If my song "Sometimes in Winter" went over well,
he would stand right in front of me, not letting me take a polite bow
and thank the audience. If I tried to move clear of him, he would
walk with me, talking into his handheld mic and blocking my view.
Again, I wanted to kill him. One night at the Troubadour, he hit on
my date, actress Sally Field's sister, right in front of me. It was beyond

disrespectful. I'd probably be in jail now for killing David Clayton-Thomas if there weren't already a line in front of me of people who would have taken the first shot at him. David was becoming an embarrassment; he was turning off promoters and promotion people, horrifying women, and pretty much anyone who walked the earth. I began to hate him.

The good thing about the original BS&T was that we were naive. If Al Kooper were a better singer, he would have lasted. At the end of the day, he was just another talented guy, and there are lots of them. But he was not a nice guy, of which there are also a lot. And there are a lot of nice, talented guys, which begs the question of why work with someone like that in the first place. In Al's case, we had history, and the fighting was part of it. You fight with family.

Unfortunately, his replacement turned out to be far worse—a great singer but a total prick, a bully, a toxic narcissist, and eventually, after stardom went to his head, a complete hack. But frankly, I didn't care as long as he could sing. Like I said, this wasn't some brotherhood the way the Blues Project was. There was a degree of professional cynicism at play. We knew what we had, and we wanted to make hit records. Not that there wasn't any joy in the music. There was, but we weren't fucking around. This was a business venture, and David Clayton-Thomas had the voice to turn a profit.

At first when he came in and was doing the Bobby "Blue" Bland stuff and really throwing himself behind the songs, believing what he was singing and delivering the soul old-school style, it was an incredible force, and the response was just as we had hoped. We became massively successful.

But after the money started rolling in and he began believing his own press clips, the worst thing you can do in this business, he turned into a parody of himself, a cartoon. It was like he was doing an imitation of Sammy Davis Jr. doing an imitation of David, doing an imitation of Sammy. If you saw them hanging out together you could see it happening: Sammy felt hip by hanging with a rock guy, and David was knocked out by Sammy's Vegas and Hollywood success, both of them reaching for worlds that were not their own. I don't know how it affected Sammy—the Vegas thing was based on schmaltz anyway, so any rock affectation wasn't going to hurt—but emulating the Candy Man sucked whatever heart David had right out of his act. David started doing this lounge-act bullshit. When he wasn't pandering, he was patronizing the audiences, and treating them as easy marks. Rubes. He had no respect for the people who were buying our records, who were keeping us in business. It made little sense. How could you have an adversarial relationship with your customers?

And he was smiling. I hate singers who smile; it's bullshit. You know, you take a sad, heartfelt song that is supposed to rip your guts right out of you and you lighten it up. Sammy did it in his act all the time. I guess at the end of the day, either he didn't have it in him to do pure soul music, or his audience didn't know the difference, or didn't care, what with the bright lights of Vegas shining in their eyes, but it wasn't real. I hung out with Sammy sometimes, and he wasn't as hip as he wanted you to believe. Trust me, it was an act. I liked Sammy, and even had a good laugh with him when he displayed his complete inability to roll a joint. Did anyone think he actually looked good in a Nehru jacket? He was just trying to capitalize on the times in which he lived. This didn't make him a bad guy, and we were probably all guilty of it, but he had Vegas and the Rat Pack too far up his caboose to ever really be free of it. That wasn't our cross to bear.

The beginning of the end was on our third record, *Blood, Sweat & Tears 3*, during Richard Manuel's song "Lonesome Suzie," first recorded by The Band. You can actually hear David smile. He ruins it. It's pretentious. It's not honest; you can feel it. I hate it so much that I haven't listened to it in forty years, but here I go, because I want to relive it and share it with you . . .

Oh, good lord, it's even worse than I remember. He just tanks the whole thing, just tosses it off like he's Dean Martin or Robert Goulet or some fucking thing, which is not what we were about, not at all. The man had lost any sense of rhythm and blues, any theology of soul. Once upon a time, he could put a song like that over. He killed with that shit, and could have gone mano a mano with pretty much any singer of our generation, but by then he was shucking and jiving. Go ahead and listen to it; you can hear him blowing sunshine. It isn't honest.

Worse, though, than David's transformation from soul singer to slinger of schmaltz was that he was a bully. When we signed him up, we had no idea of the extent of his madness. He treated everyone terribly; he abused roadies, band members, and bartenders, and he abused women, and there was no fucking way that was ever going to stand.

I regret the day we hired him and every day after that when I didn't make a move to get rid of him. I can't make any excuses except that we were caught up in the madness of rock stardom and success, brainwashed by our own circumstances, and once he was in and we were rolling and scoring hits and gold records, it wasn't so easy to make a change that would have put an end to all that. A lot of people depended on us for their livelihoods. When things are going good, besides the nine guys onstage, there are roadies and drivers and promoters and managers and record company people, all counting on you to keep it rolling. But still, I atone every day for empowering a thug.

One night he was at the Tin Angel, a restaurant upstairs from the Dugout bar in Greenwich Village, and he got into a fistfight with the cook. How the hell do you get in a fight with someone who works in the kitchen? It takes some effort. And what's the point? But apparently David didn't like the food and started yelling, and the guy came out to see what all the commotion was about, and David swung on him. He was just this little Mexican guy, but he ducked and jumped David and bit off part of his ear. They found his ear the next day on the floor of the bar, shades of *Blue Velvet*. I got called in the middle of the night to learn that David was in the hospital, and frankly, I didn't give a shit, as long as he could make the gig and sing.

Our road manager, Jim Babb, had his fun the next day when he somehow managed to sit us next to each other on the plane, which was never supposed to happen. I hated the fucker and tried to stay as far away from him as I could—not always easy, but there you have it. When I saw his ear all taped and bandaged, I couldn't help but start laughing. Now David was about ready to tear me apart, chasing me around the plane until the rest of the band stopped him. It was actually pretty funny.

I'm not very threatening, but I do have a temper. And this guy pushed my buttons. One night I was wearing a blue-and-yellow-striped shirt onstage, and he introduced me as his "little Jewish bumblebee." As soon as we were off the stage, I came after him, ready to kick the shit out of him, which wasn't very likely since I was this kid from a nice neighborhood in Queens, and he was a backwoods Canadian bully, but he backed off and cowered, and that's when I saw it was all bullshit.

Soon after that we did a gig in Las Cruces, New Mexico, and he had decided he wasn't going to travel with the band, instead taking a private plane from Los Angeles. Which made everyone in the band pretty happy, because aside from everything else, he never changed his clothes. Onstage, sweating under the lights, then off to the party, pass out in the hotel, and back the next day. The guy didn't even respect himself. We did a show in Australia, it was like 100 degrees on the stage, and he fainted from the heat. I thought he had a heart attack. Our roadies dragged him off the stage and tried to get his clothes off, but his leather pants were practically cemented to his body with sweat and gunk. It took three of them to peel them off, and when they finally did, the stench was so bad that one of them puked all over David. But at least he woke up, so they knew he wasn't dead.

We were booked on a few major TV shows. We taped the *Andy Williams Show* at NBC Studios in Burbank. Danny Thomas, the comedian from *Make Room for Daddy*, was also a guest that day. He stared me down and said, "Why don't you get a haircut?" I told him to go fuck himself.

It reminded me of the day that the Blues Project played at the Wollman Rink in Central Park. It was a hot and humid day, and before the show I nonchalantly walked past the Plaza Hotel, minding my own business, whistling "Zip-a-Dee-Doo-Dah" and admiring some colorful birds that had parked themselves in the trees at the edge of the park, when I heard someone call out "Hey you! Get a haircut!" I turned around and who did I see staring back at me? None other than that master of literature, that genius of the subtle turn of phrase, Mickey Spillane! Mickey Spillane, who wrote one of the great opening lines ever in *Vengeance Is Mine*—"The guy was dead as hell." I told him to go fuck himself, too.

We did *The Tom Jones Show* at ABC Studios in Hollywood. Tom came to one of our rehearsals and I immediately liked him. Here was a guy who had paid his dues, sang his ass off, and did it honestly and with soul. He was a great guy and I enjoyed our little conversation, although through his thick working-class Welsh accent, I didn't understand a word he said.

Bobby Darin was also on the bill. Bobby Darin, like Sammy Davis Jr., was another chameleon who latched on to whatever the latest fad was. Darin's latest persona was faux hippie. He came to the show driving a Jeep and dressed like he'd just stepped out of a Woolrich catalog. But I liked him. He was *nice*. Why couldn't *our* singer be like these guys? Why is God punishing Blood, Sweat & Tears? Why were we so cursed with our Canadian albatross? Darin and I got to talk a bit while we were in makeup. He kept pointing out how *we* were very different from *them*, which I took to mean "straight people," and as much as I liked him, I was tempted to say, "What the fuck are you *talking* about?" But I let it go.

Meanwhile, Tom Jones was about to warm up the audience before the taping, and boy, did he sing. He did a straight blues and it gave me the chills. That's how good a singer he is.

Time magazine did a front-page article on the "rock explosion," and sent an interviewer to talk to me. In that interview, I said that I thought it unfair that Janis Joplin was making so much money when B.B. King still had to struggle. B.B. had not yet reached the heights of popularity that he was about to, though in retrospect, I'm sure B.B. wasn't struggling that much. I was just trying to make the point that black people were not reaping the just rewards of the art that they had created. I mentioned Janis, but I could have been referring to any successful white blues artist at the time.

Home one evening, I turned on the TV to watch Janis on *The Dick Cavett Show*. After some introductory small talk, Cavett says to Janis, "One of your colleagues was quoted in a recent interview"—*God, no! Stop, Dick! Please don't ask her what I think you're going to ask her!*—"saying that you don't deserve to be making all this money while black blues artists are struggling." *Oh no!* "What do you say to that?" *Please, Janis, say that you're so sorry to hear about the suicide of that particular colleague who was much beloved and actually sang quite well when he didn't have his foot in his mouth.* "Yeah? You should see how much *he's* making!" was Janis's reply. Ugh. But I saw Janis after that, and she was just as warm and friendly as ever. Janis was a very special lady.

Like everyone else, we first heard the traffic reports on the radio. The New York State Thruway was jammed. Tens of thousands of people, maybe more, were headed to Bethel, New York, for the rock festival that we were about to play. We flew into LaGuardia from a gig the night before in Portland, Maine. I was wearing white pants, and although I had listened to the traffic reports hourly, I'd neglected to listen to the weather reports, which were just as bad. My white pants were about to enter the "torture test."

We packed ourselves into a couple of rented cars, got on the road, and ran into counterculture hell. It took us all day to get to the local Holiday Inn, and by the time we arrived, the rain was heavy and it was dark outside. I asked one of the girls who looked like she worked for the promoters how we were going to get to the stage area. She told me that we'd be going by car. The helicopter was reserved for Jimi Hendrix. She then added, without any prompting, "Don't you think Hendrix deserves it more than you guys?" I couldn't believe it. This was the last place I would have expected to get a bad review.

We waited around at the bar in the hotel and finally hopped in a couple of cars to the backstage area. It was already past midnight, and Katz and his white pants were about to enter a mud bath. We drove past kids who were half-naked, wet, and stoned. You've seen the pictures and know what it was like. The stage was huge, but I couldn't see the whole audience yet from our vantage point, which was a couple of picnic tables that we were sharing with The Band and Crosby, Stills & Nash. I don't know how our equipment ever got there, but one thing I have to say about our wacky roadies, they were good. I remember Stephen Stills asking me if he could plug in to my amp and I said, "Of course." I also remember that someone in The Band had some hashish that was just outstanding.

In "Woodstock" Joni Mitchell sang about being "stardust" and "golden" and getting us back to the "garden." But Joni wasn't at Woodstock. My version would have been, "We are starving, we are holding, and we've got to get ourselves back to the bar at the Holiday Inn for a stiff martini, straight up, twist of lemon." It was two a.m. when we finally went on. We were tired and stoned. We took to the very large stage. The drums were practically in another county, and the audience looked like a humongous abstract curtain, an opaque mass that I could barely make out as anything human beyond the fourth or fifth "row" of maybe 200 people. The other 399,800 souls could have been summer squash or some other kind of produce, as far as my hashish-obliterated self was able to discern. And when 400,000 people applaud in a space that could have accommodated the Battle of Waterloo, the acoustics are such that you can hardly hear anything.

Our contract, negotiated months before, stipulated that if a film were to be made of the festival, we would own a certain percentage of the rights. Not too much was mentioned about the chance that we wouldn't be in the film, and in that case, we'd get nothing, which is exactly what happened. I had noticed the cameras right in front of us, and thought how wonderful it would be when the movie of this thing came out. After about three songs, I couldn't find the cameras anymore. Years later Warner Brothers released a LaserDisc that contained the "outtakes" of Woodstock. There we were, mainly David, and a somewhat blurred view of my mud-splattered ankle. We got offstage and into our vehicles for the trip back to LaGuardia, where we stayed in a hotel in order to catch a morning flight to LA.

People over the years have asked me what Woodstock was like, and here it is: We were very uncomfortable, played a decent set for an unholy amount of people, and left. I'm sure that we weren't as uncomfortable as the kids who had to endure the bad weather, but they *chose* to be there, and probably loved the experience. For us it was a gig, slightly unusual, but a gig nonetheless. I did not mingle with the crowds or witness any births. I did not even watch any other acts. I got stoned with The Band, which was pretty cool, but if you ask me what I thought of Woodstock, I thought it was not the beginning of an era, but the end of one.

A meeting was arranged one afternoon in Manhattan at the apartment of movie producer Ray Stark. I was there, as was Herb Ross, the movie director ultimately responsible for *The Goodbye Girl, Play It*

Again, Sam, and *Footloose,* along with many more hits. We were there to discuss their upcoming project, *The Owl and the Pussycat* with Barbra Streisand and George Segal. Stark and Ross wanted us to do the score, and we were talking about what they were looking for. Dick Halligan must have been there as well, since Dick was to do most of the work.

The movie was filmed in Manhattan, and I went to see the set of George Segal's apartment, which was built on a large soundstage, an amazing replica of an Upper West Side walk-up. I was also at the filming of the last scene, which took place in Central Park. This was the scene that was underscored by a song that Dick and I wrote together. Wouldn't you know it—I write the theme song to a major motion picture, and where do they put it? At the end!

In the evenings, during filming, I would attend screenings of the daily work prints along with Streisand, Segal, Ross, and Buck Henry, who wrote the screenplay. My friend Robert Klein also costarred in the film. Bob had been a musician in his youth and played a mean harmonica. He did stand-up for a while and opened a lot of shows for us. The last time I saw Bob, we were sharing the same periodontist and ran into each other in the waiting room. Real rock-star stuff.

By the time the movie was to be released, David Clayton-Thomas was dating Portland Mason, the daughter of Pamela and James Mason, the actor. We hoped that maybe, God willing, David would finally find an anchor in his life and leave the rest of the world alone. Pamela Mason was known for her parties and social functions. She was the Perle Mesta of Beverly Hills, and now she decided to throw a party for BS&T. We had been playing some major gigs in Hollywood. We played the Hollywood Bowl, where Elizabeth Taylor came backstage to meet us with her friend Rosemary Clooney.

This was the first of many times that Elizabeth Taylor would come to see us. In person, she was amazing. Her eyes were mesmerizing. She was gorgeous. And she was terrific, friendly, warm, and funny. She later came to our Albert Hall concert in London, and even invited some of us to dinner with herself and Richard Burton. I passed on dinner. I don't know what the fuck I was thinking; I just remember that I went instead to see *Freaks* at the Paris Pullman Cinema. Or maybe I just didn't want Liz to go through all the trouble of cooking for us and then having Richard wash dishes.

I am reminded of the fast train we took from Tokyo to Osaka, where our interpreter told us we would be taking a detour to see the gardens of Kyoto, one of the most beautiful sites in the world, and the reason why Kyoto was taken off the target list for the atomic bomb toward the end of World War II. Asked if I was going to join the outing, I replied, "No, I think I'll just go to the hotel and take a nap before the sound check." A *nap*? And miss the gardens of *Kyoto*? I made a few bad calls in those days. These days I have plenty of time to watch movies and nap.

The Pamela Mason party was something I did not miss, however, and it's a good thing. Someone introduced me to Groucho Marx, and I nervously sputtered, "I once saw you coming out of Goddard Lieberson's office at CBS." Goddard was president of Columbia Records at the time, and a friend of Groucho's.

Groucho said, "Yeah, he was chasing me around his desk . . ."—a reference to Goddard's covert sexual preferences—". . . what were *you* doing up there?"

"My brother works on that floor," I said.

"He should get up and sit in a chair," Groucho said, and then turned and walked away.

Later, Lew Soloff was introduced to Groucho.

"Mr. Marx, I am thrilled to meet you," Lew said.

Groucho replied, "You should be ashamed of yourself," and again turned and walked away, shaking his cigar.

The house was studded with stars. Liz Taylor was also there. Being a movie addict all my life, I was about to have a landmark moment. I was introduced to Robert Mitchum. We talked for a while, and then the two of us grabbed a couple of chairs and sat down face to face to talk about Ireland. He had just finished *Ryan's Daughter* and couldn't stop talking about it. I don't even remember half the things we talked about.

How could this be happening? Me, Steve Katz, lower-middle-class, second son of Ann and Leo, beneficiary of a public education in Queens and Schenectady, New York, former adolescent postpubescent teen who had to read his bar mitzvah phonetically, who was almost thrown out of Dave Van Ronk's apartment for playing two wrong notes in "St. Louis Tickle," who promised a paper on Yeats and his Byzantium poems, yet could not deliver because he was having too much fun with his pregnant girlfriend, his blues band, and his psychedelic drugs—me, Steve Katz, was actually having a conversation with *Robert Fucking Mitchum!* Life does not get any better than that.

CHAPTER 9

Living the Dream

OCTOBER OF 1969 WAS A SPECIAL TIME IN NEW YORK CITY. THE Mets were in their first World Series, playing the Baltimore Orioles, and huge antiwar protests were planned all over the world on October 15, which became known as Moratorium Day.

It was maybe a month or two before the march, and although the band was booked that day, it made no difference. I announced that I would be marching on October 15, and that the band was welcome to cancel the date, get a sub to take my place, fire me, or whatever. My mind was set, and there was no talking me out of it; marching and protesting the war was more important to me than any gig. The date was canceled.

But the night before the march, I got a call from a friend: "Hey, guess what? I have an extra ticket to the game tomorrow." And so there I was at Shea Stadium, behind the left-field fence, belting out the National Anthem and watching Ron Swoboda make a classic catch out in right in Game Four of the World Series. Cleon Jones led the offensive charge, Vietnam be damned. Mets, 2, Orioles, 1, in ten innings! Tell me I didn't do the right thing.

The band, meanwhile, never found out that I had played hooky from an antiwar rally. Later I became friendly with Ron Swoboda when he was traded to the Yankees. We had talked about doing a drug clinic together on Long Island, but decided to can the idea when we confessed to each other that we were both potheads.

The year 1970 was an interesting one for Blood, Sweat & Tears. We played the Greek Theater in LA, and Cannonball Adderley sat in with us. We also hung out with Reverend Jesse Jackson and Cannonball at Basin Street West in Chicago. At the Electric Circus one night, Bill Cosby sat in with us on tambourine. We were nominated for ten Grammys, including Album of the Year. The awards ceremony was to be the last before they were nationally televised. We had this strange kind of luck and the publicity we innocently engendered was even stranger. When Arthur Bremer was arrested for trying to assassinate Governor George Wallace, Bremer's girlfriend, in an interview with *Life* magazine, stated that not long before he shot Wallace, Bremer took her to a Blood, Sweat & Tears concert where he was acting "strange." What a surprise!

William Calley was about to be sentenced for the My Lai massacre in Vietnam. The sentencing was to take place in Columbus, Georgia. What did he do the night before? According to the worldwide press, Calley attended a Blood, Sweat & Tears concert. My guess is that if we were performing around the time of the Civil War, Abraham Lincoln would surely have passed up on *Our American Cousin* at Ford's Theater to attend whatever Blood, Sweat & Tears concert was nearby. I bet John Wilkes Booth would also have been a BS&T fan.

The Grammys were hosted by the Covered Man's ex-mentor, Merv Griffin—the same Covered Man who the Blues Project had backed up, and who later, as David Soul, starred in *Starsky and Hutch*. It was the first time in my life that I wore a tuxedo. Miles Davis played, as did B.B. King. Miles did one of his more-abstract numbers, probably from his upcoming *Bitches Brew* album. When he left the stage, Merv came back to the microphone and said, "I'll bet you won't be whistling *that* one all the way home," to which I loudly booed. I guarantee you could hear me everywhere in Avery Fisher Hall (Philharmonic Hall at the time). We won three Grammys that night, including Album of the Year, and we even beat out the Beatles' *Abbey Road*. Go figure.

The Album of the Year Grammy was handed to us by Louis Armstrong—another one of life's highlights. I remember shaking his hand,

Ann and Leo Katz, Queens,
New York (1951)
STEVE KATZ COLLECTION

The roots of Blood, Sweat
& Tears: The Americana
Country Club, Plainview,
Long Island (1960)
STEVE KATZ COLLECTION

The Even Dozen Jug Band at Carnegie Hall (1963)
STEVE KATZ COLLECTION

"The Most Exciting Show Ever"—flyer for the Even Dozen Jug Band at Carnegie Hall (1963)
STEVE KATZ COLLECTION

The Gramercy Park Sheiks at the Ash Grove, Los Angeles (1964); from left to right: Stefan Grossman, Steve Katz, Ry Cooder
STEFAN GROSSMAN

The Blues Project with Emmaretta Marks, San Francisco (1966)
ALICE OCHS

Onstage with Blood, Sweat & Tears (c. 1968)
STEVE KATZ COLLECTION

Blood, Sweat & Tears promo photo (1969)
STEVE KATZ COLLECTION

Steve Katz starting off in the wrong key; Blood, Sweat & Tears in Westbury, NY (1969)

Blood, Sweat & Tears; pulling up our pants after mooning for the camera (1969)

American Flyer at Indigo
Ranch, Malibu, California
(1975); from left to right:
Steve Katz, Doug Yule, Craig
Fuller, John Mills, Sir George
Martin, Eric Kaz

American Flyer
promo portrait
(1975)

Steve Katz and Sir George Martin discussing Beatles recording tricks during the first American Flyer album
STEVE KATZ COLLECTION

Blues Project: Reunion in Central Park; Andy Kulberg, Steve Katz (1973)
STEVE KATZ COLLECTION

Steve Katz explaining to William S. Burroughs how to write a book proposal at a Mercury Records Frank Zappa release party, New York City (1977)
STEVE KATZ COLLECTION

Steve and Alison
STEVE KATZ COLLECTION

which was small and soft—interesting for a man who was a giant. B.B. King came up to me as we walked past the curtain and said, "Congratulations," and that we deserved the Grammy. I told B.B. that no, *he* was the man who deserved it. B.B. King and Louis Armstrong, within a minute of each other—what a humbling experience.

We played a few unusual gigs in the South. It would be my first time in Mississippi and I, a left-wing, pro–civil rights, urban Jew from New York, wasn't looking forward to it. We flew down from wherever we were in a couple of planes that were only slightly larger than Piper Cubs. The turbulence was terrible, and the pilot was kind enough to inform us that he didn't have too much control and would have to glide his way through it. I thought to myself that this flight was going to take the place of the lynch mob I was expecting at the airport, until I remembered that Judah P. Benjamin, another Jew, was in Jefferson Davis's cabinet in the Confederacy, and that I could probably talk my way out of the inevitable fate that awaited me—*if* we were lucky enough to land.

In order to forget the turbulence, I fantasized that I would tell the pilot that David's real name was David Clayton-Weinstein, and that he was a major contributor to the NAACP, knowing that the pilot would probably radio ahead to his buddies, who were hanging around the control tower in their pickups, tying knots in their ropes and waiting to get their hands on us, such was my paranoia about Mississippi. But I was glued to my seat, bouncing up and down, and too busy resigning myself to a violent death. I was a nervous wreck and could hardly talk by the time we got to our hotel.

We were in Jackson to play at the University of Mississippi, where we did our standard show. We were going over well until the last song—polite applause, no encore. We couldn't understand what was happening until the student promoter came backstage and asked how long our intermission would be. *What?* We just did our whole show; what do you mean *intermission?* Not having any more material, we were whisked back to our hotel while the audience waited and fumed. Some of the locals decided they might "talk" us into going back onstage whether we liked it or not. This wasn't my silly fantasy from the flight down. This was real. We were guarded all night long at our hotel by the Mississippi State Police before driving to Memphis the next morning for a concert at the University of Tennessee, where their football team was to play Ole Miss, quarterbacked by Archie Manning. Manning's fans, who were known as "Archie's Army," held a rally the night before the game, right outside our hotel. I couldn't wait to get back to the calm of New York City after not sleeping for two nights in a row.

—————

David Clayton-Thomas, a citizen of Canada, had spent some time in an Ontario prison. I don't remember why David was arrested (we never would have heard the correct version anyway), but his visa was about to expire, and the Justice Department wanted to take advantage of the situation. It was very important at that time for the State Department to find a rock band that could represent America abroad, and I don't mean people like the Young Americans, one of the darling Conservative bands of the day. Of course, with the war and all, nobody of any significant stature would do it. We certainly weren't jumping on board. That is, until some genius at the State Department leaned on the Justice Department to threaten David with deportation unless we did the State Department a little favor—and if that sounds like extortion, that's exactly what it was. It was either do a tour for the State Department or lose our lead singer. In retrospect, we should have thought it through a little more, but we stuck with David and signed on for a tour of Eastern Europe.

The countries we were to visit were Czechoslovakia, Yugoslavia, Romania, and Poland, in that order. Czechoslovakia was taken off the list at the last minute because of student rioting that was taking place there. We would have a chartered airplane at our disposal, and the tour was to be filmed for an ABC prime-time special, sponsored by Fabergé. The filming began with a reception in Washington, thrown by Under Secretary of State Elliot Richardson. In protest against the war and the Nixon administration, I did not attend.

The reasons for our going on the tour were to be kept secret, and for myself, the frustration mounted. I did an interview for the *New York Post*, then a liberal New York City daily tabloid, in which I said that the State Department should cancel the tour and give the money that it would cost to the Black Panther movement instead. Obviously this did not sit well with a lot of people. I look back on that interview today with a laugh at what balls I had to actually say this when I *really* wanted to tell the world that we were being blackmailed by the fucking Nixon administration.

The night before the first leg of our journey, a stay in London followed by the trip to Yugoslavia, David was served with a paternity suit by his ex-girlfriend, Patti. Little did David know at the time that his Patti happened to be *everybody's* ex-girlfriend. He was arrested, missed the flight, was bailed out by management, and joined us a day or two later. He also got some publicity in the New York tabloids, but it was more embarrassing than political—yet another of the many mishaps that DCT ran into, all while he protested that the mishaps ran into *him*.

In London we picked up a film crew of thirty-five people and equipment from the Samuelson Film Service. Also with us were writer Ira Wolfert, who was to document the trip for *Reader's Digest*, our director, Donn Cambern, who edited *Easy Rider*, Lorraine Alterman, a writer who was to write about the trip independently, and a representative from the State Department. Lorraine had done an article about me for a short-lived magazine called *Scenes*. The article was entitled "Blood, Sweat & Blintzes," but the subtitle, which was put on the cover, asked the musical question: "Is Steve Katz a Rock Star?" With descriptions of me taking leftovers home from my mom's house, the answer was inconclusive at best.

I had never been to Europe, and Zagreb was a hell of a way to start. I felt like I was in a time machine, on my way to the 1940s. With our very large contingent of travelers, you would think we were going to some obscure South Pacific island to find a giant ape.

There was no way I could have been prepared to be in an Iron Curtain country. Yugoslavia, under Tito's rule, was still somewhat independent, but that in and of itself certainly didn't improve the food. We were to play at an outdoor stadium, and when we arrived for the sound check, we discovered that the electric currents were completely unreliable. The organ ran a bit flat on less power than what it really needed, which whipped the horn section into a tizzy, but somehow they were able to adjust their mouthpieces so that we were relatively in tune. I tuned my guitar to the organ, but my harmonicas didn't fare very well.

Our roadies, Jon and Bob (bless their criminal hearts), told the hired help, who could not speak English, to answer any of the band's questions with "Okay, GI buddy!"

"Excuse me, could you move my amp a little closer to the drums?"

"Okay, GI buddy!" the man said as he just stood there, staring at me, Jon and Bob looking on with silly grins on their faces.

These poor guys actually had to bring David's huge gong on the road with us. David hit the gong once every show, and to this day I never saw the point in why he did it or why we brought it. No one in the audience really cared, but David thought it was hilarious.

Our next stops in Yugoslavia were Belgrade, Ljubljana, and Sarajevo. In Sarajevo, just before leaving, I informed our road manager, Jim Babb, that as an amateur student of history, I wanted to visit the bridge where, in 1914, Archduke Ferdinand of Austria was shot to death by Gavrilo Princip, a Serbian separatist. It was the spark that started World War I. I thought I had found the bridge, and as was my habit then, I shot maybe twelve rolls of film, making sure that I would capture each angle. When I got back, everyone was already on the bus, waiting for me, when I was informed by our tour guide that I'd gone to the wrong bridge. I insisted that everyone, including the poor people from the film crew and our pilot and *his* crew, wait until I found the right bridge. And they thought *David* was an asshole. I guess I have my moments, too.

Our next stop was Romania, where the food was twice as bad as what we'd had in Yugoslavia. The 1940s morphed into the 1930s, and everything was in black and white, like a bad print of an old movie. Here things got a little stranger. We were to play concerts in Constanta, Bucharest, and somewhere in Transylvania that we never got around to. We were assigned government guides who tried to keep us at the hotel or the "tourist" attractions while keeping us away from ordinary people. But there were no tourists, just plainclothes police following us everywhere.

We did, however, spy some supposed tourists in Constanta, a bunch of fat Russian government bureaucrats who were vacationing in this, their favorite resort on the Black Sea. You could tell who the police were by the newspapers they were reading, which were upside down and had a hole in the center. It would have been a flawless Cold War satire, except it was real. We drove them crazy by going wherever we wanted, even though our transportation was limited. We met a family in Constanta who surreptitiously invited us back to their home where we drank vodka, had some good conversation, and hoped they weren't tortured or assassinated after we left.

In Bucharest whatever few stores existed were empty. The place was a depressing mélange of government buildings, empty streets, and dilapidated public housing. Busboys came up to us in the restaurant at the hotel and in whispers begged us to send them Led Zeppelin albums in brown paper wrappers when we got home.

We were to play two nights at a large indoor stadium in Bucharest. When we arrived we were told that we were invited to have dinner with the American ambassador and his wife. The ambassador must have been an LBJ leftover who was punished by the Nixon administration with an assignment to one of the worst outposts in the world. And he looked it. This guy was so depressed to be in Romania and so lonely for a real conversation that I thought he was going to lock the gates of the embassy and never let us leave.

Our hotel offered a choice of bedbugs or cockroaches, no extra charge. Meanwhile, Melissa came down with a bad case of food poisoning and we had to call for a doctor, who arrived in a bloody white blouse and proceeded to inject her with a needle the size of my forearm. After that I vowed the only food I would eat for the rest of the trip was going to be Wiener schnitzel and Coca-Cola.

The first concert went well—great, in fact. We decided to kick some ass and emphasize more of the "rock" that we were capable of playing. The Romanian government was not happy with our performance. We were sent an ultimatum the next morning that we were to play more "jazz" and less "rock," and that we were to tone down our stage clothes—funny, since we hardly *had* any stage clothes, and were pretty much known for being one of the most conservatively dressed bands in rock. I take that back. I meant one of the most *poorly* dressed bands in rock.

But now we were angry. We were not going to be pushed around like that, so we decided to play even harder rock the next night. We did, and the kids went crazy, one of our best audiences ever, but when it came time to do an encore, the authorities set the police and police dogs on the audience, resulting in numerous injuries. While we thought we were being filmed, it turned out that only the audio of the night survived. The next morning, we were thrown out of Romania, even though we were scheduled to play a benefit for Transylvanian flood victims. The cancellation was especially disappointing to me. I was looking forward to getting a few shots of a vampire or two, until I found out that vampire images, just like those in mirrors, don't show up in photos. I was inconsolable.

The authorities wanted to confiscate all of our film, but the film crew was smart enough to store the film cans in boxes marked SEAT BELTS, which they surreptitiously stowed aboard the plane. Before the Romanian government people suspected anything, we were on the runway, where I spied lines of parked Russian MiGs, and kept my fingers crossed.

Our next stop was Warsaw, which seemed like heaven compared to Ceauşescu's Romanian dictatorship, from where we had just come. Journalists and fans were there to meet us, as was the staff of the US embassy, who invited us to a party on the consulate lawn, where our roadies stole the show. Though a lot more comfortable than Romania, Poland was obviously still a satellite of the Soviet Union. We checked into Warsaw's top hotel, the Hotel Krasnapolsky, where a few of us, including Fred Lipsius, went to the dining room for a bite to eat. Freddy wanted to start out with a bowl of raspberries, but when the waiter brought it, Freddy, who was about as excitable as a tranquilized sloth, noticed something walking around. "Excuse me," he said very calmly to the waiter, "there's a cockroach on my raspberries." The waiter acted surprised and said to Freddy, in his broken English, "I'm *so* sorry, sir," picked up the cockroach, and handed the bowl back to Freddy.

We bicycled around and took a tour of the old city and the site of the Warsaw Ghetto. Bombed-out buildings could still be seen all over, a marked contrast to the American consulate, which looked like a Ramada Inn amid the rubble. Up to this point, I had played Carnegie Hall, Philharmonic Hall, and many other fine venues, but I had yet to see a hall as beautiful as the one in Warsaw. The Palace of Culture and Science was located in the middle of the city. The large building, a gift from the Soviet Union, was sarcastically referred to by the locals as "Stalin's Birthday Cake." We played an excellent show there, this time with no incidents. The audience included Warsaw intellectuals and music fans, and though we all enjoyed ourselves, I couldn't wait to get back home and dive into a hamburger and fries.

While we were in Warsaw, the film producers wanted to arrange for us to take a trip to Auschwitz. I wanted to go, but I was afraid that they might do something stupid in the editing room, like put "Spinning Wheel" into the scene as background music. You never know. These guys were from Hollywood and not very high-end, so we did the wise thing and decided not to go.

We all assembled at the airport on the day we left. Though it was early morning, our manager took one last slug of 150-proof Polish vodka, immediately hit the floor, and had to be carried on board. We took a Russian Aeroflot plane from Warsaw to London, where we were to catch a plane to New York. Upon our descent into Kennedy, we were told that the hydraulic system of the landing gear had failed, and that it would have to be dropped manually. We were asked to stow all of our carry-on luggage in the bathrooms and assume the crash-landing position, with our heads down and our hands behind our heads—all this in case the landing gear refused to lock.

As Kennedy came into view, we saw flashing red lights all across the tarmac. Fortunately the landing gear locked and we landed safely. This near disaster was not as bad as what happened later, when at the very beginning of a flight back from Australia, a stewardess spilled a cup of hot coffee on my purple shirt, which meant that for the next fifteen hours or so, sopping wet, I would smell like the Dumpster behind my local coffee shop and look like a large black raspberry sundae with chocolate syrup dripping down my chest. Death would have been a better fate than that.

In retrospect, I was glad to have done the tour and to have seen what a totalitarian society actually looked like. It was a memorable experience, but there was no way that we "represented the youth of America," as the Nixon administration would have had the public believe. This was also the final straw for the "underground" press, who still had their panties in a bunch over the fact that we had played a casino in Las Vegas. We had now lost virtually all credibility.

A couple of weeks later, we had some West Coast gigs, and when we got to LA, the film's producers notified us that they had set up a press conference without our knowledge or permission. I didn't want to attend, but figuring this was my chance to once again state my position, I did. I thought they would prepare a small room, but found myself walking into an auditorium that was almost full. And the press was ready to tear into us.

We shouldn't have been put in that position, and my unprepared attempt to try to explain our way out of it without revealing the secret of why we did the tour in the first place was met with disdain, culminating in a very embarrassing and negative article that was printed in *Rolling Stone*. In the September 3, 1970, issue, David Felton, after referring to David as the group's "pudgy-faced lead singer," wrote about our criticisms of Communist society and noted that "it soon became clear from remarks by Clayton-Thomas, drummer Bobby Colomby and guitarist Steve Katz that the State Department got its money's worth."

Ugh.

At home, I even lost some friends over the controversy, people who thought we had sold out. That was the point where I just wanted to move to the countryside and hide from all the bullshit. And that's exactly what I did, but not before we recorded our third album, and made our next mistake.

The film never did come out. It was rejected by ABC, Fabergé, or both. We were so boring that they had to use animated arrows on a map to point to cities we were visiting. It looked like a World War II documentary outlining troop movements. There were lots of shots of us taking pictures of each other and even one shot of David banging his ridiculous gong. But representing the youth of America? You've got to be kidding.

A lot of people don't know what a record producer does. It's different for everyone, and changes from project to project, but basically a producer steers the ship. Think of a film's director; some have immediately recognizable styles—Hitchcock, David Lynch. Others just bring the movie across the finish line. They're professionals who might specialize in action pictures or schlocky rom-coms, but they get it done, hopefully on budget and on time.

With a record producer, it's largely the same. Some have their own thing. Phil Spector immediately comes to mind; you can tell one of his records from a mile away before the singing starts, and that's not easy to do. Jimmy Page was a master—Zeppelin had their own sound. The way the drums are recorded is epic. The producer also helps choose material and works on the arrangements. One of the first great things George Martin did for the Beatles was to make them put the chorus in front of the verse in "She Loves You" (the "She loves you, yeah, yeah, yeah" part), which turned a good song into a great record, the kind of pop rock that tickled teenage girls to tears. Later, of course, things changed as they started using strings. And as they started to get far out on drugs, the gig got a lot more complex, what with newfangled multi-track machines and expansive arrangements, backwards tapes and dissonance; but notice that George was there for the entire ride, so that should tell you right there how important a job it is.

We changed producers with *Blood, Sweat & Tears 3*. Jimmy Guercio had produced our big hit album, and he had done a marvelous job. He focused our sound, got great performances, helped keep us on course and pointed straight toward a bright future. He nailed it. Our second record sold six million worldwide, which was a lot of records. Jimmy had the magic touch with us.

But after that album, Bobby Colomby was feeling a little cocky and thought he should produce the next one. Bobby and I were friends, so I backed him on this, but it was a huge mistake. As for Jimmy, he took it out on us by going across the street and producing jazz-rock up-and-comers Chicago. They were like our little brothers or cousins. Jimmy took our magic formula into the studio with them, and they went right to the top. They deserved all of their success, but let's face it: They were the competition, and a little bit of me died when I saw what Jimmy did for them. He was the right guy, but I figured I should stay with my friend. Bad decision.

Bobby was in over his head. Our engineer, Roy Halee, best known for working with Simon & Garfunkel, is also listed as producer on the record, which certainly helped, but the record had a lot wrong with it. We had two hits on it—Carole King's "Hi-De-Ho" and "Lucretia MacEvil," a David Clatyon-Thomas original—but we were mostly hammered for our song selection, which featured (again) an abundance of covers. Some of them were already over-warmed, like James Taylor's "Fire and Rain" (to which our version added little except some cheese, thanks to what one reviewer mocked as "David Sinatra-Clayton"), and our extended, overarranged, so-baroque-it-was-almost-rococo version of the Stones' "Sympathy for the Devil," introduced with our own "Symphony for the Devil," showed a serious lack of judgment. Add to that the reviews that focused on our State Department trip, calling us traitors to the cause, sellouts, pigs, you name it. And, of course, there was our run at Caesars, which was brought up again and again as proof of our selling out.

And somehow, adding yet more to this was the fact that we did the soundtrack for the Barbra Streisand movie, which was to the hippie hordes the smoking gun that we were now in cahoots with the enemy, so blinded by Hollywood and crass commercialism that we had sold our counterculture bona fides for a bag of magic beans. It's funny, because these days, to be on a movie soundtrack is a sign of hip cachet. Now they are using punk-rock songs on cruise-ship ads and to publicize the Olympics, and even the most radical rockers are taking the checks, so really, just how square was it to be on the soundtrack of what turned out to be a pretty cool picture?

We were up against a wall, having to follow a huge album with an untested producer, and desperately looking for the hit songs that would keep us at the top of the charts. Aside from the mistake of leaving "Sympathy for the Devil" on the album, there was David's audible smile on "Lonesome Suzie" and a chorus on "Hi-De-Ho" that sounded more like they were singing Verdi's *Requiem* than what they should have sounded like—a black gospel choir. I contributed an anti-war song, but it had no place on what we thought we were trying to do. Firing Guercio was a huge mistake, and essentially sounded the death knell for Blood, Sweat & Tears.

I thought of myself as a leftist, and had been since my folk music days. I also found it hard to reconcile my politics with my newfound income, something I never expected to be doing. In an odd way, the war in Vietnam made it easy for the Left to take out their political frustrations, and to do it publicly.

By this time, we had moved north of New York, about a forty-five-minute drive up the Palisades Parkway, to a little town on the west side of the Hudson called New City. Colomby had moved there the year before, and it was where Melissa and I were married. I lived on South Mountain Road, just down the street from Lotte Lenya, who held poker games every Friday night; the great photographer Lee Friedlander; the actor and Mercury Theater alumnus John Houseman; and Kiss's manager, Bill Aucoin, who lived next door. It was a legendary leftist neighborhood where in the 1940s one would consider going to a Paul Robeson concert a night on the town.

I arranged for Lee Friedlander to shoot the cover of our third album. Lee had done a lot of photos for Atlantic Records, working with artists like Aretha Franklin and John Coltrane. We were playing in Miami where he joined us for the photo shoot. Lee asked me to let him know if I was going to any upcoming rock parties, so that he might tag along. Shortly after, I was invited to a Kinks party thrown by RCA and asked Lee if he wanted to join me. Lee came with a ring flash attached to his Leica and proceeded to get up close to people's faces for his shots—I mean, like *inches* away. I believe those photos became part of that year's "Lee Friedlander" exhibition at the Museum of Modern Art.

We were constantly being asked to play benefits, agreed to do a few, but had to turn down others, as our schedule was full. One that we took on wholeheartedly was with Neil Young in Cleveland's Public Auditorium, to raise money for the defense of the Kent State students who were indicted after the massacre. A writer friend of mine, Dotson Rader, who was also a friend of the great American playwright Tennessee Williams, called me at home one evening to ask if we would consider doing a benefit that Williams was involved with. I had to turn Dotson down, but he was persistent and said, "Okay, I'm going to have Tennessee give you a call." Oh please, *Tennessee Williams* is going to give *me* a call? No way! Ten minutes later the phone rang, I picked it up, and there was the voice I recognized from his TV interviews. Tennessee Williams—*and I had to turn him down*. Boy, that was hard. And cool. Hard and cool. It was a tough job, but somebody had to do it. And I did it with my best Brando imitation, just in case Tennessee could find some extra work for me on the side.

When we weren't on the road, I would drive into Manhattan in my little blue MGB and visit jazz guitarist Allen Hanlon for some much-needed lessons, as I was trying to keep up with the direction that the band was heading in. I'd often stop by Richard Rodgers's office to say hello to my mother-in-law and spend some time with Mr. Rodgers. The great Richard Rodgers, of Rodgers & Hammerstein and Rodgers & Hart, would sit in his office most days, mostly by his piano, with not very much to do. He welcomed my visits. The office was also where librettos were sent out all around the world.

At the time, there was never a day when a Rodgers & Hammerstein or Rodgers & Hart musical was not being performed somewhere around the world. Librettos of *Carousel*, *Oklahoma*, *The Sound of Music*, and *The King and I* were being shipped out daily. I loved spending time with this legend of American music. He would tell me jokes, like the one about a writing session he had at Larry Hart's apartment, where Hart greeted Rodgers at the door, naked, and proceeded to work that way for the rest of the day. At the end of the session and halfway out the door, Rodgers turned to Hart and said, "By the way, Larry, your fly is open."

When I asked Richard Rodgers if he had ever listened to covers of his songs, he told me that he rarely did, and so one day I asked him if he wouldn't mind listening to a few tracks and giving me his opinion. He agreed, and so I brought him "My Favorite Things" (Rodgers & Hammerstein) by John Coltrane, "My Funny Valentine" (Rodgers & Hart) by Miles Davis, and "Little Girl Blue" (Rodgers & Hart) by Janis Joplin. He took the records home over the weekend and called me that Monday.

"What did you think, Mr. Rodgers?" I asked.

"Sorry, Steve, I didn't like any of them—too modern for me. Remember, I grew up with Jerome Kern; he was my idol, and I don't think I ever veered away from that old style."

Wow. At least he got to hear some brilliant musicians paying him the homage that was due him, and I was glad I had the opportunity to have him listen. It answered one of those great theoretical questions: If Richard Rodgers ever heard John Coltrane doing "My Favorite Things," what would he think? Well, now we know.

Musically, I felt that we were heading toward a place where I no longer fit in. And this is when I began to work my way out of the group. There was no way I could play the jazz licks and insanely stacked chords these guys wanted to perpetrate. Back in the day when it got jazzy and I found it difficult to learn a guitar part, or even *read* one, I would say, "Hey, this could really use a harmonica." And it used to work. How big a part of "And When I Die" is the harmonica? But now our songs were getting so far out, there was no room for anything that earthy.

And there was another problem. We had been doing so well for so long that we were getting lazy and entitled. Like *Blood, Sweat & Tears*,

Blood, Sweat & Tears 3 had been mostly cover songs, and when it came time to do the follow-up, we hadn't even bothered to learn any new covers, let alone write our own stuff, which was going to be imperative if we wanted to stay competitive. Beyond all the politics, staking our rep on other people's stuff got us in hot water with the critics, and we weren't going to be able to sustain another barrage of bad reviews.

We went to Clive Davis and asked that he build a studio for Roy Halee and BS&T. Roy had his own clout from working with Simon & Garfunkel, and lo and behold, he got the studio, which is where we went to write the next record.

Do you have any idea how absurdly expensive it is to write songs in a studio? Just because the record company owns it does not mean it's free, and those bills add up faster than spending a week with, say, a phalanx of lawyers, plumbers, and call girls.

The response to our third album was not good. It became clear we needed someone else to produce, or Bobby needed some help to get us back on the right track. We called on Don Heckman, a writer who had shown a fairly profound understanding of BS&T, and someone we thought we could trust to right the ship, and at least maybe get David to temporarily stop his idiotic crooning. Heckman was the rock critic for the *New York Times* and had written a scathing review of *Blood, Sweat & Tears 3*. Thing was, though, Don was absolutely right. Bobby protested Don's involvement, so as a compromise, the album was to be a three-way production steered by Don, Bobby, and Roy Halee.

We were totally unprepared to make a record. For one thing, we didn't have enough material. After noodling in the studio and not coming up with much, I would run back to the apartment to write instead of doing it on the band's tab. A few new songs I came up with were "High on a Mountain," "Valentine's Day," "Mama Gets High," and "For My Lady."

"For My Lady" was originally titled "For Melissa," but it was decided that David would do the vocal. I wrote a song for my wife, a love song, and *David* wound up singing it. I was mortified, and thinking that it wouldn't be long before I was out of there.

Santana was recording in studio B, only a few yards away. We would hang out at each other's sessions. Santana would come to the studio late in the morning and start recording. Family members would trickle in, and by the end of the day, most of the band members were in the control room while the band's cousins, second cousins, uncles, and aunts were in the main room, recording. I'd stop by periodically to say hello, listen to some fabulous music, and smoke a joint or two, while back in studio A, members of BS&T were still trying to figure out what to do. There was definitely a marked contrast to the way each of us recorded, the main difference being that Santana was actually having *fun*.

I loved the Tracy Nelson song "Down So Low," and thought it would be a perfect song for us. And it would have been, had Bobby and Don not hired Jimmy Giuffre, the clarinetist and avant-garde jazz arranger, to do the chart. The chart was so off the wall that I even pitied David, who had to sing it. It took him an hour just to find the first note. We hired a few of the male voices from the Edwin Hawkins Singers. I was laughing my sides off when the track was played for them and, instead of doing their vocals, what I heard in the control room were these guys going *What the fuck?* It was a disaster and would have been a total waste of time if it weren't so funny.

That track was scrapped, but someone did make a couple of smart decisions. One was to ask Al Kooper to give us a song, and Al did. "John the Baptist" came out great. Good chart, good vocal, good performance, good politics. We also did "Rock Me (For a Little While)," the Isley Brothers song that was also covered by the Doobie Brothers. That track also came out well. My song "Valentine's Day" worked, with some beautiful trumpet playing by Lew Soloff. The artwork was excellent, and the photos were taken by South African émigré Norman Seeff. All in all, I liked *BS&T 4*, and I still do. It was a better album than its predecessor, but, as expected, did not sell nearly as well as the previous three.

In October of 1971, we were asked take part in a PBS series called *The Great American Dream Machine*. I was also asked to write the theme song. Our segment included a PBS film that was to be done at a gig where we were to play at Chino Prison in California. The gig was outside, and the audience that greeted us was made up of black prisoners on one side and white prisoners on the other, and lots of tattoos all over. There was an obvious tension, and, of course, David was in his milieu.

In his autobiography, David states that I was afraid to get off the bus, and that when I saw *him* get off and dive into the crowd of convicts, the first thing I thought was "what a man" he was, and that I knew he'd protect me. *Where does he come up with this shit?* This is the same DCT who said recently in an interview on Canadian television that the kids at Woodstock came there to protest the shootings at Kent State. Somebody forgot to inform him that the Kent State shootings happened *after* Woodstock.

Regulars on *The Great American Dream Machine* were Albert Brooks, Chevy Chase, Andy Rooney, and Marshal Efron. In our episode, Albert Brooks was to do a film entitled *The Albert Brooks School of Comedy*, which included a class on the "Danny Thomas spit-take," where someone is informed that so-and-so's uncle had just died, and the person drinking from a coffee cup spits all over the floor. I was at the filming, and when I passed the classroom at UCLA where filming was taking place, there was coffee all over—seats, tables, the floor. Classic stuff.

Albert and I got to be good friends. He would stay at my house in New City when he came east to play the Bitter End. In the mornings, Albert, still in his robe and playing on the couch with my malamute, would ask me to put some light classical music on the turntable. Then he would break into a "travelogue" voice and have me on the floor laughing—"As we enter the beautiful white cascades of the Alps . . ."

My theme song for the show was taped with a chorus of sixteen people dressed as different Americans—laborers, doctors, motor-cyclists, hippies, etc. They would speak lines, talk about statistics in American life, such as how many TVs there were, and how many murders a year. The vocal arranger was Bob De Cormier, whose name I had heard previously from his association with Harry Belafonte. My song was never released commercially, but as I was trying to write about the times and to fit it in with the theme of the show, I've included a couple of verses:

If I gave you today
A tax-free holiday
Would you want to go away
To Southeast Asia

An interstate dream come true
What do you think you'd do
Could you take a look at you
Or wouldn't it phase ya

The kids are gettin' crazy now, you better believe it
Papa says to son, you got to love it or leave it
Drinks on me, America, if you must

And livin' in the city's like dyin' in a cage
You got your bouffant hair and your minimum wage
Ten free rides, America—come by bus

A month later, in November of 1971, we taped *The David Frost Show*, a nationally syndicated interview and entertainment program. Frost gave us the whole hour, and we were even able to pick our own opening act, Howard Johnson's Tuba Band. Dave Bargeron, our trombone player, was also in Howard's band, so we thought it would be a good fit and a nice novelty; here were some of the greatest tuba players in the world, in one group. Later they also performed with The Band on their album *Rock of Ages* and made an appearance in The Band's *The Last Waltz*. Howard himself is still one of the most respected names in jazz. Say what you want about the tuba, it's a very underrated instrument—a lot hipper than most people think.

As with most of these shows, we were interviewed by a member of the staff who would then be able to better direct questions for Frost to ask. You have to watch out for this. My interviewer was taking notes and had asked me how I started my career. I said that I used to sing at weddings and bar mitzvahs in Schenectady. Bad enough, but then he put his notebook down, convincing me that anything I said after that would be off the record. He smiled at me and said, "Wow. Just between you and me, what songs *did* you sing at weddings and bar mitzvahs?" I began to trust the son of a bitch and laughingly went down a list of songs that included "My Yiddishe Momma."

"Great! Thanks, Steve!"

I was chosen to do "panel," along with David, Bobby, and Lew. We played a couple of songs, including what I thought was the best version of "I Can't Quit Her" that we'd ever done. We slowed it down a bit and leaned hard on the two and four. It had balls. After playing a couple of songs, we walked over to where Frost was sitting and he started interviewing us. I had brought out my acoustic guitar because I was going to play a new song I had written, solo.

Frost's questions revolved around how we all got started playing music professionally. Lew told a funny story about jumping in and almost missing the "pit" at the Rockettes show in Radio City Music Hall. David was next. "Oh, I started out in lumberjack camps in Canada, where my only possessions were a beat-up Telecaster and a Gideon Bible." Again, where the hell does he come up with this shit? Did he actually *believe* it?

So Frost asks me the same question and I say that I also sang in Canadian lumberjack camps—I did the bar mitzvahs there. And then Frost says to me, "Really, Steve—and what songs did you used to sing at bar mitzvahs?"

It was at this point that I wanted to get up from my seat, on national television, find the cocksucker who interviewed me, and wring his neck.

" 'My Yiddishe Momma.' "

"Wow, Steve, maybe you'll sing it for us [turning to the audience]. Folks, wouldn't you like to hear Steve sing 'My Yiddishe Momma'? Steve, let's hear you do 'My Yiddishe Momma'!"

I then did something that you don't see happening much on TV, especially when your stage fright has already kicked in and there's a red light on the camera that's slowly turning a semicircle around your head. I looked at Frost and said, "No."

Silence.

"But since I happen to have my guitar right here, I wouldn't mind singing something else."

It was the best segue of my life; talk about dodging a yiddishe bullet. The lights dimmed and I began a song I called "M," not to be confused with the Fritz Lang film. We recorded a version of "M" with BS&T, but it was never released until recently. I later recorded the song with American Flyer, accompanied by a George Martin orchestral arrangement.

We were getting further away from the sound that made us successful. The only good thing that came out of all this was that David finally left the band.

It was fairly uneventful, as these things go. One day at a band meeting, he just told us he was moving on to make his own records, and I remember everyone being incredibly happy about it. We tried to keep straight faces when he told us, but the second he left the room, everyone in the room was laughing and crying tears of joy, maybe even dancing. We hadn't liked him from day one. I don't think there was ever a time when most members of BS&T didn't regret hiring him, and then having to wear what amounted to golden handcuffs because we were so successful, we couldn't really fire him despite everything.

David was convinced that BS&T was holding him back, and so he was going to leave us and begin a lucrative solo career, which, of course, he did not. He even thought at some point that he was going to get the role of Johnny Valentine in *The Godfather*. It was actually kind of sad, he was so unaware, such a complete sociopath that he really believed his bandmates would be upset to see him go, that he actually had friends in that room.

For the rest of us, the show kept on rolling. *Blood, Sweat & Tears Greatest Hits* came out in February 1972 and sold faster than loose joints at a Jethro Tull concert. Unfortunately, *Greatest Hits* was our last gold record.

Without David, I decided to give the band another try. The guy we got to replace David was Jerry Fisher. Bobby Doyle was singing for a hot second, but Bobby, who was blind, had a lot of personal problems of his own.

Fisher was good, a strong Oklahoma R&B singer who had actually once been in a bar band that did BS&T covers—kind of funny, if you think that years later, a few big-time arena bands like Judas Priest and Yes actually hired new singers from "tribute" bands.

Right around then, Fred Lipsius also left, which is when Joe Henderson came in for a spell, before "Blue" Lou Marini, best known for his part in *The Blues Brothers* film, settled into the gig. And then Dick Halligan left, replaced by Larry Willis, who had done some time in the Cannonball Adderley group.

We did one concert when Larry first joined the band where, backstage, he asked me in a whisper if I wanted to go into a stall in the men's room at the far side of our dressing room and do some blow. Of course I did. While we walked to the restroom and as he took out his accoutrements, Larry kept saying to me, "Please, nobody in the band can know about this. I really don't want to get fired from this gig. Please make sure that nobody finds out we're doing this," on and on, over and over. "Don't worry, man," I assured Larry, "nobody will know a thing."

We're on. Showtime. Larry and I come bounding out of the men's room and get up on a dark stage in front of maybe ten thousand people. Larry's skin is very black, and I mean, *very* black. So the lights come up, I look at Larry, and there they are, two white rings around his nostrils. No, Larry, I won't tell a soul.

The new group, locked and loaded with jazzers posing as rock stars, began pushing away from the roots of the band and toward jazz. The version of Herbie Hancock's "Maiden Voyage" especially was a sign that we had gone over the cliff into some dark netherworld of autoerotic jazz-rock horseplay. Why we even tried to improve on Herbie Hancock's version is a mystery to me.

We still had some gigs to play before I would depart from the band, including some more TV. In October of 1972, we taped what was to be the first of Dick Clark's *New Year's Rockin' Eve* shows with us, Three Dog Night, Billy Preston, Al Green, and Helen Reddy, and we were to tape it on the *Queen Mary*, docked in Long Beach. The tape would then be interspersed with live cuts to Dick Clark in Times Square on New Year's Eve night. At rehearsal I reunited with my old friend Danny Hutton, who had left a solo career and was now in Three Dog Night. Danny saw me from across the rehearsal space, came running over, slipped on the floor, and flew into me, his head crashing into mine, knocking us both out. When we came to, we gave each other a hug and Danny insisted I hang with him at his house that night. Lew Soloff came with me. Danny's girlfriend had just left him and he was lonely and depressed, and he also had some great cocaine, so we stayed up the whole night. We didn't have any choice—Danny wouldn't let us leave until five a.m.

We were to be at the *Queen Mary* at nine a.m. I was in a daze, but being a rock 'n' roll veteran by now, this was not something that I was unused to. The audience of kids was actually Dick Clark's ensemble hirelings. They would cheer like lunatics for each act, throw hats and balloons, and blow noisemakers until their faces were blue, but as soon as the red lights were off and the cameras stopped, you could hear a pin drop. We all sang "Auld Lang Syne" at the faux midnight hour (actually around two in the afternoon), and in between takes, I asked Al Green for his autograph. He was confused, but since this was the greatest soul singer since Sam Cooke and Otis Redding, I wanted proof for the ages that we had actually worked together.

My last TV appearance with the band occurred about a month after the Dick Clark taping. In November of 1972, we were booked on *Don Kirshner's Rock Concert* at Hofstra University on Long Island with Poco, Alice Cooper, Curtis Mayfield, Chuck Berry, Seals and Crofts, the Allman Brothers, and Bo Diddley. The lineup was pretty astounding; we probably all could have hung around for a couple of days to start our own rock festival.

The actual night of December 31 rolled around, and we were to headline a New Year's bill at the Capitol Theatre in New Jersey with B.B. King and his band, while our *New Year's Rockin' Eve* show was to be telecast nationally. I drove down to Paramus in my little blue MGB and left my keys in my attaché case just before going onstage. I could not find my case when we finished our show. It was stolen. Somehow I had to get back home. By now it was one a.m., and I managed to hitch a ride to New City, where I was so pissed-off that when my friend Bruce Johnston of the Beach Boys called to wish me a Happy New Year, I practically hung up on him. I had to take it out on somebody, and Bruce was the first one near. Bruce didn't let it hurt our relationship, thank goodness, as a couple of years later when my divorce had rendered me penniless, Bruce called to recommend that I invest in Krugerrands. The Beach Boys lived in a much different world than I did.

To be clear, "jazz fusion," is the worst music ever created in the history of, well, music. Blood, Sweat & Tears was "jazz-rock," which is a label I never liked in the first place, but was more accurate in that we were doing soul and rock and blues with some jazz influence, basically just working the horns into the sound. The guys who started this band, Al Kooper and me, were rock 'n' rollers. We were blues hounds. We came up on Chuck Berry and Muddy Waters while we were in the Blues Project, the same formula that produced the Rolling Stones. Do you think jazz fusion had anything to do with that? Listen to the Mahavishnu Orchestra and everyone who followed them—Weather Report, Return to Forever, and a million other jazzers who plugged in and played endless solos over increasingly boring rock and funk vamps. There was no blues in that, no swing. It was a big jerk-off session for soloists. Now take a look at Muddy Waters playing one note, riding his Telecaster from bottom to top with a sawed-off bottleneck ...*Brrrrrrrrrrrtwannnnnng!* There is a lot more sex in that than the five million notes played by show-offs like so many of the jazz musicians who think they can solo for half an hour and actually get away with it.

Part of the problem was that jazz guys looked down on rock and roll. They thought it was easy to play, which it may be, in theory, but it's like pizza: Even though you only have a few ingredients, not everyone can do it right. Why? Because it takes a lot of heart and feel and an understanding of tradition. All those Juilliard graduates who said the Ramones couldn't play because they only played barre chords and slammed 4/4 time were lost the first second they tried it. Maybe they could play the notes, but it was a joke, because the Ramones had the touch, the feel, and the heart, and that's why they were so great. They believed what they were playing, which is why it was so beautiful. The jazz guys disdained the less-is-more, play-it-like-you-mean-it approach. They never got it.

And so I announced that I was leaving. See ya.

Usually there's great acrimony when someone leaves a successful band, for whatever reason. Brian Jones left The Stones and ended up facedown in a swimming pool. Mick Taylor quit The Stones, and for all the career success he had after that, he probably wished he was dead, too. There wasn't so much drama when I announced that I had finally had enough of Blood, Sweat & Tears and was walking away. We were in Florida and had just had a band meeting when I told them it was time for me to move on, and frankly, no one gave a shit. We promised to stay in touch. No one cried. One stoned jazzer may have even yawned. Twenty million records after the band started, and that's what I got.

I had gone through periods of insecurity before—when I'd left the Blues Project, when Al had left BS&T and we had to put it back together without the record company's blessing. Now I felt it was time to stand on my own. My friendship with Bobby Colomby had taken a turn for the worse, as Bobby saw BS&T as an opportunity for himself, a vehicle to further his own security as his career pointed more and more toward a Hollywood lifestyle. In saying good-bye to BS&T, I did not have any personal misgivings. I was never close with those guys like I was, in an odd way, with the guys in the Blues Project. Now I just had to figure out how to pay the mortgage.

I had recently recruited a second guitar player for BS&T, Georg Wadenius, who was recommended by Stefan Grossman, so there was no reason for me to be there anymore. He could comp all the fancy jazz chords and read the crazy fly-shit the horn players called charts. And anyway, with all the hot air they were blowing, empowered by a couple of *DownBeat* awards and a *Playboy* jazz poll that fanned the flames of their anti-rock ardor, there was hardly room for one guitar player, let alone two.

There's a lesson here for anyone who is planning to work with a horn section: don't. Horns are great, and obviously they were at the heart of the success of Blood, Sweat & Tears—at least while they acted like a horn section. But once they were exposed to the radioactivity of acceptance on a jazz level, they turned into hepcat Godzillas and wanted to take over, blowing solos all over the place. And if there is one thing rock fans hate, it is jazz solos.

There was a reason even giants like Mingus and Coltrane didn't play stadiums. Occasionally they might be on a big stage for some kind of festival, but in New York City, where there are more jazz fans per capita than anywhere in the world, they generally played tiny rooms like the Village Vanguard. Even when the Miles Davis electric band of the early 1970s—which was, despite his proper upbringing, more like an out-of-control acid-rock act, and undoubtedly the most popular "jazz" band of its day, what with the breakthrough of *Bitches Brew*—played the Fillmore East, they were down on the bill; usually they were second, below the Steve Miller Band, or else they were playing club dates. One of the biggest dates they did was opening for us at Madison Square Garden, but that was strictly a one-shot deal, riding on whatever synchronicity a gig with us offered, and by then the electric guitar had pretty much taken over that group, and whatever jazz Miles was playing was whacked half to death through a wah-wah pedal.

Unfortunately the jazzers in BS&T wanted it both ways. They figured once they snuck into the stadium hiding under the coattails of the BS&T formula I had begun with the long-gone Al Kooper, they could gravitate toward their high-minded bebop idealism and the kids wouldn't notice. Well, it doesn't work that way, and the more jazz that got floated into the set, the more the crowds drifted away from us.

I was shocked when Joe Henderson wanted to join BS&T, and even though he never made it onto a record, he was with us for a few months. I couldn't believe it. Joe is a monster sax player, one of the best ever, highly regarded by anyone in the know as playing in the same league as John Coltrane. In fact, the band he used on some of his greatest Blue Note sides was basically Coltrane's quartet, which is like a guitar player hiring Jimi Hendrix's band to back him up—it's musical hubris, and takes a lot of balls, except in Joe's case he had it covered. He was a phenomenal, dominating tenor player. So what the fuck was he doing in our horn section? He told me straight up, it was for the money. He wasn't deluding himself; he knew exactly which side of the toast the butter was on.

Speaking of jazz greats, Bill Evans came up to the studio one time when we were covering his song "Time Remembered." I didn't play on it because there were about four hundred chords I didn't know, and you know with him, it's all about voicings and subtlety, and has about as much to do with rock music as a teapot has to do with a tractor. Bill was a nice guy, but the band was making mistakes, and he sorted them right out. He wasn't mean about it, but he cut them zero slack. They thought they were climbing out of the cesspool of juvenile rock music, but the fact was, that was where this band lived, and their pretensions were going to kill the goose that had laid the gold records.

The thing was, BS&T wasn't even so much a group as it was some oddball corporate entity. It was pasted together—here's a trumpet player, here's a trombone player, a sax; you play this, you play that. It wasn't exactly the Stax/Volt band or the Memphis Horns, but it wasn't supposed to be Sun Ra's Arkestra, either.

Looking back, it was the beginning of an odd trajectory for the band. They never had another hit record. There is an old philosophical quandary: What if while you were out one day someone snuck into your house and replaced everything you owned with exact replicas. How would you know, and would it make a difference?

Well, this wasn't that; not quite. They called it Blood, Sweat & Tears, but it's not like a baseball team where people are still going to root for you based on the color of your shirt. The fans always know when it ceases to be real. And the crazy thing is that right now, today, as of this writing, Blood, Sweat & Tears is touring without any original members, working what we politely like to call the "legacy circuit," and their manager claims that this is the best lineup ever! I'm not sure whether that counts as toxic postmodernism or what, but it's just kind of fucked-up. You look at the history of the band: 134 people have been in BS&T over the years, but mostly all after I left. It became an employment agency for horn players. The four records I worked on were pretty steady—I mean, you can swap a second trumpet now and again and it doesn't make a difference, and there is always a horn player who is better at selling pot than showing up on time for the gig, but mostly we had a steady working band.

Anyway, all of a sudden I was out on my own. I had wanted out, but after eight years of the Blues Project and BS&T, what now? I used to spend six months of the year on the road, and I didn't think I'd miss it—not the hassles, the infighting, the crappy DC3s with no cabin pressure, or the lifestyle. And that's how it was. I liked the lifestyle, but at the end of the day, I was a giant nerd.

My marriage, for the moment, was stable. Melissa was mellow; in fact, she didn't say too much at all. Now I can look back and say that something was bubbling inside her, because before too long she'd become paranoid and terrified, and it would all come out, but right then, things seemed good.

Leaving BS&T was working out well. Earlier, I was able to get some money from the group, enough to buy a new house. The deal was that I would give up future royalties for a one-time payout, but here's the thing: We weren't collecting royalties the way we should have been, with Sony later on deducting CD production costs from the royalties—what was later called a "misinterpretation of our contract." We threatened to sue, along with Simon & Garfunkel and the Janis Joplin estate, among others, and things got straightened out.

Before we brought the lawsuit, however, Columbia copped to their "mistake," at which point Bobby Colomby (who was once on staff at Epic/Columbia and still knew people in the royalty department) did a nice thing and said, "Hey, Steve, it's been a while; you should be getting royalties again." And so now I do. (For the years I wasn't collecting, it didn't amount to a lot because of the way Columbia was interpreting the contract.) Anyway, Bobby's generosity could also be seen as payback for when I stuck by him and helped jump-start his production career.

Meanwhile, someone I knew over at Columbia asked me if I wanted to produce a band called El Roacho. He knew the manager, and figured correctly that if they got my name on the project, he'd be able to sell them to his bosses and sign them. I was thrilled. They were an actual rock 'n' roll band who didn't know how to read music! Well, except for the bass player, who had played oboe in the New Orleans Symphony until he freaked out and left to join this cosmic cowboy stoner band. (I can imagine his parents were thrilled: "Hi, Mom, good news! I'm leaving the philharmonic to join El Roacho!")

It was a real breath of fresh air. BS&T rehearsals had become unbearable toward the end, and all El Roacho wanted to do was play and have fun. They were from Oklahoma and along the lines of Leon Russell, just an old-fashioned stoner medicine show of a band. The record I produced for them was called *The Best of El Roacho's Biggest Hits*, but of course, there were no hits. Good songs, though, and I had a lot of fun doing it.

There arose an opportunity for the Blues Project to do some reunion concerts. Al Kooper had started his label, Sounds of the South, and had signed an unknown band out of Florida called Lynyrd Skynyrd. Al thought it would be nice to do some Blues Project recordings and maybe release one on his new label, so we were booked into Ron Delsener's Central Park concert series at the Wollman Rink and recorded the show. Al took the tapes down to Atlanta and, with Andy Kulberg, mixed them, while replacing any of his unacceptable vocals. Typically, Al didn't ask me if maybe *I* wanted to fix a vocal or two, and so the album, *Reunion in Central Park*, was released with my out-of-tune vocals, while Al's vocals were so improved that they sounded almost human. We also played Philharmonic Hall, with Lynyrd Skynyrd opening. Al asked me to do a jug band–like harmonica solo on Lynyrd Skynyrd's first album, which I did on a song called "Mississippi Kid."

Our reunions were to continue through the early 1990s. In later years I received a phone call from New York promoter Ron Delsener, who asked me if I would be interested in working with the Blues Project again in a reunion tour with the Lovin' Spoonful and The Rascals. I told Ron that Kooper and I would never work with each other again, and he said that each member of the tour would get approximately $150,000. My answer: "For that much money, I'd tour with Adolf Hitler." The tour never happened, and as it turned out, Hitler wasn't available either.

So, from Bill Evans to El Roacho to the revitalized Blues Project. It felt great. I was back in rock and roll. But it certainly didn't prepare me for what was about to come next—the amphetamine psychosis of the Dark Lord, Lou Reed, and the *Rock 'n' Roll Animal* show.

CHAPTER 10

Rock 'n' Roll Animal

Sometimes I just wanted to scream, "Is *every* lead singer an asshole?" And if not, *how come I always wind up with the ones who are?*

But things were about to change. In 1973 I had left Blood, Sweat & Tears. I needed to get off the road and build up my studio chops. No more puffed-up, self-serving, vanity-driven lead singers. No more ego-maniacal prima donnas and woman-hating Neanderthals; this time, I thought, my luck would be different.

Most of the time, I had enjoyed the music I was making, with both the Blues Project and Blood, Sweat & Tears, but personalities and the music business always had to be addressed. I thought that on my own (and this would be the first time I would really be on my own), I would have the aesthetic freedom to choose whom I wanted to work with and how I would approach any given situation. I wasn't going to suffer egos and assholes. That is, until I met Lou Reed.

I first met Lou—or, to put it more accurately, we first inhabited the same space—in 1966 when he was with the Velvet Underground.

When I had started out with the Blues Project, we were terrified of the Velvet Underground. We were suburban hippies; they were junkie warlocks. We balled girls in skirts and sandals. They were all about leather boots and whips and furs; God only knew what kind of dark sex magick they practiced. It was intimidating. We'd run into them all the time over at Max's Kansas City, which is where everyone would hang, but we kept our distance. The back room was where the avant-garde stars of the New York art, fashion, and music underground hung out. Andy Warhol would hold court with his coterie. We would eye each other suspiciously, but Lou and I weren't to formally meet until a few years later.

Meanwhile, as I was evolving from Greenwich Village progressive blues rocker to pop-radio darling, my brother, Dennis, had gone from personal management to the legal department of Columbia Records, and from there to head the Artists and Repertoire Department at RCA Records. In that capacity he signed David Bowie, Lou Reed, and Elliott Murphy, and was responsible for John Denver, Hot Tuna, The Kinks, Harry Nilsson, and Bruce Johnston from the Beach Boys, who was about to embark on a short-lived solo career.

Harry Nilsson and I were friends. I introduced him to my brother, as I did Bruce Johnston and Don Everly, which precipitated my brother's signing the Everly Brothers. Nilsson and the Everlys eventually had major disagreements with my brother, and Lou was to fall out with my brother later on as well, but that falling-out would be cataclysmic in comparison.

Lou had recorded three solo albums for RCA. *Lou Reed*, his first solo album, was produced by rock critic Richard Robinson. *Transformer* was produced by David Bowie. It gave the world the classic single "Walk on the Wild Side," made Lou a star, and, technically, a "one-hit wonder." When Lou got to his next album, he chose Canadian producer Bob Ezrin, who would later produce Kiss and Alice Cooper. Reed and Ezrin came up with an idea for a concept album called *Berlin*.

Berlin was a rehash of some of Lou's earlier songs and set in a rock-opera context. Its themes were suicide, depression, drugs, and, to my ears, a pretentious load of Lou's latest faux persona. The album was overproduced, though beautifully wrought, and played by some of the finest musicians of the day. I can understand why Ezrin had to take control of *Berlin*. I can't imagine the mess it would have been without him.

I had the same problem producing *Sally Can't Dance*, Lou's next studio album. What do you do when the artist is not the god that he and the rest of the world think he is? You do the best you can and hope that you'll get a decent vocal out of the son of a bitch, and not have a nervous breakdown over it, like Ezrin eventually had.

Berlin was a bomb. It sold hardly any copies; although it's well-respected now in certain circles, especially by those prone to rock revisionism and worshipping the emperor's new clothes, it was a stunning disappointment coming off the heels of *Transformer*.

It was the spring of 1973, and I was still in Blood, Sweat & Tears, rehearsing at our space in Dobbs Ferry, New York, just up the Hudson River from Manhattan, when my brother left RCA to manage Lou, along with one of the BS&T staff, a fast-talking ganef by the name of Fred Heller. Dennis and Fred had Lou rehearse at our Dobbs Ferry studio with his new band of child rock 'n' rollers, local kids aptly called The Tots. That was how Lou and I were first introduced. It was Lou's post-heroin, pre-speed period, an era when rock critic Lester Bangs referred to him as a "bibulous bozo." Lou was drinking heavily then, confused about his sexual orientation, and shaking like a leaf.

The question for Lou now was: "What do you do after coming off of a bomb album?" Luckily someone asked my opinion, and I replied, "You put Lou together with a great band and immediately record a live album of mostly Velvet Underground songs." That way all those people who first heard Lou through "Walk on the Wild Side" would now be exposed, in a modern context, to some of the best material he ever wrote. The Tots were dismissed and replaced by an excellent band, some of whom played on *Berlin*. Steve Hunter and my old friend Dick Wagner, both from Alice Cooper's band, were the guitarists, In my opinion, it was their heavy sound, even more than Lou, that helped *Rock 'n' Roll Animal* become a classic album.

Lou was doing epic amounts of speed at this time. His drug of choice was methamphetamine hydrochloride (brand name, Desoxyn).

He was losing weight and his shaking hands got worse. I was curious as to what Desoxyn felt like. One day, on a visit up to my house in New City, I asked Lou to leave me a pill before he left. Taking a break from my daily weed regimen, I swallowed half of it. I couldn't get to sleep for three days. Nor could I properly form a chord on my guitar or press the PLAY button on my tape deck. My wife had to change the channels on the TV. I was a zombie. My first thought: "How does he *do* this shit?" My second thought: "How do I come *down* from this shit?" That's when I switched to decaf and smoked another joint, and I haven't looked back since.

Lou was probably too intelligent for his own good, but he could be one of the funniest people I had ever known, a refreshing change from the studio guys in boring old Blood, Sweat & Tears. That was the good side of him.

Babysitting Lou was the responsibility of my brother and Fred Heller; I did not have to deal with it, which left Lou and I more or less on equal ground to make a record. Lou respected that I was a musician and that we had a shared history in the New York underground, even if the Blues Project had been abjectly terrified of the Velvets. Lou and Dennis, fully aware that I was looking for a way out of BS&T, liked my idea for a Lou Reed live record and asked if I would be interested in producing it. I had already produced one album, but I jumped at this chance to produce someone with a track record. My new career was about to take a giant step forward. I was getting back to rock and roll, and overjoyed at the prospect of producing a possible hit album. I hadn't even considered the fact that the compromises I would have to make producing this artist would make my role in the previous two bands seem like a walk in the park.

During the summer of 1973, Lou and I started spending more time together. I was mostly able to see beyond the arrogance and the drugs and learned that much of what Lou did was an act. We were sitting in Max's Kansas City together once and Lou ordered a Singapore

Sling, but he wouldn't touch it. He turned to me and said, "Watch what happens. People are looking at me and waiting for me to drink this, but I won't." It was then that I realized people had different priorities in life; Lou's was to observe and torture, to find a person's weakest point and go in for the kill. He was a pro at it.

His questionable bisexuality during this period also lent him a mystique that he himself helped to foster; however, I knew that when you took that much speed, you probably couldn't even get an erection, and thus it became a moot point. In a perverse way, it probably meant that his relationships, whether with males or females, were less threatening, but the illusion certainly fed his fans and critics alike. Earlier that evening, Lou had asked me to pick him up and hang out. We decided to go down to Max's for the aforementioned Singapore Sling, but Lou had to make a stop first. He needed to see a Dr. Freyman, aka Dr. Feelgood, who was to give Lou his "vitamin" shot. I couldn't believe he dragged me up there, so back in the car I turned to Lou and asked why he did that shit when he knew that eventually it could kill him. He told me that he would rather be dead than not do it. End of argument; Max's, here we come.

The live concert that we decided to record was actually two back-to-back concerts at Howard Stein's Academy of Music on Fourteenth Street and Irving Place in Manhattan, on Friday, December 21, 1973. The band had rehearsed long enough on the road to keep the music fresh, yet not so long that it got stale. Enough cocaine was supplied for the musicians to give it that extra sparkle, something I would advise young musicians not to try at home. We hired the Record Plant remote, mic'd the band, ran the wires, did the sound check, and were ready to go. Lou, as always, was the unknown factor. His performance depended not on any sense of professionalism, but on whatever his mood was at the time, natural or artificially induced. Thankfully, in this case, it wouldn't make too much difference. The band was that good.

With his skinny amphetamine physique, newly close-cropped dyed hair, leather jacket, and basically looking like a Hitler youth who had just emerged after twenty-eight years in a Berlin bomb shelter, Lou was about to take the stage after the Hunter/Wagner overture and begin his classic "Sweet Jane." Forget praying that Lou would sing in tune that night—I would have been happy if he came somewhere close to a melody. But he did, the band was terrific, and the night, a success.

When it was time for postproduction, thankfully, Lou was still on tour, so I was able to mix the album without the artist in attendance, a producer's dream, especially with this artist in particular, just starting his descent into amphetamine-induced psychoses. He would take speed for a month or two and then clean out his system for another couple of weeks. This was when he was the most difficult to be around—not when he was high, but when he was in remission. This was when you did not answer the phone if Lou called. This was when I had to take two aspirin every time I had to speak with him. Maybe, I thought, being a musician in a band was not so bad after all.

RCA had a union rule: If you were an RCA artist, you had to use an RCA engineer. The way around this was to record outside the country. *Rock 'n' Roll Animal* was recorded in New York, so I had to use a staff engineer. I lucked out with Gus Mossler, who, with his short hair and Archie Bunker–like demeanor, turned out to be a treasure. I would use Gus for the mix as well. We ran into only one problem: It's usually wise to record the audience track separately, in stereo on two tracks, which we thought we had done until we listened to the playback and found that one track was missing, probably due to a faulty cable at the venue. It was still possible to "fly" an audience track in, so Gus came up with the idea of using someone else's applause from the RCA vaults. So Gus went to the vaults, came back, and asked if I minded borrowing the audience track from a John Denver concert. Mind? Could I have been any happier? *Be still my beating heart!* It was an absolutely brilliant idea.

The *real* fun part was, just like with laugh tracks in sitcoms, you could play with the volume. Loud laughter can make a bad joke sound funny, and loud applause can make a mediocre performance sound positively virtuosic. Halfway through "Sweet Jane," when the band is still playing the overture, and Lou begins his entry onstage, we beefed up the applause. We turned up the volume so that it sounded as if the Pope had just entered Vatican Square. It was beautiful, and that's the way it stands to this day.

Rock 'n' Roll Animal was released in February of 1974. The album got great reviews, tons of airplay, and sold well, picking up new fans and confusing the old ones without alienating them, which was good, since that lot generally seemed to thrive on confusion.

With *Rock 'n' Roll Animal*, we got away from the high-minded stuff and made a decidedly excessive guitar romp aimed right for the heart of the beer-drinking American rock concert–going public. But Lou could never escape pretense and was a victim of his own junkie gimmick, pretending to shoot heroin onstage, actually tying off and hitting himself in the arm with a syringe while crowds of stoned kids cheered him on, as if shooting dope in front of an audience for kicks was actually cool. They ate it up like candy.

That same month we began preproduction of Lou's new studio album. It was one thing to work with Lou on a live album. You record it one night, and if your artist is a problem, you don't have to spend too much time with him. In a studio situation, you have to live with the artist. My dream was to work with somebody I liked and respected. This would not be that kind of situation. I shamelessly convinced myself that Lou could be a great artist when, in fact, the closer I worked with him, the more I regretted it.

Whenever the subject of Warhol or Bowie came up, Lou became reverent and submissive. Andy was everything to Lou. In fact, Andy was everything to so many fucked-up characters that I was almost afraid to meet him. I had this image of an evil puppeteer pulling the strings of a bunch of innocently deranged marionettes. But when I finally did meet Warhol one afternoon at The Factory, I was surprised at how gentle and affable he actually was. It was then that I realized that Warhol—accused of so many things behind his back by so many in his circle of manipulation—was actually a reasonably normal person. Unfortunately, he surrounded himself with sycophants who could barely dress themselves in the morning, Lou Reed included. This was part of Warhol's art. *They* were Warhol's art, from the Velvet Underground on up. If they weren't created by Andy, they were certainly propagated and nurtured by him.

One evening a gang of us, including Lou and Warhol, went to Lincoln Center to see comedian George Burns in concert. We had been invited backstage. On the way to the greenroom, Andy and I got separated from the others and started walking down the hallway, just the two of us, when a young fan saw us and came running over, pen in hand. I moved aside a step or two so that Andy could sign the kid's program, but the kid passed Warhol and said, "Mr. Katz, could I have your autograph?" Andy had a smile on his face while I stood there, embarrassed.

I was now living a second childhood within the Warhol milieu, but only on the periphery. At night I would look forward to going home to my life in the country, a far cry from Lou and the crowd at Union Square. My house was my retreat, where I could pick up my guitar and not worry about Lou Reed demanding my attention, where I didn't have to answer the phone if I didn't want to, and where I could gather the strength to deal with the next round of Lou's psychological missiles, which were becoming more tedious by the day.

Lou's career was back on track, but his personal life was going through changes, not the least of which was his relationship with women. Lou married Bettye Kronstadt in January of 1973. Bettye, a sweet and gentle person, was devoted to Lou. She accompanied Lou to Europe on the *Rock 'n' Roll Animal* tour, but he'd dumped her by the time we got to Paris. I didn't know why, and I made it my business not to know, as I felt it would be wise for me to stay out of Lou's personal life. But to me, it was definitely official—Lou Reed was an asshole.

As his producer, I was part of Lou's entourage for his 1973 European tour. It was in Paris that I was first introduced to Nico, who stopped by to say hello.

We were staying at L'Hotel, the former residence of Oscar Wilde and Marlene Dietrich. L'Hotel was considered to be one of the greatest hotels in the world. Nico would stay over as well, so I volunteered to sleep on the floor and give her my bed. Let it be said that no matter how luxurious the hotel, a floor is a floor, and the one in L'Hotel was just as uncomfortable as it would have been in a Motel Six in Iowa. The only difference was that I never woke up in a Motel Six and saw the gorgeous Nico wafting around the room.

On to Amsterdam, where Lou was to play the legendary classical venue, the Concertgebouw, where I had played a couple of years before with Blood, Sweat & Tears. On the morning of the gig, I called Lou's room. He answered the phone in his little-girl voice, a timbre heard by most of the people he's tried to humiliate over the years. I asked if I'd woken him up, although I knew that, like most nights in those days, he probably hadn't gotten to sleep at all. I stretched the point and told him that we were, after all, nice Jewish boys, that we were in Amsterdam, and that we were going to see the Anne Frank House.

The Frank family hid in one of those charming canal houses that line the Prinsengracht Canal when the Nazis occupied the Netherlands during World War II. It was where Anne wrote her famous diary, and where the family was finally found out and shipped off to various concentration camps, where they ultimately died. The exception was Anne's father, Otto Frank, the only one of the family to survive the camps. The house was opened to the public as a museum in 1960.

I mistakenly thought that underneath Lou Reed's crass exterior lay a somewhat compassionate human heart. Even Lou Reed, dressed in leathers and sporting his cropped, androgynous *Rock 'n' Roll Animal* haircut, would understand the solemnity of this visit—or so I believed. Anyone who has been to the Anne Frank House knows that you can almost feel the spirits that once shared these five hundred square feet. This was my second visit, and tears filled my eyes, as is usual for all who visit here. You could hear a pin drop between the near-silent sobs of the tourists and visitors from all over the world. The museum was always packed, but the mood was never less than serious and dignified, as if you were in a church or synagogue.

I told Lou that it would probably take about twenty minutes to tour the apartment, and that I would meet him downstairs in the information center. When I got downstairs, Lou hadn't yet arrived. I felt proud of him. He must have been taking the time to soak in the experience and to feel the suffering and humiliation that this very sad episode in human history had evoked. He would, as a Jew, relate to the experience of how horrible it must have been for families to have been torn from each other and killed in the death camps. This time, I thought, this morning, here in Amsterdam, Lou Reed will set aside his newly created speed-freak punk persona and return, if for only a few minutes, to his roots, and do it with the dignity and respect that the occasion warranted. I expected to see tears in his eyes.

I was at the far end of the room when Lou came down the stairs. Between myself and Lou, there must have been thirty or forty people, and as in the apartment, you could hear a mouse breathe. That is, until Lou, from halfway down the stairs, caught my eye across the room and said, in a moderately loud voice that all could hear, "Who the fuck is Anne Frank?"

Around this time Lou had met Rachel, a transvestite who would tape razor blades across her chest to defend against bullies who would try to abuse her in reform school. That's all I knew about Rachel. I have no idea where Lou found her, what happened to her, her last name, or anything else about her, except she was tall, dark, quiet, and gorgeous.

I was in the studio in Toronto producing an album by Rory Block when Lou came up for some preproduction work. Rachel was with him. We went out for dinner, and halfway through our meal, a group that looked like the Police Christian Benevolent Society walked in and asked for a table. Of course, the maître d' stuck them near us.

They couldn't take their eyes off Rachel, and I knew at that moment that I was about to die, along with the rest of our motley yet somewhat fashionable party. But nothing was said, no slander, no curses, no threats of having a late circumcision, nothing. Then I realized that these guys weren't looking at Rachel, the freaky transvestite; these guys were ogling what they thought was a beautiful woman. I almost warned them to keep their eyes off of my friend's girl, but I valued the bones in my fingers too much to take the leap.

Later that winter a bunch of us spent a weekend at a friend's farm near Beacon, New York. Lou and Rachel were there. Everybody thought Rachel was a woman until the last morning at breakfast, when it was evident that her beard was starting to grow. Rachel's was a face that launched a thousand paranoid fantasies.

I booked Electric Lady Studios on Eighth Street in Greenwich Village from March 18 to April 26, 1974, for our next project. The extraordinary guitarists, Hunter and Wagner, had to rejoin Alice Cooper. I kept the *Rock 'n' Roll Animal* rhythm section and replaced Hunter and Wagner with Danny Weis, a great Telecaster player who had been in Rhinoceros and had done a stint with Iron Butterfly. I added Michael Fonfara on keyboards.

Sally Can't Dance was to be a mélange of styles. I was still trying to avoid the concept album route that had already been a commercial failure. I even added a horn section on two tracks led by my old bandmate Lew Soloff and a Dizzy Gillespie protégé, John Faddis, both on trumpet. The two horn tracks, the title song, and "Ride Sally Ride" were R&B influenced. "Kill Your Sons" was pure Lou Reed hostility with a little metal thrown in. "Ennui" and "Billy" could have come from a folk-rock, singer-songwriter repertoire, and "Animal Language" could have appeared on a children's comedy album. The album had no real thread running throughout—mostly intentional, to avoid setting it too deeply into one niche, which had led to the commercial ruin of *Berlin*.

The one thing that *Sally Can't Dance* lacked was Lou himself. He was at the sessions and contributed rough vocals when we needed him to, but otherwise, we had to work around him. Mostly he was just getting high. We would be working on tracks until four a.m., and Lou would come out of the bathroom after shooting up and ask what "we" were going to do next. The rest of us, of course, had been done for hours.

There was a time in the late '60s when homes were allowed to be built using aluminum conductors for electricity. One day, while changing blown bulbs in the lanterns at the end of our driveway, I noticed that the leaves around both lanterns were charred. I immediately called the electrician who had installed the wiring and told him of my discovery. He said he'd come out in two days to take a look. Meanwhile, the next day, I received a call from my mother who asked if I would listen to a tape by a relative of a friend. It happens; the tapes are almost never any good, but it's nice to be nice, so why not. The people delivering the tape didn't live far away, and it shouldn't take too long. They came to the house at about nine, but I ended up liking them, and they stayed longer than expected.

It was around one a.m. when I heard Melissa screaming from upstairs. I left my guests and ran up and saw flames coming around the corner of our bedroom and swiftly entering the hallway. It's hard to describe exactly what this feels like. The flames are like a monster invading your home, your privacy, and violating all you hold dear. But it was also time to think fast. The first priority, after Melissa, was our three dogs; I immediately put them out back in their pen, away from danger. Our guests, meanwhile, were smart (and good) enough to help by putting our cars in neutral and rolling them far enough down the driveway where they wouldn't blow up.

The top floor burned completely in what felt like minutes, before the fire engines even arrived. A couple of rooms on the downstairs level were not fully destroyed—until the firemen hosed down whatever was left, meaning most of my record collection, posters, gold records, and memorabilia. It was all over in moments.

I was barefoot and wearing only a T-shirt and pair of pants. Melissa had on a little more, but not much. Our cat died in the fire. All we had left was what we were wearing, our two cars, and our three dogs.

We moved into my brother's house in Chappaqua, on the other side of the Hudson. Staying there for a little while was better than living in the charred remains of our house, but not by much. My brother never missed a chance to make us feel that we were somehow at fault, or that this was the fate of anyone who dared live outside of the corporate rat race. Although he was a muckety-muck in the music industry, he had no respect for the musicians who made the records that kept him in business. It was maddening at worst, unkind at best. We had to get out of there or we'd lose our minds, which wasn't an option, since we had already lost everything else.

After we were informed that insurance would only pay for half of our losses, we found a house rental and began to put our lives back together. It appeared that Melissa had suffered severe psychological damage, believing that God was punishing her by burning down our house. This is when all of her demons started to appear. Although it was later determined that her issues were mostly caused by a chemical imbalance and not the fire itself, Melissa was about to begin a journey from which she would never really return, affecting our marriage and her well-being, with tragic results.

We still had some overdubbing to do on Lou's record. Most of the recording was done, but Lou had yet to do *any* of his vocals, which caused its own fair amount of dread for everyone involved. And when we returned to Electric Lady after the fire, once I had calmed down enough to get back to work, Lou decided that he not only wanted to do all the vocals in one take, but he also didn't even want the tape to stop in between. He just wanted to go from one song to the other. I had to explain to him that we needed time to change tapes, that headphone mixes had to be brought up for each song, that vocal tracks were never necessarily the same in terms of levels, and that I would have a nervous breakdown if he had his way.

We reached a compromise: We were allowed to change tapes if he just did one vocal per song. I was fine with this as long as my engineer was fine with it. It wouldn't have made much difference anyway—Lou's vocal takes were never very different from one another. This was not a case of dealing with phrasing, timing, or pitch. With Lou, none of those things mattered. Ray Charles, Lou was not. But to his credit, beyond the posturing, Lou had his own vocal style, so I agreed. You'll never hear criticism of Lou's vocals on the albums I produced. The production, yes; the choice of material, maybe; the concept, probably. But the vocals? They were uniquely Lou's, and thus beyond criticism.

Lou, Rachel, and Nico came up to my new house at Turner Drive in Chappaqua to hear a test pressing of *Sally Can't Dance*. We had just moved. I was planning to soundproof a music room for myself, but because I hadn't yet begun, my stereo was temporarily placed in the living room. Nico went crazy over "Kill Your Sons" and played it over and over at top volume. Windows and doors to our back lawn were open, so before you could say "Andy Warhol," the police stopped by to tell us to keep it down.

You can just imagine what the cops must have thought when they saw Nico, Lou, and Rachel. I thought for sure that I would be the first lynching victim of this lovely upper-class suburban town, the future home of Bill and Hillary Clinton. Thank God Officer Jim Baines was not only a music fan, but also a Blood, Sweat & Tears fan. He understood rock and roll and was truly happy to meet me.

After the police left, I opened an unlocked bathroom door to find Lou shooting up.

"Now you know," he said.

Seriously. As if Lou's drug habit was some kind of state fucking secret.

"You've got to be kidding!" I said to him, genuinely incredulous. "You actually thought that nobody knew? Or did you just think *I* was the only schmuck who didn't know?"

The cop was hip, but I was glad he hadn't seen this, or his visit wouldn't have had such a sunny ending.

Sally Can't Dance, released in August 1974, was Lou's only top-ten album, though *Rock 'n' Roll Animal* was his biggest seller. Years later Lou denounced both albums as being his least favorite, probably for three reasons: First, because my brother, Dennis, was managing him at the time, and he had learned to hate Dennis. Second, because they were his most commercially successful albums (not something that Lou's automatic self-destruct mode could easily accept). And third, he didn't have the complete aesthetic control that he would have liked. I could agree with the last point, except that Lou was not in any state at the time to take that kind of responsibility and expect any positive results. I wish that he were.

In December 1974 we were to begin preproduction for his next album, *Coney Island Baby*. Lou Reed was now behaving like a full-blown asshole. Everything he did was contrary and spiteful. He began treating everyone he knew, including those who had the misfortune to like him, with contempt and arrogance. He was abusing his privileges and everyone around him. It was at this point that Lou Reed's most ridiculous act of grandeur was about to take shape, or, I should say, *non*-shape, and he was going to inflict it on his record company.

Lou brought home two reel-to-reel tape decks, shot enough speed to run the perimeter of Central Park in under six minutes, and in two weeks "created" a feedbacked monstrosity called *Metal Machine Music*. This horror had nothing to do with music, no matter high-minded claims to the contrary. It was a kid playing with his toys on amphetamines, and it produced nothing too different than if one had recorded the whistle on a teakettle for an hour and a half. Lou had reached the height of absurdity. He tried to get RCA to release it on Red Seal, their classical imprint. It didn't come out on Red Seal, but RCA, not realizing the joke was on them, released it anyway. It reminded me of Terry Southern's cynical materpiece, *The Magic Christian*—Lou threw a bunch of shit into a tape box and RCA jumped in for a swim.

At the time *Metal Machine Music* was received as something between a prank by a churlish child who could never get enough attention and an act of hubris by an artist so convinced of his own greatness that he believed he could put out any sort of shit and expect the listening public to bow down before him. At least Lester Bangs had some fun writing about it, declaring it the "greatest album ever made," explaining that "If you ever thought feedback was the best thing that ever happened to the guitar, well, Lou just got rid of the guitars," adding, "I realize that any idiot with the equipment could have made this album, including me, you or Lou. That's one of the main reasons I like it so much."

Over the years *MMM* has become the ultimate version of the emperor's new clothes, adopted by minimalists and hipsters as some sort of powerful art statement, even as a legit composition, but I defy anyone to listen to it without irony and detect any sort of merit. Terry Riley and La Monte Young, it ain't.

I booked session time again at Electric Lady in January of 1975, but by this point Lou had truly become impossible to work with. I told Bruce Somerfeld, my A&R contact at RCA, that the sessions had to be called off because Lou was hostile and uncooperative. I had planned to pare down the sessions and have Lou play on his songs with minimum input from outside musicians, but it made no difference. I wanted Lou to be naked on this one, an honest attempt to scale back to a purer version of himself, to let his voice and the songs shine through, but he was out of control and the sessions were called off. RCA agreed with the canceling of the sessions until Lou could get a better grip, but in the interim they needed a Lou Reed album while Lou was on "leave," so I mixed some outtakes from *Rock 'n' Roll Animal*. It was released as *Lou Reed Live* in March 1975.

I never returned to the studio with him again.

I ran into Lou one time since, at a party at Studio 54 in the late '70s. We said hello and continued on our separate ways. By then Lou had sued my brother. From what I understood, Lou had accused Dennis of not paying his withholding to the IRS, a problem that I myself had to confront later on when my brother and I were partners in our own production company.

I never listened to Lou's albums after working with him; I wasn't really interested, just like I was never interested in listening to any Blood, Sweat & Tears albums after I left the band. The one thing I did tune into, though, was a scathing song on his album *Street Hassle* that he wrote about my brother. It was called "Dirt." I believe that Lou's termination of our relationship was due in part to collateral damage from what happened between him and Dennis.

I never went along with the popular consensus—that post-Velvet Lou was a great genius. After the Velvet Underground, Lou's real genius was being able to fool the world into thinking that he was important and talented. In the end, and as far as I was concerned, Lou Reed turned out to be just another asshole.

Soon after Lou, I produced an album by Elliott Murphy called *Night Lights*. It was a very good album that should have done better. Elliott, much like his friend Patti Smith, was a poet and spent some time as a rock journalist. His band consisted of Ernie Brooks from the Modern Lovers on bass, Jerry Harrison, soon to join Talking Heads, on keyboards, and Andy Paley on drums. There was one session where I wanted the sound of a children's chorus, so we bused down my niece's third-grade class from Chappaqua. There are very few things more beautiful than the sound of a children's chorus.

We also held a midnight session for a song called "Deco Dance." Some of the musicians on the date were Billy Joel on piano, the great bass player Richard Davis, and a horn section featuring Lew Soloff, Lou Marini, Michael Brecker, Howard Johnson, and Tom Malone. The only thing that was overdubbed on that session was a tap dancer, Cheryl Clark, who was a friend of my wife's from the old days. When Cheryl went out into the studio to dance, I had to convince her that nobody was watching—that all we needed was the audio, so she didn't need to fling her arms all over the room like she was doing a solo in *A Chorus Line* at the Winter Garden.

CHAPTER 11

The Fifth Beatle

One roadie was assigned to the end of my driveway. His job was to alert us when the limo made the turn toward the house. As soon as he signaled, we would start singing a fully rehearsed country song where the vocal harmonies were perfect, so well oiled that we still sounded like we were informally jamming. The record company president would enter my house and walk into the living room, where anybody could have confused the four of us with a choir of angels, possessing enough commercial potential to go public on the New York Stock Exchange. We would stop in mid-song and the record company president would inevitably say, "No. Please. Continue. Don't let me stop you." Money signs were already flashing across my living room walls like I had just hired some capitalist version of the Joshua Light Show.

So far, I had been in a jug band, a psychedelic blues band, and a jazz-rock band. It was time to try country-rock. Before we finally fell out, my brother and an associate staff producer from RCA, Bob Ringe, wanted to help form a new band.

Bob had produced Pure Prairie League and was still working with Craig Fuller after Craig left the group. My brother was representing Doug Yule. Dennis and Bob wanted to put Doug and Craig together and asked if I would be interested in producing. I thought about it and said no, that I'd rather be *in* the band. So it was me, Craig Fuller, and Doug Yule. I felt we needed some outside material, so I called Eric Kaz, with whom I had played years before in a trio with Stefan Grossman. Eric had been in the Blues Magoos, did one solo album for

Atlantic, and was now earning most of his living from writing songs for Bonnie Raitt and Linda Ronstadt. Eric also wanted in, and so we had a fourth member. We decided to call ourselves American Flyer.

We rehearsed both at Eric's mother's house in Woodstock and at my house in Chappaqua. Not long after, we were ready to play for the record people. We invited the heads of four companies—Jerry Greenberg at Atlantic, Clive Davis at Columbia, Al Teller, recently hired as president of United Artists, and Ken Glancy from RCA. Although we hadn't even played a gig yet, we were asking for a lot of money. Clive sent up a remote recording truck from the Record Plant and we demo'd six songs.

Al Teller showed the most exuberance. He had come from Columbia Records and wanted to sign his own flagship act at UA, so he asked us, "Aside from money, what can I give you guys to have you sign with United Artists?" We told Al, half-jokingly, that if he got George Martin, the Beatles' producer, to produce us, that we would sign with UA. And that, in 1976, was that. Not the best company in the world, but between the money, Al Teller's excitement, and George Martin, we signed with United Artists Records.

Recording was to take place at George Martin's choice of studio, Indigo Ranch in Malibu, on the coast and hills west of LA. Doug and I stayed at the Chateau Marmont on Sunset Boulevard and commuted every day, but first we had to rehearse. George had pretty much picked all the songs before we even met, but he had not yet picked all the musicians, so we held auditions for the rhythm section, and some pretty amazing people auditioned: Jim Gordon from Derek and the Dominoes, Ron Tutt, who had been Elvis's drummer, and my ex-bandmate Jim Fielder, just to name a few. George was not happy with any of them until he found Alvin Taylor and Fred Beckmeier, a couple of unknowns. We did have guest stars on the album: Rusty Young on pedal steel, Larry Carlton on guitar, Joe Sample on keyboards, Ernie Watts on sax, and Lee Sklar, also on bass.

George Martin was amazing. Tall and handsome and aristocratically British, he was a living legend and a great person to boot. No wonder the Beatles stuck with him for every album but the last. I followed George around like a puppy, constantly badgering him with questions on how he did what with the Beatles. I must have been a huge pain in George's ass, but I probably wouldn't be any less curious if it all happened again today. George had his Tannoy monitors delivered to Indigo Ranch.

"George," I said, "are these the same monitors that—"

"Katz, leave me *alone!*"

The first day of recording, I followed directions out to Malibu, thought I had found the right address, and walked inside to make sure. There in the living room I saw a bunch of instruments, so even though the place was small and obviously ill-equipped for a professional studio, I brought in my guitars and proceeded to make myself at home, until Garth Hudson's wife came in and asked what I was doing in their home. Oops! I was politely thrown out and sent down the road to where I was supposed to be, sitting on my ass while basic tracks were being recorded.

I loved working with George Martin. On the way to the studio one day, I stopped at a record store and found a pirated copy of *Let It Be*. But it wasn't Phil Spector's mix, the one that was released commercially. It was George's mix, before Spector got ahold of it. I brought it to the studio and showed George, who immediately asked if he could borrow it. I never saw it again.

George's fee was very high, and one of the reasons we were so happy about our deal with United Artists was that they were willing to pay it. One day, during a lull in recording, George said to me: "I wonder if the people who own this studio would give us a break if we called the album *Indigo*. Why don't you ask?"

Me—"Good idea, I'll give it a try."

So I go up to the owner in the studio kitchen and I say, "Richard, how would you feel if we called our album *Indigo?*"

Richard—"Wow. I would be honored."

Me—"I mean, a little *more* than honored?"

Richard—"No, I'm afraid I couldn't do that."

Me, back at the studio—"George, I have a great idea. How about we call the album *George Martin?*"

I don't think George was too pleased with my suggestion.

I wrote two songs for the album. One was called "Back in '57" and the other was called "M." Both were recorded earlier when I was still in BS&T, but never released, thank goodness. George asked me how I wanted to hear "M," and I told him that I would love to hear a George Martin orchestration with oboe, and that's what he did.

One day during overdubs back in LA, Craig Fuller had brought his little dog to the studio. I was talking to George in the hallway when David Crosby, who was recording down the hall with Crosby, Stills & Nash, noticed Craig's dog and, thinking it belonged to George, said to George Martin, "Get that fucking dog out of here!" I couldn't believe Crosby had the nerve to insult *George Martin*—and dogs—all at once. What kind of human was this? I was mortified, and whenever anyone has asked me over the years, of all the people I met, who I disliked the most in rock and roll, the answer is easy.

American Flyer was released in 1977. Stupidly, we didn't perform behind it; we just did a promotional tour and a lot of half-assed publicity, like the time I was asked to do an interview for what I remember as Radio Sheffield in England.

Someone from UA's publicity department called me and asked if I was available the next morning at eight a.m. on the dot for a live radio interview. I said I was, figuring I would just wake up when the phone rang. I was usually pretty good at feigning alertness under those conditions. But not this time. I had been up late and had smoked a lot of weed the night before. When the phone rang, promptly at eight a.m., I picked it up and said, "Hello?"

British-accented voice—"Well, *hello*, Steve Katz, this is Radio Sheffield. Steve, what time is it over there?"

Me—"Just a second."

I fumbled around for my watch, figured I'd left it downstairs, so I headed down to get it, stopping for a glass of water on the way. When I got back to the phone, I was able to give the fellow a solid answer.

Me—"It's ten after eight."

British-accented voice—"Well, *thank you*, Steve Katz!," and he hung up.

The record didn't do well. We didn't get behind it enough, which was sad, because it was a good record. Contractually, we still had one more album to do. We decided to produce it ourselves, and to record it in Toronto at Eastern Sound Studios. We used Whitey Glan and Prakash John, the same rhythm section I had borrowed from Bob Ezrin and Alice Cooper. I'd used them with Lou Reed, and also on an album that I had produced with Rory Block. Guest appearances were supplied by Linda Ronstadt and Tracy Nelson.

About halfway through recording, we saw that Bobby Keys, the great sax player, was in town with The Stones and asked if he would lay down a solo on one of Eric's songs, "Keep on Tryin'." We supplied a bottle of Jack Daniel's for him and told him to just keep doing solos on the empty tracks, erasing whatever he didn't like and doing it over until he was happy.

Meanwhile, we received an urgent call from management. They had to have an emergency meeting with us. They were at the airport and on their way over. The meeting concerned the firing of Al Teller from United Artists and the hiring of Artie Mogull—not the best choice as far as we were concerned. This was sure to be our last album, not only because of the probable impending problems with Mogull, but also because we were having problems of our own within the band. Eric and Craig were getting along great, but they both had problems with Doug Yule. I was too lost in my own personal problems to get involved, and wound up spending at least some of my time with my old friend David Steinberg at a TV studio outside of Toronto, where he was taping his show then.

We had our meeting, but were so involved in our future plans with United Artists that we totally forgot that Bobby Keys was still in the studio, doing his solos. We ran back to the control room where we saw that very little was left of the Jack Daniel's, and a staggering Bobby Keys was about to record his twenty-seventh solo of the day.

That was the end of American Flyer. The album, *Spirit of a Woman*, did even worse than the first one. Sad, because like the first album, I thought it was pretty good, and like the first American Flyer album, I still listen to it today. But I did learn a lesson: You are not a real band unless you go out and play.

CHAPTER 12

The Suit

After American Flyer I began going through a very painful divorce. Melissa had been withdrawing from me *and* from reality day by day. Inspired by Chuck Winfield and his wife, Sandi, she had decided to join Bible study as a Jehovah's Witness. Needless to say, this limited our marital conversations both at dinner and in bed. She began seeing a psychiatrist, who decided that it would be best if Melissa's problems were kept between the two of them, without my knowledge or input. The marriage ended one evening when Melissa, unbeknownst to me, packed her bags, got into our station wagon, and left.

I was devastated once again, but it was different this time than when Mimi left. In a sense, I was Mimi's boy toy, an innocent and inexperienced kid subjected to a world that was way above me. I had treated Melissa, on the other hand, as *my* toy, a possession more than an equal—not really a friend so much as my own sexual object. The marriage was destined to fail, and it was time for me to grow up and better understand the meaning of "relationship" and "marriage," and even "friendship." But it wouldn't be long before I would try to get my toy back—with disastrous results. I was still such a child.

I had already made a deal, through Dennis as my attorney (mostly because he was able to expedite the deal), to take what turned out to be a modest advance from RCA in return for giving up record royalties from all of my RCA productions, an incredibly stupid act that I regret to this day; but I needed the money. My brother recommended a divorce lawyer friend of his who did such a bad job that not only did

I lose everything, including my house, but my ex-wife gained absolutely nothing in the final decree. The lawyers got it all.

Dennis came over to my house one day during this period, ostensibly to soothe my depression, but what he really wanted to say, even as I was pretty much broke, was that he felt he deserved some of my royalty settlement since he had hired me to produce Lou Reed. Not only had he been complicit in making one of the worst business decisions of my career, but now he was actually asking for a part of the only financial resources left to me, aside from the dwindling publishing checks I was receiving from BS&T. Stupidly, and without outside legal advice, I let him lay guilt on me and bully me and I gave in to his request. I was one confused guy at the time. First the fire, then the divorce and the loss of my house. I wasn't thinking straight. I had to start piecing things together once again.

Through a corporate headhunter, I interviewed for a job at Phonogram Records. I had never heard of Phonogram until I was told that it was Mercury Records, now part of the Polygram Group, which was owned by Philips in the Netherlands and Siemens in Germany. I immediately recognized Mercury from all my old Patti Page records. Phonogram's American headquarters were in Chicago, and so I was flown out for an interview with Irwin Steinberg and Charlie Fasch, the two record-business veterans who ran the company. Irwin was president. His background was in accounting; Charlie was the record guy. Their first question to me was "What do you think of new wave and punk music?" I answered, "I don't think too much of it." I was their man, hired.

What they didn't know was that I didn't think too much of it because my head had been up my ass for the past few years, and I didn't even know what new wave or punk *was*. But they were so impressed with my "candor" that I was offered the job—East Coast director of A&R, Phonogram Records, answerable to Irwin, Charlie, and all the Dutch guys at Polygram. In retrospect, I'd probably already won the job before the interview; Irwin and Charlie just wanted to make sure that I had two good ears and didn't dress like a Hasid. The boys at Siemens wouldn't have liked that.

I moved back to Manhattan from my Chappaqua retreat and got a place on Horatio Street, pretty close to my old apartment on Jane Street. That was where I would walk my two dogs, dogs that were used to country life and afraid of city streets.

The first day at my new office on West Fifty-Seventh Street, I met the staff and my secretary, Cynthia. I'd never had a secretary before and didn't know what to do with her, so I sent her down to the Village to walk my horrified dogs. Later, my old friend Richie Havens, who lived down the street, recommended that I hire his niece to walk my dogs while I was at the office. I had to find other things for my secretary to do, so I began drinking coffee. "Cynthia, a coffee, please."

At first I listened to demo tapes while the artist sat in my office, in front of me.

Big mistake.

There was the psychology major who asked me to listen to his tape and honestly tell him whether he could have a career in music, or whether he should stay in school. I asked him whether he'd be able to handle it if my reaction was negative. He replied with a calm smile, "Of course. No problem—I just need to know." After one song, I told him he should stay in school. He began to sob like a baby.

After a very pleasant and funny conversation about the business with one fellow, I mistakenly thought he had a good sense of humor. He handed me the tape and I just put it up to my ear and ribbed him that I didn't like it, at which point he yelled "Fuck you! What do *you* know!" and stormed out of my office. If he had laughed at my joke, I would have played it within the next thirty seconds, and who knows? Oh, well.

That was it. To hell with the proletariat! There were too many wackos out there. If they had a tape, they could send it through a lawyer or manager. I didn't have time to waste. I was already much too busy listening to twelve-minute-long conga breaks, now that disco was king. It is a crazy fucking business that puts nerds like me in a position of power. But at least I knew how to play an instrument; a lot of the cats running the show knew nothing about music.

As I settled into my A&R power-broking role, I had to spend more and more time making Solomon-esque decisions about the future careers of musical wannabes. I got to know most of the important managers and lawyers in New York. I would constantly get called upon to see an act at a club or at a rehearsal hall. Some of these "auditions" were carefully staged and sort of embarrassing, but that was my job, so I couldn't complain too much if I had to go to a club to hear a band that didn't go on until midnight. But if I was going to do this, there had to be some rules.

It was in that spirit one day that my secretary received a request from a lawyer friend that I go to see his band downtown at the Ritz. I didn't really feel like doing this, but I knew it would be bad politics to say no, so I asked my secretary to call down to the club, reserve a table for me, and make sure my name was left at the door.

Secretary—"They won't leave your name at the door. You have to pay to get in."

Me—"No way! Call them again and tell them that I will never, *ever* enter their club again if I don't get comped!"

Secretary—"Called again. They said they can't leave your name at the door."

Me—"*Don't they know who I am?* I don't do this for *fun*, for chrissake; *this is my job*. Mercury Records will never sign an act out of their club, *ever*, if my name is not left at the door!"

Secretary—"Called again. They said they can't leave your name at the door."

This went on and on until I came up with the obvious solution.

Me—"Okay, call them back one last time and tell them that if they comp me at the door, I'll pay for my own drinks."

Secretary—"Called them back. They gave in—said they'd comp you at the door."

So at eleven p.m., I begrudgingly took a cab down to the Ritz where I saw a huge banner out front that said:

TONIGHT—A BENEFIT—ROCK AGAINST WAR—
ADMISSION $2—FREE CIDER

I took a crash course from the head of business affairs on how to negotiate a contract. I would fly to Chicago every couple of weeks for A&R meetings and to Hamburg or Baarn, outside of Amsterdam, for international meetings. I had an expense account and a decent salary, most of which went to legal bills and divorce-related ephemera, but I was honestly not happy in my role of judging other people's music. Leave that to the guys who couldn't play; I actually missed being a musician.

I found I had no time to play or to practice, but I did get to spend two incredible weeks in Europe on the road with Paco de Lucia, the world's greatest flamenco guitarist. Paco was signed to Phonogram worldwide, except for the United States, so I was sent as the US Mercury Records emissary to travel with Paco and make an assessment. My assessment was that Paco was too good a musician to be ruined by a shitty label like ours, but that wasn't how I put it to my bosses, so the only records that Paco put out in America were the ones that he did with Al Di Meola and John McLaughlin for Columbia.

The most fun I had was when a Broadway play was about to go into production and the composers would give a synopsis of their work and play samples of songs to sell to record companies for original cast-recording deals.

I spent an evening at Betty Comden and Adolph Green's apartment listening to songs from their upcoming show, *On the Twentieth*

Century. Comden and Green had written the music for *The Bells Are Ringing* and collaborated with Leonard Bernstein for *On the Town* among other shows. What can I say? For all the rock and roll I was always surrounded with, I have a soft spot for musicals. So what if I can't get the theme to *Raintree County* out of my head, even while cranking up my Super Reverb amp.

One day I got to hang out again with Richard Rodgers, but this time in a professional capacity. Martin Charnin played and sang some songs from their upcoming show, *I Remember Mama*. It was good to see Mr. Rodgers again, and I was delighted to know that he felt the same about my visit. We had to pass on these shows because Mercury had a hard enough time in those days breaking a rock act, much less an original cast recording.

One day when I returned to my office after yet another two-martini lunch, I noticed that there was an unusual amount of commotion and anxiety. My secretary informed me that a crisis was brewing. The indomitable Jerry Lee Lewis, now a successful artist on our country roster, had gotten into a serious car accident, and we were awaiting word as to his condition. By the end of the day, we found out that Lewis, who had just finished his new album, had been driving his Rolls-Royce on a downtown Nashville street at a ridiculous speed. When he tried to make a turn, the Rolls had careened and turned over on its side with Jerry Lee at the wheel. When the police and ambulance came, Lewis, still laying on his side, refused to be extracted from the car until he was finished listening to a test tape of his new album.

I signed NRBQ, recognized by those in the know, or at least by Elvis Costello and Keith Richards, as the best band of all time, brilliant musicians who could turn in Beach Boys–pretty pop next to authentic roots and country music. They made a fabulous classic album called *NRBQ at Yankee Stadium*. The album had a pile of potential hits, yet Mercury could not break it for love or money. They remained a well-respected cult band.

I also signed a bunch of kids from Mississippi, the Cryers, who were sleeping on floors in the East Village during the day and playing at CBGB's at night. They also did two very good albums. I produced one of their singles, a song called "Heartbreaker." Unfortunately, Irwin Steinberg spent most of his time trying to break acts like Demis Roussos, a big Greek with a near-falsetto voice who wore flowing robes and owned a pet lion. This was Polygram Europe shoving flamboyant international bullshit down our throats, but no one in America cared.

Between trying to peddle global effluence and not being able to break some truly great American rock bands, it got to the point where I knew that if any lawyer or manager was hawking an act to us, the likely reason was that they had been passed on by everyone else. Despite my getting outside employment offers, I naively stuck with Mercury, not realizing at that point how impermanent the music business was and how fickle it could be. Eventually I applied for a vice presidency, and when Charlie Fasch asked why I would want one when so many other people in the company had one, I told him that that was exactly the reason why. Why not? So I was promoted to vice president and given a raise and a company car. For a while I actually believed there was a future in A&R. Boy was I wrong.

I spent a lot of time in clubs and on the road, checking out bands that I might be interested in signing. One of the bands was a Rochester, New York, group called Duke Jupiter. I flew up to Rochester where the band's manager informed me that the latest version of Blood, Sweat & Tears was performing at a local club, and that we should go see them.

That was the *last* thing I wanted to do, especially since David was now back in the band. But that night, after a few drinks, I thought it might actually be fun. David didn't know I was in the back of the audience when I yelled out a request—one of my songs, and something that the band couldn't do without me. "'Sometimes in Winter'!" I called out, and I continued calling out throughout their set, all the while watching DCT getting redder and redder and angrier and angrier. I should have taken into consideration what the rest of the band would have to suffer through when they got offstage, but at that point I was having too much fun.

Years later what I heard from ex-BS&T members was that these guys were peeing in DCT's coffee or dumping Ex-Lax into his cup when he wasn't looking. I'd have given anything to see a show when the Ex-Lax took effect. I later signed Duke Jupiter and produced their first album. I am guessing you never heard of them.

—◆—

It was 1977, the summer of Son of Sam. There was plenty of paranoia to go around. I received a call from Melissa's brother. Melissa had attempted suicide in a motel room in Stroudsburg, Pennsylvania. She had been in a coma for a short while and then was transported to White Plains Hospital, where she took up residence for a few months until I picked her up, so that we could marry each other for the second time.

After all the craziness, I still missed her.

And so we took up residence together again the weekend she was released, the weekend that she said she was seeing flying saucers picking up people on the streets of New York.

She was far from well and should not have been released at all. My decision-making processes where she was concerned were far from reality—I should have been institutionalized myself for being such an idiot. Had we both been a little saner and done the right thing, we could have avoided much of the bitterness and pain that was to come. One of the side effects of Melissa's illness was coming to the surface in the form of the anger that she had sublimated for most of her life. Being the closest person to her also made me the perfect target, but her anger was never overt. It was quiet, thoughtful, and ultimately terrifying.

When I had to travel to Ireland to work with the band Horslips, my latest signing, I thought I'd take her along. I was hoping that a change in scenery would do her some good.

We took the red-eye from New York, making the obligatory stop at Shannon Airport along the way. In order to get to Donegal from Dublin, the band's roadie was to meet us at the airport and drive us through Northern Ireland.

At the first border crossing, British soldiers were pointing rifles at us and asking us to get out of the vehicle. Because I felt that the Irish "troubles" were none of my business, my first reaction was to jump out of the car, raise my hands above my head, and shout "Don't shoot! I'm Jewish." I bit my tongue, and we were allowed to continue on our journey north through Ulster.

Rehearsals were to take place outside a sleepy little village called Glencolumbkille. Glencolumbkille wasn't far from Donegal, but it was a world away from the second half of the twentieth century. The hotel was charming and old, like something out of an early David Lean film. From the hotel we could see the sheep that dotted the windswept treeless hills that overlooked the Atlantic. Every few days a bus would drop by the hotel's pub with old retirees from the Republic who would order an ale or two and in unison sing sad old ballads amid the yellow shafts of afternoon light before departing, quiet and ghostlike, as if they were never there. It might sound a bit too poetic, but what I witnessed those afternoons *was* poetic, and I wouldn't know of any other way to describe it.

No matter the bucolic scenario, Melissa's hallucinations only got worse. Her medication was hardly working, and she had become so attached and dependent on her psychiatrist that the rest of the world almost ceased to exist around her, including myself.

Nonetheless, rehearsals went well. Horslips had become an Irish national treasure and, along with Thin Lizzy, were one of the first rock bands to really gain that sort of status, long before U2. Their albums up until then had been influenced by traditional music, what one would catalog as folk-rock, a genre in which I was well versed. This time around, however, Horslips was going through some artistic changes and wanted to reach a wider audience with a bigger sound.

The band and I had first met at a concert that they were playing in Armagh, north of Dublin, in British Ulster. I had just finished a distribution deal with Dick James Music in London. Dick had a hit record in England in the 1950s, the theme song of the TV series *The Adventures of Robin Hood*. He parlayed that hit into a publishing and recording company and had a huge success with the early Beatles catalog and Elton John. Two of the acts that were part of the deal with Mercury were bluesman Johnny Guitar Watson and Horslips. And so I flew to Ireland to welcome Horslips to the label. We partied that night, and the band requested that I produce their next album. I jumped at the chance to get out of the corporate world for a while and back into the studio. I had had enough of disco Greeks with pet lions and needed a break.

In order to gain that wider audience for Horslips, I felt I would have to bring the band into more of a guitar-oriented, hard-rock direction, but I didn't want them to lose any of the Irish folk quality that identified them. To get the band to sound more commercial, I would have Johnny Fean, the band's guitarist, add natural overdrive to his guitar and double, or sometimes triple, his parts for a thicker sound, and with the keyboard player, Jim Lockhart, doubling on flute, the band would sound a little like Jethro Tull. Not a bad thing.

Sessions were to take place in Dublin at Lombard Sound, located on Lombard Street. Lombard Sound was a wreck, a fleabag of a facility that was lit by a forty-watt bulb and a bag of candles. The one good thing going for it was a nearly new Studer twenty-four-track machine, which, unfortunately, broke down intermittently. The first time this happened was about one a.m., and we had to call the studio maintenance guy, who walked up to the Studer, kicked it, and pronounced it still not working until, with a little encouragement, he would actually take out a screwdriver and somehow manage to get the thing going.

Michael Deeney, the band's manager, had arranged for Melissa and I to stay in a half-finished apartment, a new construction in the

Sandymount section of Dublin, close to one of the Martello towers that served as a backdrop for James Joyce's *A Portrait of the Artist as a Young Man.* We had a car at our disposal, with a not-American-friendly stick shift.

One night after a session, I came back to the apartment to find my wife and the car missing. I was astonished to learn that, although she didn't know how to drive a stick, she had driven from the passenger side *and* on the "wrong" side of the road to the airport and boarded a plane to New York. In one sense I was saddened that she had left, and in another sense alarmed at *how* she'd left. But I was relieved that I could get on with my work and not have to worry as much about what I might return to every night.

At session breaks I would run downstairs to call Melissa. I some-how had to make it to the phone booth, at least a block away, before my pants would fall down from the weight of the very heavy and large pre-euro Irish coins I needed to pump into the phone's coin box. Every night I spoke to the same friendly long-distance operator. After about a week, he felt familiar enough to say, "Oh, Mr. Katz! How are you? And how's the missus? Feeling any better, is she?"

Welcome to Ireland.

We were recording on Irish Racal-Zonal tape. Our engineer, a Derry lad by the name of Dec O'Doherty, noticed that there was a small pile of oxide droppings by the heads of the Studer. The tape was peeling, and we had to stop the session immediately before any-thing was lost. Luckily, the basic tracks were mostly finished, but over-dubs had to be done somewhere else, after we had transferred all the tracks to fresh tape. This meant that at least half of the album would be mixed from second-generation tapes. The next day we were able to book immediate time at Advision Studios in London, where Dec was also on staff.

We left for London the day after. I was put up in a hotel, the band in an Indian B&B. As I unpacked, I noticed that I had yet to wear one of my favorite shirts, a red sports shirt that was still neatly folded at the bottom of my suitcase. I pulled the shirt out of the cellophane bag my launderer had provided. The sleeves fell off. Horrified at the thought that I'd been sleeping all this time with a woman who could actually take a pair of scissors and snip the sleeves off of my favorite shirt, I was even more horrified that she had taken the time to fold it back up and perfectly install it back into the bag, sleeves and all.

The London sessions progressed smoothly. My only fear was that Horslips's *The Man Who Built America* was going to be on Mercury Records. True, I worked for the company, but the company couldn't break a glass at a Jewish wedding while its sister label Polydor was having hit after hit, mainly with the Bee Gees. The top two acts on Mercury were Rush and Kool & the Gang, but they were licensed acts, borrowed from subsidiary labels, one from Canada and the other from De-Lite Records in New Jersey. Although we could boast a few good record people at Mercury, like Charlie Fasch and an excellent radio promotion staff, most of the company was run by people who really didn't care about music, and the Europeans who ultimately called the shots were totally ignorant of the American market. I was worried, rightfully so in retrospect, that Horslips would fall into the abyss.

Typical of the day, I got a memo from Irwin Steinberg. He loved sending memos, more than actually talking to someone. "Gabe Vigorito, owner of De-Lite Records (Kool & the Gang), will be making an appointment with you to play a new record that he strongly believes in." So Gabe makes the appointment and comes in all the way from New Jersey to play it for me. It's called "Roller Skating Disco." I had to sit and listen to this horror through to the end; what with Kool & the Gang selling so many records, Gabe practically owned us then. I told Gabe that I wasn't crazy about it and had to pass. The next day I get a memo from the memo king: "Why did you pass on 'Roller Skating Disco'?" I let that one go. I didn't want to have to remind Irwin that that's what I'd been hired for—to say "no." Years later I ran into

Irwin Steinberg at restaurant near me. I said hello, but Irwin had no idea who I was.

The Man Who Built America registered, predictably, mediocre sales, but the band wanted me to produce their next album, this time in Dublin at the new Windmill Lane Studios, a block or two from the quay by the River Liffey. We rehearsed at a cottage in Killarney and entered the studio as two separate bands. Charles and Eamon became so infatuated with underground punk and new wave that they veered off from Barry and Jim, who were still the traditionalists and, as it turned out, the realists of the band. It resulted in a schizophrenic album entitled *Short Stories / Tall Tales*.

During the recording a friend of Michael Deeney's, Paul McGuiness, would drop by the studio along with a group of four kids he was managing. U2 looked up to Horslips and liked hanging around the recording sessions. Paul would give me demo tapes of the band, hoping I would sign them to Mercury. I wasn't that excited about the tapes, but the real test was when they played a gig at a club called McGonagle's. These kids were too young and the music was too raw. I passed. Now, please pause for a second or two and think about what I just said—I, Steve Katz, representing Mercury Records, passed on U2. And to think, they could have been *huge*.

After *Short Stories / Tall Tales*, Mercury had taken on a new president, Bob Sherwood, who I knew from the promotion staff at Columbia Records. What I didn't know was that Bob would be bringing in his own A&R guy and that my days at Mercury were numbered.

No one ever informed me about the corporate way of getting an ex-executive out of the building—as fast as possible, locking down his office and sequestering his files. What a barbaric and humiliating thing for anyone to have to go through. I felt like a criminal. I guess working for a big record label, after a fashion, I was.

Fortunately, despite being tossed from the Mercury offices, I was asked to do a live album by Horslips, who had decided that their schism was insurmountable and that they would break up, but, bless their hearts, not without a bang. So we took a train from Dublin to Belfast where the concert was to be held at Queens University, recorded the show, and mixed it back at Windmill Lane. It was the last time I would work with the band, and it was sad to say good-bye. My only regret is that they never achieved the fame in the United States that they so deservedly earned.

By now I was a firsthand witness to the death of rock and roll. The major contributor was a company called Burkhart/Abrams. These guys came up with a formula for airplay that made rock radio uniform across the country based on demographics, and computerized without regard to locality. They were not a household name, but Burkhart/Abrams were the Walmart of radio and affected the cultural landscape of America. Most, if not all, rock stations subscribed to their service, and within a few years, airplay in America became homogeneous. Radio was losing its soul. It was Lee Abrams himself who once said that '60s radio was programmed by "some guy in a basement in Brooklyn, burning incense and playing whatever he pleased." Well what the fuck is wrong with that? Corporations had co-opted rock music and there it was, ubiquitous, all over TV; it had become hard to tell the difference between a record and a radio commercial.

Something strange and awful happens when you live with a mentally ill person every day, twenty-four hours a day. You want to help them, but you can't. You create your own universe, an unreal bubble where you look at the world, like your partner, as though the walls are slowly closing in. And all you want to do is help, though you're not capable of doing so. You become like a version of your mate, and then you feed on each other's psyches like cannibals. It's unhealthy and destructive, and that's how we lived for nearly three years.

Melissa and I moved back to the country, to Yorktown Heights, near Croton-on-Hudson. I was frozen, afraid of going out and working, doing projects, or even playing music. I kept wanting to make sure that Melissa was okay—that *we* were okay—all the while soaking up her unhappiness and feeding my own. At one point she had taken my Les Paul guitar and thrown it off our deck. I had no idea why. She would sit on our living room couch, threaten to overdose on her medication, and, on the brink of giving up, I would say, "Go ahead. Please!" I knew she needed more than I could ever give her—that any quest to save her was not just selfish, it was self-destructive.

In my quest to reestablish my own identity, I had just begun a production company with my jet-set friend Mimmo Ferretti. Mimmo wanted to fly me to Ibiza for the summer where his family owned a sprawling mansion on the western coast of the island. I jumped at the chance to get away from the horror that my home life had become. I did not want to be a nurse to Melissa, and certainly did not want to become any more belligerent toward her than I had found myself becoming. I paid whatever bills were around and gave Melissa the credit cards to use while I was away.

My summer in Ibiza consisted of staying up all night in the island's discos, then staring at gorgeous naked girls by the pool during the day. The soundtrack for the summer was The Clash, Phil Collins, Tears for Fears, and especially "Enola Gay" by Orchestral Maneuvers in the Dark. For a moment I had successfully escaped. The problem was that nobody spoke English in Ibiza, or at least nobody that I could find. Most people spoke either Spanish or Italian, or both. I got to jam with some pretty interesting musicians from South America, but the Euro jet-set lifestyle was really not my thing. I needed suffering in my life, and Ibiza was certainly not the place for it.

I had asked Mimmo if I could stay at his place upon my return that autumn, a beautiful Park Avenue apartment with an Ethiopian butler by the name of Russom. The day after I got back, I went to the bank for some cash and was told that I had none. My bank account had been emptied and my credit cards had reached their limit. Melissa had gone into Yorktown Heights and walked up to the second-floor office of the local sleazy ambulance chaser. He had advised her to turn all my assets into cash and to charge as much jewelry as possible on credit cards, and then sell the jewelry for cash, and cheaply, if necessary, at jewelry stores and pawn shops. Either this asshole was taking advantage of a sick woman, or I had overestimated my wife's illness.

Melissa's lawyer successfully had her take out an order of protection against me. I could not even retrieve my winter clothing without breaking into my own home, which is exactly what I did one night when I knew Melissa would be at her weekly Jehovah's Witnesses meeting. Eventually her lawyer was castigated in court, the judge saying that he represented everything that was bad about divorce in New York State. I had to start putting my life back together, yet again—broke, but alive.

The order of protection was reversed, and I was able to move back into my house when Melissa was evicted. I took some production jobs while Mimmo and I sat on our asses by my fireplace, trying to figure out what to do with our new company. I wanted to sign Cindy Lauper, and spent a lot of time on the phone with her, but Mimmo wasn't excited about the idea. Instead, he wanted to sign a group from New Zealand who were living in New York at the time and who called themselves the Drongos. Though I loved Mimmo, he was financing the company, and I didn't have the freedom to sign acts like I had thought.

Meanwhile, I was asked to produce a band called Blue Rose in France, not far from Paris, at a quaint little studio in the village of Longueville. The songs were basically already worked up and the studio was inexpensive, so I flew back to Europe and checked in at Longueville. The sessions went smoothly, though not speaking each other's language made communication with my engineer practically nonexistent. On our dinner breaks, women would come from all over the village and cook amazing meals, not the least of which was Coquilles St. Jacques, with scallops the size of baseballs. We would watch *Tom and Jerry* cartoons all through dinner, get back to the studio, usually by ten p.m., and record for the rest of the night. There was still some romance in the business, after all.

I had been doing cocaine in Ibiza, and when I came home from France, I was alone and not thinking clearly. My temper was easily aroused and I wasn't making any new friends. A job came up in Sydney, Australia, and although I wasn't crazy about the material, I needed the work and wanted the trip, and so I flew to Sydney and began working with a band called Full Marks, for Columbia Records. I was still doing my share of cocaine and did the band a disservice, so much so that we parted ways before the album was finished.

I flew home, alone, almost broke, and in bad shape. I also had no representation. When I tried to get management, people would say, "Oh, doesn't your brother represent you?," and they passed. Luckily, my friend John Scher, the New Jersey promoter, called and asked me to play at a folk festival where my friend Jorma Kaukonen was also going to play, and I was thrilled. I practiced like mad, played the festival solo, and got an encore. I wanted to do this full-time; I wanted to be a musician again.

CHAPTER 13

Ashes to Ashes

I wasn't feeling like a rock star. I had lost my home, my wife, and my money. I could hardly get any work, and the times that I *did* work were fleeting and unsatisfying. But at least I still felt like a musician, probably more than I had in years. I immersed myself in writing, playing my instrument, and learning new recording techniques. I took advantage of home multitrack recording and began coming up with fresh ideas that, even though they mostly never saw the light of day, kept me sane enough to get me to the next phase of my life. I felt humbled, and, like Job, I began to think that I might be running out of opportunities. Whether I was a "rock star" or not, I was too busy walking through life with my head up my ass to even give it a second thought. And to add insult to injury, I received a call from *Rolling Stone* magazine, who wanted to feature me in one of those "Where are they now?" articles. I had to do something.

Moving is a drag, but it also signals to the universe that you are ready for new things. Sometimes it is as easy as that. I recruited a few friends to help me move to a new place in North Salem, New York, not far from Yorktown Heights.

Before we started loading the van, we all met at a diner in Katonah. A friend of one of the movers was there, just getting a cup of coffee to go, and stopped by our table to say hi. As down as I may have been in my life, I saw something radiant in Alison Palmer. The second I saw her I felt like a schoolboy, and somehow thought it would be a good idea to ask her to come watch a video of *Repo Man* with me, camped out among my cartons of stuff. She was sane, so she turned me down, which only made me more attracted to her.

I soon found out that she was a ceramic artist and worked out of a studio in Croton Falls called "The Schoolhouse," a converted elementary school that was now home to a group of artists, including filmmaker Ralph Bakshi, the creator of *Fritz the Cat*.

I courted Alison, visited her studio, insinuated myself into her small party of friends at the local hamburger pub, and basically made a pest of myself until we'd spent enough time with each other to precipitate a decision that involved her moving in with me. She moved in one morning while I was out, but by the afternoon she had moved back out, another case of sanity prevailing.

But a little more convincing and she was back in the next day, and this time for good. Alison was attractive, bright, talented, and goofy in a Gracie Allen kind of way. She had studied at the Kansas City Art Institute, and when I met her had recently returned from California, where she had studied ceramics with Viola Frey at California College of Arts and Crafts. We fell in love. We really had nothing to our names—no money or real estate or safety nets. Nothing.

The fact that I had once been a "rock star" meant very little except that there were people who wanted me to produce their demos, so I got out my four-track cassette machine, some midi equipment, a keyboard and a sampler, and worked with some very nice but naive people who were never going to get anywhere. I had no choice. For me, it was torture, especially when I knew that most of them were going to be disappointed with rejections as they tried to get their tapes to the "right" people. I didn't have the means to get my own legitimate production company off the ground so that I could work with artists who I actually believed in. I was submerged and desperately trying to keep my head above water. The only good thing in my life was Alison—she kept me alive, healthy, made me laugh, and kept me from calling it quits.

One day I attended the CMJ independent music conference in Manhattan. I was talking to an old publicist friend who had mentioned that she knew the owner of a little record company in Connecticut called Green Linnet Records. Green Linnet had once been owned by my old friend Patrick Sky and specialized in Celtic folk music—not the Dubliners kind of music, but the real thing, hard-core and Gaelic: fiddles, bodhrans, acoustic guitars, and concertinas. This was the music that Horslips had turned me on to during my trips to Ireland, and I fell in love with it. I made an appointment to meet Wendy Newton, who ran Green Linnet. Wendy was funny, incredibly bright, and a totally out-of-her-mind red diaper baby. She was having a hard time being an "executive," although the company was so small, you would hardly know it existed. But it had an audience, fans who were obsessed with Celtic music. Wendy offered me a position, one I desperately needed and was very happy to find.

I worked at Green Linnet for five years, mainly doing A&R, artist relations, and oversight of some questionable business dealings that were conducted through Warner Brothers Ireland, Warner Brothers UK, and an independent record distributor in England before I had signed on. Aside from that, I spent most of my day doing data entry, learning computer skills, and desperately trying to convince artists that there was no money to be made in Celtic folk music, that having delusions of stardom and financial rewards was unreal and, in the end, could even be quite destructive.

Working for a small independent label was an education. Most of the time, we found ourselves caught between manufacturing costs at net-zero and billing at net-thirty. You were lucky if you got paid on time because everyone else was having to deal with the same never-ending cycle. Celtic folk music was never going to have the same success as the bluegrass or blues labels.

One of the problems was that most of the acts were from overseas, which made many prospective tours prohibitive. I signed two great young bands, Capercaillie from Scotland and Altan from Ireland. If any of the Celtic acts were going to be successful, these two were the ones. They sold as many albums as there was an audience for, but barely enough to pay the bills, including royalties. Most of the Celtic musicians couldn't really grasp this concept, and so, just like the "majors," tension developed between the acts and the record company. On the plus side, the music never got old. If the music is good, and so much of it is, the records could sell for years to come, albeit in limited quantities.

Alison and I were married in February of 1988 on a Tuesday afternoon in Katonah, New York. We only had a few close relatives and friends at the "ceremony." My brother couldn't make it. Not that he had anything better to do, he just didn't care.

Alison and I had a strangely unique idea. We thought of starting a business where we would sell Alison's canisters to people whose pets were dead or dying—handmade funerary urns. We called our company Ashes to Ashes and even printed up business cards, but after the fourth or fifth depressing phone call from our friends with old or dying pets, we had to give it up. It was just too sad.

We did do a homemade catalog and a small mailing of Alison's stuff, and the response was terrific. Along with her bowls, salt and pepper shakers, and cookie jars, Alison had come up with the idea of creating handmade whimsical spoon rests that we could sell to galleries at an affordable price. It worked. We were soon inundated with orders. It was nice for a change to just make something and sell it—minimum manufacturing costs, no middlemen or distributors, and no royalty issues. Except for the schlepping of our booth to various retail and wholesale shows, this was going to be fun.

Alison needed me to work more in the studio while taking care of marketing and bookkeeping at home. The computer skills that I'd learned were essential to what we were doing, from databases to artwork, from billing to design and communications. Not quite as romantic as playing at Woodstock, but we were in business, and I welcomed every new day. I stayed on at Green Linnet for another year as consultant while Alison was accepted to some high-end wholesale shows. The orders poured in. At one point in the 1990s, we had seven people on staff with reps all over the country. We were selling to over 1,200 galleries, museum shops, and catalogs, and were working our asses off, especially my wife, who, as it turned out, was a workaholic.

One of the pieces in our line was an Alison Palmer menorah shaped like a dachshund. *I had become a menorah salesman!* From twenty-eight million records worldwide, this was my new life—I was selling *menorahs*. I wonder what my ancient relatives would have thought about that?

In March of 1993, Al Kooper organized a *Child Is Father to the Man* reunion concert at the Bottom Line in New York. Ironically, Al was not allowed to use the name Blood, Sweat & Tears. It was owned by Bobby Colomby, and there was no way that Colomby was going to give Al permission after their falling-out, when Al had accused Bobby of stealing his royalties.

It was a fun gig, though dampened a little by a late-winter snowstorm. We played the entire album live, just like it was recorded, string section and all, and in chronological order. The only strange thing about the gig was that we wore tuxedos, the only time for me since the Grammys. Randy Brecker, Lew Soloff, Tom Malone, and Fred Lipsius were the horn section, with Will Lee on bass and Anton Fig on drums. I had hardly played in recent years, and felt slightly uncomfortable until Randy Brecker, saint that he is, encouraged me by telling me that I had my own style, and it worked, so there was no reason to be intimidated—even though these guys were some of the best musicians alive.

I got a call from Al after the gig saying that he hoped I wouldn't mind, he wanted to take the *Child Is Father to the Man* show on the road, but he wanted a different guitar player. I said that it was fine with me because I was so busy with Alison, but what I *really* wanted to say was *Fuck you, Al.* It was typical Kooper bullshit. Once upon a time, Al played with Bob Dylan, and after that he thought he *was* Bob Dylan—or at least some variety of superstar—and nothing could be further from the truth. He had been dining out on the work of others for years, and a BS&T reunion was no different. He got what he wanted and didn't care who he pissed off.

The next year Kooper decided to throw himself a birthday party, also at the Bottom Line. He called me and said, "Hey, I want to throw a big party, a show at the Bottom Line for a couple of days to celebrate my fiftieth birthday. I'd like to have a *Child Is Father to the Man* band reunion *and* the Blues Project, with special guests. Do you think you could come?"

I am a chump, and actually wanted to celebrate our bands, so I said, "Sure, I think it would be fun." We rehearsed for a couple of nights at SIR rehearsal studios. And then the night before the gig, Al handed out papers to each of the musicians. *What the hell was this? Contracts? Recording contracts? Wait, I was invited to a birthday party, not a recording session! What the fuck?*

Al had done it again. Without asking anyone up until the night before his "birthday party," Al was actually handing out recording agreements. And if that wasn't mortifying enough, Al had booked a remote video truck to tape the show for possible TV and video distribution. I went ahead with the concert, but I wasn't happy about the way Kooper had gone about suckering us. It was low-down bullshit.

On top of that, Al took the only good dressing room at the Bottom Line, where he held court, entertaining guests like he was the godfather at his daughter's wedding. It may seem like a petty complaint, but the lowly musicians were relegated to a trailer out on the street. This included the author Stephen King and John Sebastian, who were our special guests. It was just more pompous crap.

I was on the brink of driving back home. I had visions all the while of what Al's album cover was going to look like—his name in large letters, and "The Blues Project" in small print—and that's exactly what happened. Al's ego was out of control. I wanted no part of it, and if I *did* agree to eventually lending my name to his project, I would at least have to get paid for it. That's only fair business, right?

So don't be surprised that his *Soul of a Man* album, recorded that night, came out with my guitar parts replaced. I also would not give him the rights to the video without some sort of compensation. I mean, he was getting paid, and you would think that after everything, Steve Katz was worth some consideration. Once upon a time, Al and I shared one of the most famous marquees in the world. Then again, even back then I'd had to fight to get my name next to his. I had come to the absolute end of putting up with this sort of hustle. It's too bad; it could have been a fun party. The music could have gone on and on.

CHAPTER 14

Epilogue

WORKING IN THE CRAFT WORLD WITH ALISON, I'VE MET SOME really great people, all involved in the visual arts on a very high level, and most with lifestyles that brought me back to everything that was good about the '60s. These were artists who worked with their hands and earned barely enough money to keep their kilns warm, but they were real, they struggled, and they were honest, and I was happy that my life had taken the turn it had.

You get to a point where it becomes important to impart the things that you've learned over the years, just as you begin to understand that there are people who are really interested in what you've done and what you are doing. I've gone through periods of bitterness—you've read about it—but I am happy and content right now, in the present. I was part of something very special, and the fact that I've finally acquired the confidence to understand the rest will turn out to be just as good.

For me, Blood, Sweat & Tears was both a blessing and a curse. Many of my peers and even some of my so-called friends felt that I had sold out to an overcommercialized, middle-of-the-road milieu—that having hit singles and playing Las Vegas was politically incorrect. I had sometimes felt the same way myself, and agonized many days over the blessing and the curse of bearing bad reviews while depositing some pretty decent royalty checks into my bank account. My peers thought that I had shed my urban folk roots. I never did, but I felt stigmatized for decades. Not that it bothered me much, but there were books in which I should have been included, festivals I might have been invited to, venues I could have been booked at. And so, to this day, I am not really viewed as a folksinger, a blues musician, or a singer-songwriter. Rather, I was part of an organization that was lucky enough to have been successful at making hit records and creating some very respectable music. I was part of an experiment that worked, but deep down, I never lost the love I have always had for roots music.

In 2008, I returned to Blood, Sweat & Tears and toured with them for three years. I was the only original member in the band. My new role was to make the introductions, play harmonica, sing, and smile like I was enjoying myself. Honestly, I did it for the money, and although I was not happy doing most of the gigs, smoky run-down casinos and outdoor civic barbecues, I did have a good time traveling to places like Russia and Korea—places that I otherwise would never have had the opportunity to see. But by the third year, I felt like an employee, and the humiliation of being treated like that in the band that I had started was just too much. I began to dislike and lose trust in the people that I was working for, the mercenaries who had licensed the band name. We were selling snake oil and I wanted out of the midway.

Now I play solo, acoustic, pulling out my favorites, the stuff I learned from Van Ronk, Mississippi John Hurt, or my own songs—the stuff I wrote and played with the Blues Project and Blood, Sweat & Tears—basically, whatever I love.

So, is Steve Katz a rock star? These days a good show for me is thirty people. Just a few weeks ago, I played at a chapel in a cemetery in Brooklyn and the pews weren't even filled. Occasionally I play with some of the original guys and some of the bigger places, but mostly it's just me, and if there is any insanity left, I have no one else to blame. I used to rock stadiums, but my mailman has no idea. Life is good like that.

Acknowledgments

Large portions of this book were the result of a collaboration between myself and Mike Edison, author of *Dirty! Dirty! Dirty!* and *I Have Fun Everywhere I Go*. I am grateful to Mike for lending his voice to my life. His contributions were an essential addition to my story.

Keith Wallman, my editor at Lyons Press, took this book to a higher level and showed me possibilities that I didn't even know existed. Also, thanks to Keith for believing in this project from the beginning and suffering through it while his workload became almost too much for one human being.

Thanks to all the folks at Lyons Press, including Meredith Dias, Melissa Hayes, Brett Kerr, and Jessica Plaskett.

Bruno Ceriotti did an amazing job of research, helping to put my dates and places in order; his contributions were invaluable. And thanks to Mike Fornatale, who devoted much of his time early on to transcribing the audio interviews that we did together.

My agents, Jane Dystel and Miriam Goderich of Dystel & Goderich Literary Management, believed in this project from the outset, and guided me through it with their wisdom, savvy, and intelligence. This book could not have happened without them.

Special thanks to Margo and Robert Schneider for putting us up—and putting up with us in the Yucatan, where I finished the second half of the book. I will be eternally grateful to my manager and attorney, Alex Rubin, for doing the impossible. Also, special thanks to my old bandmate Roy Blumenfeld, Steve Morrell, Terry Ellis, Lauren Abramo, and Wendy and David Newton, for their sound advice;

Sheila Weller, for the coffee and for letting me bother her every now and then; and to my artist friend Tomas Savrda, because I promised to put his name here.

A special thanks to my friend, the great and beautiful Judy Collins.

And finally, I could not have done any of this without the massive input and advice from my beloved wife, the wonderfully talented Alison Palmer.

Index

About the Author

Steve Katz and his wife, Alison Palmer, live in Kent, Connecticut, with their two dogs, Mickey and Henry; their two African gray parrots, Tutu and Kuku; and the remains of their beloved guinea pig, Sid.